Sigmund Freud

Sigmund Freud

His Personality, His Teaching, & His School

By

Fritz Wittels

Translated from the German by
Eden and Cedar Paul

BOOKS FOR LIBRARIES PRESS
FREEPORT, NEW YORK

1971

First Published 1924
Reprinted 1971

INTERNATIONAL STANDARD BOOK NUMBER:
0-8369-5869-1

LIBRARY OF CONGRESS CATALOG CARD NUMBER:
79-161001

PRINTED IN THE UNITED STATES OF AMERICA

Il faut admirer en bloc !

PREFACE

I MADE Sigmund Freud's personal acquaintance in 1905, but I had been influenced by his writings for some time before that. In the summer of 1910 I had a personal difference with Freud, and left the Psychoanalytical Society. I consider, however, that during the years from 1905 to 1910 my relationships with this great man were sufficiently intimate to justify me in writing his biography. I have never ceased the study of psychoanalysis, which is a scientific method independent of its discoverer's personality. My own aloofness from Freud since 1910, my detachment from his overshadowing individuality, has perhaps been an advantage. Of unquestioning disciples he has more than enough; but I would fain be a critical witness.

CONTENTS

		PAGE
PREFACE		7
FREUD'S OPINION OF WITTELS' BIOGRAPHY		11

CHAPTER

I.	EARLY YEARS	15
II.	CHARCOT	27
III.	BREUER AND FREUD	36
IV.	ANXIETY NEUROSIS	46
V.	DREAM INTERPRETATION	59
VI.	REPRESSION AND TRANSFERENCE	85
VII.	SLIPS, MISTAKES, AND BLUNDERS	98
VIII.	EROS	105
IX.	FREUD'S PERSONAL CHARACTERISTICS	129
X.	ALFRED ADLER	145
XI.	THE CASTRATION COMPLEX	160
XII.	CARL GUSTAV JUNG	176
XIII.	NARCISSISM	197
XIV.	WILHELM STEKEL	216
XV.	FREUDIAN MECHANISMS	234
XVI.	BIPOLARITY	249
	GLOSSARY	261
	BIBLIOGRAPHY	272
	INDEX	279

FREUD'S OPINION OF WITTELS' BIOGRAPHY

THE English translation, although substantially from the printed German original, contains a number of emendations made by the author at Freud's suggestion. Some of these relate to matters of fact, and others to matters of opinion. Shortly after the work was published, Wittels sent Freud a copy of it, and on December 18, 1923, Freud wrote Wittels a letter of acknowledgment from which, with Freud's express authorisation, the following extracts are here translated:

"You have given me a Christmas present which is very largely occupied with my own personality. The failure to send a word of thanks for such a gift would be an act of rudeness only to be accounted for by very peculiar motives. Fortunately no such motives exist in this case. Your book is by no means hostile; it is not unduly indiscreet; and it manifests the serious interest in the topic which was to be anticipated in so able a writer as yourself.

"I need hardly say that I neither expected nor desired the publication of such a book. It seems to me that the public has no concern with my personality, and can learn nothing from an account of it, so long as my case (for manifold reasons) cannot be expounded without any reserves whatever. But you have thought otherwise. Your own detachment from me, which you deem an advantage, entails serious drawbacks none the less. You know too little of the object of study, and you have not been able to avoid the danger of straining the facts a little in your analytical endeavours. Moreover, I am inclined to think that your adoption of Stekel's standpoint, and the fact that you contemplate the object of study from his outlook, cannot but have impaired the accuracy of your discernment.

"In some respects, I think there are positive distortions, and I believe these to be the outcome of a preconceived notion of yours. You think that a great man must have such and such merits and defects, and must display certain extreme characteristics; and you hold that I belong to the category of great men. That is why you ascribe to me all sorts of qualities many of which are mutually conflicting. Much of general interest might be said anent this matter, but unfortunately your relationship to Stekel precludes further attempts on my part to clear up the misunderstanding.

"On the other hand, I am glad to acknowledge that your shrewdness has enabled you to detect many things which are well known to myself. For instance, you are right in inferring that I have often been compelled to make detours when following my own path. You are right, too, in thinking that I have no use for other people's ideas when they are presented to me at an inopportune moment. (Still, as regards the latter point, I think you might have defended me from the accusation that I am repudiating ideas when I am merely unable for the nonce to pass judgment on them or to elaborate them.) But I am delighted to find that you do me full justice in the matter of my relationships with Adler. . . .

"I realise that you may have occasion to revise your text in view of a second edition. With an eye to this possibility, I enclose a list of suggested emendations. These are based on trustworthy data, and are quite independent of my own prepossessions. Some of them relate to matters of trifling importance, but some of them will perhaps lead you to reverse or modify certain inferences. The fact that I send you these corrections is a token that I value your work though I cannot wholly approve it."

SIGMUND FREUD

CHAPTER ONE
EARLY YEARS

SIGMUND FREUD was born in 1856, his birthplace being Freiberg, a small country town in the north of Moravia.[1] His mother was quite a young woman, and he was her first child. His father, who had been married before, was already a grandfather. Thus little Sigmund had a nephew, John, who was a year older than the uncle. Inasmuch as Freud's development was notably influenced by the conflicts between the two boys, this peculiar relationship is worth mentioning. German was the ordinary language of the domestic circle, but the child was also familiar with the sound of Slavic speech.

Like Goethe, Freud came into the world black of hue. But whereas in Goethe's case this was due to the cyanosis of impending suffocation, we learn from Freud that as far as he was concerned he was covered with such an abundant black down that his mother called him " a little blackamoor." The biographers of Goethe like to dwell on the paradox that this

---

[1] Most of the biographical details in the text are taken from Freud's Die Traumdeutung. For the editions, see Bibliography. My page references are to the second edition, 1909.

"Lucifer" came into the world dark-tinted. There would be as much, or as little, justification for regarding Freud's "darkness" at birth as symbolical of the part he was destined to play in the world, a part which to many has seemed satanic. He, himself, does not wholly deprecate the charge, seeing that the motto he has chosen for his book *Die Traumdeutung* is: Flectere si nequeo superos, Acheronta movebo (If I cannot influence the Gods of Heaven, I will stir up Acheron).

Late one evening, when I was reading Freud an essay, he suddenly jumped up, saying: "Let's see what old Goethe has to say about it," and took down a copy of the second part of *Faust*. Noticing the affectionate way in which he handled the volume, and his eagerness to hunt up a quotation which did not seem to me specially apposite, I realised that he stood in a peculiar relationship to Goethe. In *Die Traumdeutung*, immediately after his account of how he was born a little blackamoor, Freud writes (p. 243): "Birth and death, as in the dream of Goethe I had shortly before this . . ." In this way Freud brings the legend of his own birth into touch with the one Goethe relates in *Dichtung und Wahrheit*. His journey to Paris, which was to exercise a decisive influence upon the remainder of his life, took place in the years 1885-6, precisely one hundred years after Goethe's Italian Journey. In this connexion, Freud's persistent yearning towards Italy, and especially towards Rome, is noteworthy.

We have excellent reason for assuming that Freud had a good conceit of himself, and an ardent longing to give practical proof that his favourable opinion was deserved. An old peasant woman had

EARLY YEARS

told his mother that she was about to give birth to a great man. Subsequently, in Vienna, an itinerant fortune-teller informed Sigmund's parents that the boy was destined to become a minister of State—an incredible prospect, in the Austria of those days, for any one who was not of noble birth. Such prophecies are common enough. The remarkable feature in the case is that, forty years later, Freud should have dreamed of the childish trifle.[1] This indicates that the lad's ambition had been something quite out of the common.

When the little boy was three years old, the family removed to Leipzig. A year later, the Freuds settled in Vienna. Ever since the days of Maria Theresa, the capital of the sometime Austrian empire has exercised a strong attraction on the cultured section of the Moravian population. Sigmund's elder brother, or rather half-brother, went to live in England. The second family grew in numbers, and in Vienna was no longer so well off. For a long time the Freuds lived in Kaiser Josef Strasse, now renamed Heine Strasse. Freud tells us that the name Josef has always played a great part in his dreams, his view being that in dreams of emperors and kings these potentates symbolise the father. On the other hand Stekel, Freud's most distinguished pupil, considers that in such dreams there is condensed with the signification of the father an ideal of power and splendour. Since 1848, Joseph II has been regarded by the liberal bourgeoisie as the finest flower of the Habsburg dynasty; as an exemplar of wisdom, benevolence, progress, and devotion to duty. In reality, this emperor was a despot who paid lip-service

[1] *Traumdeutung*, p. 135.

to the ideals of the French enlightenment. His progressiveness was an ill-digested Voltairism, his benevolence was capricious, and his wisdom was a fable. We may, however, admit that he was devoted to what he believed to be his duty. In 1848, his statue was decorated by hanging the flag of liberty to one of the arms. His notion of freedom was embodied in the maxim: Everything for the people, nothing by the people.

Long residence, during the impressionable years of boyhood, in a street whose name carries such associations, cannot fail to have an influence! Freud has become an emperor, one around whom legends begin to accrete, who holds enlightened but absolute sway in his realm, and is animated by a rigid sense of duty.[1] He has become a despot who will not tolerate the slightest deviation from his doctrine; holds councils behind closed doors; and tries to ensure, by a sort of pragmatic sanction, that the body of psychoanalytical teaching shall remain an indivisible whole.

Freud attended the Sperl Gymnasium in Vienna, and throughout the eight years of his studies was always the leader of his class.[2] We rarely find that these model pupils attain distinction in adult life, but Freud was one of the exceptions. There are, in fact, two kinds of model pupils. Some of them are exemplary because they are docile, because they know nothing of the revolutionary stirrings of youth. They never waste their energies in protests against the educational authorities. Those of the other type resemble the youthful Lessing, of whom it was said

---

[1] For an instance of strict devotion to duty see Traumdeutung, p. 162.   [2] Traumdeutung, p. 109.

EARLY YEARS

that he was one of the horses that need a double allowance of fodder. In Sigmund Freud's case, keen ambition was obviously the motive force, for his was certainly not one of the sheep-like natures. He has always been of a combative disposition, as shown in his early bickerings with the nephew who was his senior,[1] and by numerous incidents down to our own day. When he was fourteen years old, someone made him a present of Börne's Works, and he still possesses this book, more than fifty years later, as the only relic of the library of his school days.[2]

For a long time, Freud hesitated in his choice of a career between law and natural science. His skill as a dialectician, his eloquence, his interest in universal history and in humanism, seemed to mark him out for the study of the abstract sciences. Shortly before leaving the Gymnasium, he made up his mind to become a medical student, but he tells us that this choice was uncongenial.[3] In another place [4] we learn that Goethe once more influenced his decision. In class, Freud became acquainted with Goethe's " incomparably beautiful essay on Nature," [5] and he declares that this awakened in him an enthusiastic desire to become a doctor. The statement arouses the impression of being a screen-memory. I do not know what the real determinant was. Goethe studied law to begin with, and then natural science, though his main interest was always given to imaginative literature. Freud told Stekel (so I learn from the latter) that at one time he had an inclination to

[1] Traumdeutung, p. 259.
[2] Sammlung kleiner Schriften zur Neurosenlehre, vol. v, p. 144. (In subsequent notes, this will be called Sammlung, for short.)
[3] Sammlung, vol. iv, p. 4.   [4] Traumdeutung, p. 270.
[5] Fragment über die Natur. See Bibliography.

become a novelist, in order that he might be able to leave to posterity all that his patients had told him.

"Naturam expellas furca, tamen usque recurret."

Freud declares to-day that medical knowledge is superfluous for the practice of psychoanalysis, and that his best pupils have been outside the ranks of the medical profession.[1]

One who chooses natural science for his life occupation may make this choice because of a constitutional fondness for the study of natural phenomena, because of a longing to be perpetually examining them and admiring them. On the other hand, he may be one whose bent towards abstractions is so powerful that he is afraid of being mastered by it, and feels it necessary to study concrete science as a counterpoise. Certainly that is how it was with me. I became a medical student in order to keep my feet firmly planted on the solid ground of fact. I fancy Freud may have been influenced by similar motives. He studied assiduously and perseveringly in the school of facts.

Raphael would have become a great painter, even if he had been born without hands. In like manner, Freud would have become a great psychologist even though he had never studied medicine. The danger of psychoanalysis lies, however, in this, that it may lead those who practise it away from the world of concrete reality. Philosophers and men of letters may devote themselves to it; and may falsify it by the introduction of mystical, that is to say, suprasensual, ingredients. Psychoanalysis is still a rock on which the troubled waters of our

---

[1] I learn this from private information.

EARLY YEARS

epoch are breaking; it is an invasion of reason into that which seems, but only seems, to be unreasonable. I do not know whether Freud is destined to make further notable discoveries. I am confident, however, that, despite some of the indiscretions of recent years, he retains unimpaired the critical spirit of the true man of science, and that this will enable him to safeguard psychoanalysis (even in its world-wide development) against a lapse into mysticism and scholasticism. There is no danger so long as he lives and retains his leadership. Freud's decision to study medicine, to study concrete science, has been of immense advantage to the world.

On leaving school, Freud went to England to visit his half-brother, who was quite twenty years older than himself. This journey expanded his outlooks greatly. In Austria he had never been able to escape the sense of inferiority which early affected him, as it does all Jews in German-speaking lands, and especially those who move in intellectual circles. In England, Freud renewed acquaintance with members of his family who had escaped this danger. Furthermore, conversations with his half-brother gave Sigmund a fuller and more affectionate understanding of his father. Thus the journey was important in that it put a term to some of those conflicts which none of us escape during adolescence.[1]

Young Freud had no patrons. It was due to his talents and his remarkable diligence that he was not merely able to continue his studies with success, but soon began to play a notable part in the scientific

[1] Zur Psychopathologie des Alltagslebens, ninth edition, 1923, pp. 264 et seq.

world. While still an undergraduate he became demonstrator under Ernst Brücke.

At that date, the medical faculty of the University of Vienna was at the climax of its fame, or had but just passed the climax. Brücke (ob. 1892) was professor of physiology from 1849 to 1890, and was one of the teachers who, in conjunction with Hyrtl and Rokitansky, established the theoretical foundations on which the great Viennese physicians were to build their practical successes. The scientific investigators of this epoch had an amazing competence for the observation and description of natural phenomena, and among them Brücke was preeminent.

What we regard as characteristically scientific is, not so much the brilliant flash of insight that leads to a discovery, as the work of methodical demonstration. The achievements of the investigator must be expounded in such a way that they can be tested by all who use the scientific method. Those who had worked under Brücke might subsequently become interested in fields remote from physiology, but they could never forget what they had learned about scientific method. Freud's training in this respect was of inestimable value to him, and its results distinguish him from many of his pupils. The memory of Brücke's " formidable bluc eyes "[1] may often have acted as a restraint when he was preparing to make too bold a leap in the world of subterranean investigation.

In Brücke's laboratory, Freud had to dissect rare fishes, whose simple structure could throw light on some of the problems of biology. Another of Brücke's multifarious interests at this epoch was the

[1] Traumdeutung, p 258.

study of the assonances of speech. Before his appointment to the professorial chair in Vienna, he had published a careful study of the structure of the eye, and had only just missed being the discoverer of the ophthalmoscope. He had noticed the way in which the black aperture of the pupil lights up when luminous rays are projected into it in the line of the observer's gaze, and he knew that this red reflex came from the retina. The book on the structure of the eye was published in 1849. The discovery of the ophthalmoscope, from which modern ophthalmology dates, was made in 1850, by Helmholtz in Heidelberg. The point which Brücke had missed was that a lens must be placed in front of the illuminated pupil in order to make the retina visible to the observer.

As luck would have it, Freud, too, was to come very near to an important ophthalmological discovery, and was just to miss it. In 1884, when he was assistant physician at the General Hospital, he procured from the Darmstadt firm of Merck a sample of cocaine, in order to study the properties of the drug. The effect of the coca plant as an invigorant, and its power of producing euphoria, were already known, but that the alkaloid extracted from coca leaves could anæsthetise the mucous membranes had not yet attracted attention. Freud had ceased working in Brücke's laboratory two years earlier, and was content to write for publication in Heitler's " Zentralblatt für Therapie " a report on cocaine, which was chiefly concerned with the history of the coca plant in Peru. Some experiments upon the internal use of the drug were also recorded, and references were made to the work of other investigators. Freud noted that the tongue and palate are benumbed after drinking a solution of cocaine. The closing words of the essay ran as follows: "We may presume that this anæsthetising action of cocaine could be utilised in various ways."

The young surgeon, Karl Koller, one of Freud's colleagues, read this essay, betook himself to Stricker's Institute for Experimental Pathology, and remarked to Gustav Gärtner, Stricker's assistant: "I gather from what Freud writes that it ought to be possible to anæsthetise the eye with a solution of cocaine."

Koller and Gärtner at once made some experiments to ascertain whether this theory was correct—at first on frogs, rabbits, and dogs; subsequently instilling the solution into their own eyes. In the summer of 1884, Koller read a paper upon the new use of cocaine at the Ophthalmological Congress in Heidelberg, and the report of the discovery was cabled all over the world. A new era in operative ophthalmology had been inaugurated, and ere long the use of cocaine anæsthesia for minor operations found applications in all departments of surgery.

Robert Koch's first sight of the tubercle bacillus, an organism that is so minute but so terrible a scourge of humanity; Karl Koller's discovery that when he had instilled a drop or two of cocaine solution into his eye, the cornea had become insensitive to the prick of a needle; Röntgen's first sight of the bones of his own hand; Galvani's experiments on the muscles of the frog's leg; Pythagoras' measurements of the squares on the sides of a right-angled triangle —all these were stepping-stones established in the ocean of error and darkness, destined in due time to join up into a bridge leading to the shore of knowledge. The aim of natural science and its

EARLY YEARS

charm are to be found in such researches. It is hard luck for an investigator to come so near to great discoveries as Brücke did in 1849, and Freud in 1884, without reaching the goal.

Freud pondered long in the endeavour to account for his failure. As late as 1906, when I was attending his lectures, this cocaine incident was still a good deal in his mind. Koller, said Freud, had had, as it were, a fixed idea that he would make an ophthalmological discovery, and had endeavoured to apply to the ophthalmological field all that he heard and all that he read. That was why Koller, though not a man of any marked ability, had rushed off to drop some cocaine solution into his eye the instant he had read Freud's essay. Now I do not deny for a moment that Koller, whose name has not been noted for any other researches, cannot be compared with Freud in point of genius. Nevertheless, so mechanical an explanation of a discovery seems to me inadequate. Koller did not become an ophthalmologist until after his achievement. Before that, his aim had been to study general surgery under Albert. Freud's explanation does not explain the mystery of a creative act.

In the eighties, Freud followed in the footsteps of Theodor Meynert, the renowned psychiatrist and cerebral anatomist. He worked in the children's clinic of Max Kassowitz, who subsequently acquired fame as a biologist, and as a critic of some of Darwin's teachings. Traces of Kassowitz' views concerning the upbuilding and disintegration of protoplasm are to be found in Freud's *Jenseits des Lustprinzips*, published in 1920. Kassowitz had a keen, speculative intelligence, and he took delight in running atilt against prejudices both old and new. He did good service by his vigorous campaign against alcohol. To the end of his days he refused to admit the value of Behring's antitoxic serum for the treatment of diphtheria. Though an able investigator, he is now almost entirely forgotten.

CHAPTER TWO

CHARCOT

FROM the autumn of 1885 to the spring of 1886 Freud worked in Paris under Charcot, the most famous neurologist of the day. Freud's financial position was far from easy, and I have no doubt that he was often on short commons while in Paris. His favourite resort when not at work was the top of the tower of Notre-Dame. He could be alone there. He had sacrificed fine possibilities in Vienna in order to make this visit to Paris.

It was not surprising that the famous name of Charcot should act as a lure. But the journey had another aspect, for it was also a flight. Just as Goethe's Italian journey had been a flight from the philistinism of Weimar, so Freud felt that it was essential to break with all his previous activities. At first, he had been perfectly satisfied with his occupations in Brücke's laboratory. But, as we have learned, he had abandoned this post even before leaving Vienna, and it does not appear that after his return from Paris he ever resumed relationships with Brücke. Theodor Meynert, his clinical teacher, who had at first made a protégé of him, subsequently, he tells us, took a dislike to him.[1]

Young Freud had friends enough, and had enjoyed

[1] Traumdeutung, p. 267.

a fair measure of success. But this measure did not satisfy him, for he had the feeling of those who believe they carry a field-marshal's baton in their knapsack. If we would know the young man's opinion of himself, we may read it in the motto he " half-jokingly " designed to use as the title of a chapter on " Therapeutics " : Flavit et dissipati sunt. What are scattered ? Presumably the neuroses; but we might think of rival investigators ! The phrase is from the medal that was struck in England to commemorate the defeat of the Spanish Armada, and in full it runs : Flavit Jehovah et dissipati sunt. In the reproduction of the motto, Freud has suppressed the word Jehovah.[1] But he cherishes it all the more in his heart.

The larger moiety of the years devoted by Charcot to scientific study was that in which he worked as a pathological anatomist. He was over fifty before he was at liberty to follow his bent, was free to lay down the scalpel and discard the microscope that he might concentrate upon the study of nervous diseases. At the Sorbonne, the philosopher Paul Janet (not to be confused with Pierre Janet, the neurologist, one of Charcot's pupils) was then engaged in an attempt to counteract the predominance of materialism in philosophy. There was a similar idealistic trend in contemporary Germany, the classic land of idealist philosophy. Perhaps it was in the wards of the Salpêtrière that this swing of the philosophical pendulum first showed its influence in the medical domain. Charcot taught that hysteria is psychically engendered; that the disease is not due to any tissue changes, but arises from purely spiritual

[1] Traumdeutung, p. 151.—The Interpretation of Dreams, p. 180.

causes, which are not recognisable under the microscope. This conception of "psychogenic" disease seemed incomprehensible to the doctors who regarded themselves as modern at that date. Though it was recognised that the term hysteria must be used to denote a special group of symptoms, most medical observers were inclined to look upon the disease as a form of malingering, so that the disgrace of being regarded as a humbug was superadded to the sufferings of the unfortunate hysterical patient. Even those who took a more lenient view, were none the less materialistic in their outlook on the ailment. They considered that, although the pathological anatomy of hysteria was still unknown, improved technique and more powerful microscopes would, in due time, enable pathologists to ascertain the organic causes of the disorder. At that epoch, nothing was yet known regarding internal secretions. To-day it has been proved that neurotic symptoms are connected with disturbances in the composition and relative proportions of the incretions. But we also know that the glandular secretions are influenced by unconscious ideas.

Charcot showed that in a hysterical subject it is possible, under hypnosis, to arouse ideas—with the aid, perhaps, of some trifling physical impression, such as a tap upon the skin—which lead to a paralysis of one of the limbs, a hysterical paralysis. This paralysis will last for some time after the awakening from hypnosis. Anæsthesia could be experimentally produced, as well as paralysis. Charcot thus proved that ideas can induce bodily changes. But if an idea deliberately introduced from without into the subject's mind can have such an effect, does it not seem even more likely that the subject's own unconscious ideas can work in like manner? To-day, of course, we no longer hesitate to speak of " unconscious ideas."

It is not easy to draw a sharp line separating the end of Charcot's work from the beginning of that of his pupils. Suffice it to say that the psychogenic character of hysteria was established by Charcot towards the year 1883. In Leipzig, J. P. Möbius was not slow to profit by the discovery. But, generally speaking, Charcot's theory came into sharp conflict with the views which were then, and still are, dominant in Germany.[1] This is plainly shown by the fact that another of Brücke's pupils, the distinguished physiologist, Sigmund Exner, published in 1894 a work entitled *Entwurf zu einer physiologischen Erklärung der psychischen Erscheinungen* [An Attempt at the Physiological Explanation of Psychical Phenomena]. This book appeared almost contemporaneously with Breuer and Freud's *Studien über Hysterie*. Ten years after Charcot had proved that bodily diseases can arise out of ideas, Exner was still maintaining the antagonistic view that mental happenings can be explained in material terms, thus lining up with the naturalist philosophers Büchner, Moleschott, and Haeckel, to whom it seemed that there was nothing mysterious in the workings of the mind and the consciousness—no problem at all. With stupefaction we read in Exner again and again: " having cut off a frog's head "; or " having laid

[1] As late as 1906, almost five-and-twenty years after Charcot's discovery, we find the following bland statement by C. Fürstner, one of the contributors to the collective work Die deutsche Klinik edited by Leyden and Klemperer (vol. vi, § 2, p. 157): " The theory of the psychogenic origin of various symptoms still lacks confirmation. How, for instance, can an idea cause unusual nervous symptoms in children ? "

the headless body of a snake upon glowing charcoal." The investigators of the old school imagined that, guided by such bold experiments, they could run the soul to earth in the body. Schopenhauer speaks of the human mind as the supreme enigma. Exner cannot see that there is any enigma.

Hard indeed is it, in a materialistic age, to make people reverence the saying : " The spirit builds the body for itself."

Thus the sometime assistant physician at the Vienna General Hospital moved through the courts of the Salpêtrière, surrounded by old and grey two-storeyed buildings very like those of the Vienna hospital. He came to study under one who, like Freud's teachers in Vienna, had graduated as pathological anatomist, and had therefore been well grounded in the field of natural science. This man maintained, and could prove, that mere ideas were able to cause disease. It is probable that Freud was not slow to realise that he was learning something which would bring him into collision with the Viennese School.

The physicians of Vienna made light of hypnosis. Meynert declared that it was nothing more than a means for the artificial production of imbecility. Of course, this is not an explanation, but merely a quip expressing the irritation of one who is loath to admit the existence of a phenomenon that does not fit conveniently into his pigeon-holes. Forty years later, the alienist Wagner-Jauregg, a man of first-class intelligence, remarked to me : " The trouble with hypnotism is that you never know who is pulling the other fellow's leg." The jest shows that those who would fain account for everything in terms of organic disease, are no less perplexed now than were their forerunners of Meynert's day when confronted with a purely psychical mechanism.[1]

The hostility to Charcot's teachings was so marked that, in the Medical Society of Vienna, Freud aroused an outburst of laughter when he reported that male hysterics could be seen in Paris. Meynert said that the notion was preposterous. One of the pundits present interposed with: "But my good sir, 'hysteron' means the uterus!" Every one knows to-day that hysteria is just as common in men as in women, but that, owing to differences in the social position of the sexes, it shows itself in men under a different form. On his death-bed, Meynert said to Freud: "Really, you know, I have always been a typical instance of male hysteria!"[2] The remark explains, to those with true understanding, why Meynert and his contemporaries were so reluctant to admit the existence of hysteria in the male.

Freud writes concerning Charcot: "He was not a thinker, but a man of artistic temperament—to use his own word, a 'seer.' He told us about the way he worked. It was his practice with things that were new to him to look at them again and again, intensifying the impression of them from day to day, until suddenly and spontaneously understanding would come. Before his mental vision, chaos would change into order, and the change would

---

[1] These two witticisms, and especially the latter and livelier of the two, illustrate Freud's theory that wit is something which economises thought, and pleases us because of this economy. Wit economises thought by diverting attention from the fundamental problem. Cf. Freud, Der Witz und seine Beziehung zum Unbewussten, 1906.

[2] Traumdeutung, p. 267.

always occur along the same lines. He would grow aware of the existence of new types of disease, characterised by the constant association of symptoms in particular groups; the well-marked, the extreme instances, the 'types,' emerged to take their places in a system; he would say that the greatest delight a man could experience was to see something new, that is, to recognise it as new." [1]

Freud seems to have developed his own talent as a seer after this example. But, though a "seer," he is not a "visualiser" to a notable extent, his mind being rather of the intellectualising type. He certainly does not think in auditory images, being unmusical.[2] The important thing in the seer's gift is that one should have the courage to confide in it. The gift resides in the will to accept one's own visions. By some this is termed "intuition." Every one might have the daimon of Socrates, an inner voice that whispers truths, would he only be bold enough to cherish so mysterious a power. But those who study natural science hesitate to employ methods that dispense with weighing and measuring. Natural science is "charged with hidden poison." [3]

In the manner above described, Charcot had repeatedly visualised the attack of major hysteria, and he divided its course into four phases. The influence of his school was so great that for a time every one accepted the subdivisions. Before Charcot, no one had distinguished four phases in the hysterical paroxysm; and, to-day, Charcot's classification of the phases has been forgotten. There is no regularity in the hysterical paroxysm. The chaos cannot be

---

[1] Sammlung, vol. i, p. 2.   [2] Traumdeutung, p. 147.
[3] Goethe, Faust, I, l. 1986.

reduced to order by simple contemplation, and the seer's vision was false. Even more fugitive was the vogue of Charcot's subdivision of hypnosis into major hypnosis and minor hypnosis, with its detailed description of the three stages of hypnosis. We shall see that Freud took over from Charcot some of the questionable elements in the seer's gift; and that both he and his pupils are often led astray by their fondness for classification, by their love for a tripartite subdivision. Those who sit at Freud's feet are constrained by the power of the master's personality to see things with his eyes—just as Charcot's disciples accepted folly as well as wisdom from the hands of their teacher. Thus it has come to pass that some of Freud's pupils who have diverged a little from their master are better in a position to direct and purify the splendid current of his teaching than are the more reverential apostles whose critical faculties have been scorched by the fire of his genius.

When Freud came to Paris, it was with a mind filled with the details of cerebral anatomy, though he was certainly in search of deliverance from this unduly physical outlook. At the Salpêtrière, he acquired a new conception of the neuroses, one he was to continue to hold throughout life. Hysterical phenomena had become explicable to him as due to a dissociation of consciousness. A study of the works of Delboeuf, Binet, and Pierre Janet had led him far into the domain of the unconscious mental life. Confronting the familiar ego, the ego known to consciousness, there must be another ego, at times hostile to the other, at times assuming a threatening attitude towards the " official " ego.

To the orthodox adherents of the Viennese School

of medical science, such an outlook could not but seem a relapse into medievalism, a relapse into the errors of those for whom hysteria had been the outcome of demoniacal possession. But young Freud was undisturbed by the prospect of a fight, for he loved contest, and was a born revolutionist. A case of Faust and Mephistopheles! (The positive principle and the negative principle.) Freud delighted to play the part of devil's advocate.[1]

Thus the roots of the Freud of later days reach back to 1886. On the other hand, the studies of the earlier Freud, the young man who had been a cerebral anatomist, continued to bear fruit for several years after his visit to Paris, for in 1891 he published a monograph on Aphasia, and in 1893 a monograph on the Cerebral Diplegia of Childhood. They are excellent accounts of their respective subjects, conventional accounts, which now have rather an old-world flavour. The monograph on Aphasia, dedicated by Freud to his friend Josef Breuer, is the abler of the two. There is nothing in either monograph to foreshadow the storm which Freud was already brewing.

[1] Jenseits des Lustprinzips, p. 56.

CHAPTER THREE

BREUER AND FREUD

FREUD's days shortly after his return from Paris seem to have been filled with scientific controversy. He cut loose from the teachings of the Viennese School. A great impression was made upon him by the failure of the hopes which Erb had held out in his famous treatise on Electrotherapeutics. For a long time, Freud kept up communications with Paris, since this gave him a firm ground to stand upon. He translated some of Charcot's lectures, and subsequently a work by Bernheim.

Solid support was secured by Freud in his collaboration with Josef Breuer, who was an old family friend. Breuer was an excellent and thoughtful physician. He is still living in Vienna, being now well up in years, but both the literary and the personal ties between him and Freud were severed long ago. Freud was too intimate with Breuer for the friendship to last. The younger man's volcanic nature could not long endure such an intimacy.

Breuer was one of those successful practitioners who find that the claims of a growing practice divert their energies from the science they love. The two friends must have enjoyed fascinating hours when Freud was pouring out the story of his Parisian experiences—was telling of Charcot, hypnotism, and the psychogenic theory of hysteria. Breuer was, on the whole, opposed to such theories, and he never went so far as to repudiate the anatomists and physiologists. As early as 1888, J. P. Möbius had enunciated the following definition: "Hysterical, are all the morbid manifestations which are caused by ideas." Breuer held that this assertion went too far. Nevertheless, it was from Breuer that came the push which was to start the psychoanalytical avalanche. In 1881 and 1882, Breuer had under his care a girl suffering from hysteria. She was affected with paralytic symptoms, disorders of speech, and somnambulist tendencies. Breuer applied a new method of treatment, which relieved her of all these troubles. He hypnotised the patient, and in the hypnotic state she was able to remember a great deal which in the waking state she had forgotten. Among the details thus recalled, were the causes of the symptoms from which she suffered. Here are some of these reminiscences:

a. Not able to hear when anyone came into the room, absence of mind on these occasions, 108 detailed instances, mention of persons and circumstances, often with the date; the first instance given was when she failed to hear her father coming in.

b. Failure to understand when several people were conversing, 27 instances, the first being failure to understand her father and an acquaintance.

c. Failure to hear when a single individual spoke to her, 50 instances. Origin, that her father had vainly asked her to fetch some wine, etc.

As soon as the patient had traced back the thread of her memories to an origin, the symptom vanished. According to the terminology then introduced by

Breuer and Freud, it had been "abreacted." The record does not show whether Breuer had treated any other cases in the same way. For a time, he looked on benevolently while Freud was making use of the newly discovered "cathartic" method in the treatment of a female patient under hypnosis. In an interim report published in the year 1893,[1] and in the major work of 1895,[2] Breuer and Freud affirmed that the newly discovered method was fruitful, and that by its use hysterical patients could be freed from their symptoms. But by 1895, Freud was already abandoning the use of hypnotism.

Breuer's discovery supplemented Charcot's; or it may be regarded as Charcot's discovery inverted. Charcot had shown that by instilling suitable ideas it was possible to cause hysterical symptoms. Breuer showed that hysterical symptoms vanish when the pathogenic idea can be disinterred from the unconscious.

In 1889, Freud made another journey to France. Instigated, presumably, by the idea that the application of Breuer's method demanded an expert knowledge of hypnotism, he went, not now to Paris, but to Nancy, which was at that time, under Liébeault and Bernheim, the chief centre for the study and practice of hypnotism. Bernheim's explanation of hypnotic phenomena was extremely simple. "Il n'y a pas d'hypnotisme, tout est dans la suggestion."[3] But he made no attempt to explain the nature of suggestion.

Freud never became a very successful hypnotist,

[1] Ueber den psychischen Mechanismus hysterischer Phänomene (now included in vol. i of the Sammlung).

[2] Studien über Hysterie.

[3] There is no hypnotism; suggestion explains it all.

and for years he has ceased to make any use of the hypnotic method. Nevertheless, strangely enough, many people imagine that psychoanalysis is a kind of hypnosis, or is at any rate a form of suggestion. Freud's main purpose in developing the psychoanalytical technique was to render psychotherapeutics independent of hypnotism. Public displays of "hypnotism" have aroused a very natural prejudice against the method. Results gained by the use of hypnotism are not durable, simply because, in a profound sense, they are dishonest gains. The relationship between hypnotism and psychoanalysis is akin to the relationship between passive immunisation and active immunisation. There is something essentially artificial and superficial about the results obtained by hypnotism, whereas psychoanalysis goes to the root of the matter.

During Freud's stay in Nancy an enduring impression was made upon his mind by the following experiment of Bernheim's (Experiment A) :

A posthypnotic suggestion is remarkable enough per se. "You will wake up, and five minutes later you will take that umbrella in the corner and open it." In due course the subject acts on the suggestion. The operator enquires : "Why do you open an umbrella indoors ? " We should naturally expect the answer : "That is what you told me to do." Or perhaps the answer : "From an inward impulse which I am unable to account for." Instead of giving either of these answers, the subject becomes embarrassed, hesitates, and at length furnishes an explanation which everyone, except the subject, knows to be false. We get some such answer as this : "I wanted to see whether it was my own."

The subjects of Bernheim's experiments were healthy persons for the most part. Such experiments show that in certain circumstances we all act under the stress of motives very different from those which we believe to be at work. The real factors are in the unconscious. We lie without knowing it. At Nancy the collapse of the theory of free will and the victory of determinism, which philosophical considerations had long led us to expect, were made directly visible in Bernheim's experiment.

Thus three noted men are grouped round the cradle of psychoanalysis: Charcot, Breuer, and Bernheim. The first and the last have a world-wide fame, quite independent of this association. Breuer, on the other hand, would have been practically unknown had not Freud so persistently trumpeted his name, acclaiming him as the real founder of psychoanalysis. Others share my surprise that Freud should place so much value upon Breuer's collaboration. Breuer was likely to have forgotten his " case " before long, for its significance had not become manifest to him prior to his conversations with Freud, and he had never thought of publishing it. After Charcot's experiments, the next step was obviously to invert the order of the enquiry, and to ask: " Why do you suffer from paralysis, and how long have you had this trouble ? " Indeed, the step was so obvious that it must have been taken sooner or later quite independently of Breuer, and was taken in France by persons who had never heard of the Viennese physician. It is true that Freud brought the news of Breuer's case with him to Paris, but Charcot took no interest in the affair. Moreover, we shall soon see that Freud's real discoveries, those which form the content of what is now known as psychoanalysis, have nothing to do with Breuer.

Even if, before going to Nancy, Freud had been unable to devise for himself the reversal of Charcot's experiment, there can be no doubt that he would have hit upon the notion after watching Bernheim at work, and would have done so if Breuer had never existed. Take, for instance, Bernheim's subjects who acted on posthypnotic suggestions, opening umbrellas and the like. In a second experiment with such a subject (Experiment B) Bernheim would show that by suitable remarks he could bring the unconscious idea into the patient's consciousness. He would say : " Excuse me, but you are making a mistake. The reason you give is not the real one. Think the matter over. Try to recall what happened." He would go on saying things like this until the apparently forgotten incidents of the hypnotic trance rose into the subject's conscious memory, and the suggestion was recalled to mind. In Paris, Freud had learned how hysterical symptoms could be induced under hypnosis ; in Nancy he learned that without hypnosis, and simply by reiterated persuasion, the subject could be induced to trace back a symptom to the idea out of which it had originated.

Inasmuch as Freud was disinclined to practice hypnotism, his researches were, so I believe, hindered rather than helped by Breuer's collaboration. Already in 1895, when the two men were still working together, Freud had abandoned the use of hypnotism and had moved on to the practice of psychoanalysis. Breuer's contribution to the discovery of psychoanalysis was no more important than Brücke's contribution to the discovery of the ophthalmoscope. Breuer caught sight of the reflex from the unconscious, much as Brücke caught sight of the reflex from the retina. But Freud supplied the lens through which the images disclosed in psychoanalysis become visible. Breuer, in the record of his case, has nothing to tell us of the young woman's fixation upon her father, not a word about the transference of affect upon the physician, not a word anent sexual symbolism. It was inevitable that the dynamic of repression should elude him, seeing that he practised hypnotism. The whole " conflict " was left in the dark. But these mechanisms constitute the essence of Freud's teaching, and that is why we have to dissent from Freud when he makes so much of the part played by Breuer. At times, indeed, Freud realises that Breuer's contribution was not very important, after all.[1]

Shortly after the publication of the Studies concerning Hysteria, Breuer began to find it impossible to accompany Freud farther along the new path. When sexual explanations came to play a larger and ever larger part in Freudian theory, and when Freud began to interpret dreams, Breuer withdrew from collaboration. He returned to his early love, the study of organic disease. Not for him the role of interpreter or magician ! He was content to be a faithful student of such natural phenomena as can be scrutinised through a microscope or analysed in a test-tube.

Freud married in 1886, shortly after his return from Paris. His wife was born in Hamburg and grew to womanhood in a cultured environment. She has always been an admirable helpmate—not perhaps

[1] Sammlung, vol. iv, pp. 1 et seq.

an easy task for the wife of a man who is such a demon for work. Even to-day, Freud receives patients from nine in the morning until eight in the evening. His literary tasks—writings for publication, and an enormous correspondence—occupy him till about 1 a.m. Then he sleeps for seven hours. He is a remarkably good sleeper, and this probably explains his marvellous power of sustained work.

Six children, three boys and three girls, were born to the Freuds between 1887 and 1895. He is a good father, just as he is a good son. (His mother is still living, now nearly ninety.)

I mention these details because those who know Freud only by repute might perhaps be disposed to think of him as a rebel in conduct as well as a revolutionist in ideas. His writings have undermined the credit of the conventional code of sexual morality. Personally, he walks straitly, resembling in this his forerunner Nietzsche.

All who have entered Freud's immediate circle have derived the impression that he is a man with a well-balanced and strongly moral personality. He is austere towards others, and anything but indulgent where his own case is concerned; and, for all his severity, he displays that old-fashioned Austrian courtesy which is now threatened with extinction. He is almost more liberal in his benefactions than his circumstances might seem to justify. If my account makes it plain that there are flaws in his character, the reader must be good enough to remember that we owe our knowledge of most of these flaws to the man's amazing frankness. In his writings, and especially in *Die Traumdeutung* and *Zur Psychopathologie des Alltagslebens*, he has, as he phrases it, depicted himself as the only rogue in a company of immaculate individuals. The usual practice of us all is to conceal our weaknesses with the utmost care, and to conceal them from ourselves as well as from others. The wolves wear sheep's clothing. Pride apes humility; envy wears the mask of good will. But confession is followed by absolution. Freud has analysed himself, and has given the results to the world in the two books just mentioned. These are the royal gifts of a man of genius. Assuredly the world that receives this largesse would be most ungrateful to don a pair of critical spectacles and to read from these books: " Oho! you are one of these envious wretches, a man who detests those whom he calls friends, a fellow whose main desire in life was to become a professor—and so on, and so on." We shall do better to admire the genius, to value the man with all his faults—the man whose talents are so intimately intertwined with these alleged faults that the defects become merits. Genius is perforce solitary. This consideration explains all the questionable traits in Freud's character. For my part, I have only one complaint to make of him, he smokes too much. But even this fits into the picture. He can only think in a cloud of tobacco smoke!

Here are Freud's own conclusions regarding himself: " It has always been necessary to my affective life that I should have both an intimate friend and a cordially detested enemy. I have invariably been able to satisfy my needs in this respect, getting a new friend and a new enemy as required. Often enough, the method of childhood has been so persistent that the same individual has been both friend and enemy—though not now, of course, both friend and enemy at the same time, or alternately friend and enemy several times in succession, as may happen to one in early childhood."

This peculiar tendency towards attraction and repulsion is one which Freud shares with the magnetic pole. He refers it to his early struggles with his nephew John. Since John was a year older than Sigmund, the latter was unable to enforce his avuncular authority. At first the friends who had to be repelled were older than Freud; they were fathers, so to speak. Brothers came next in the series. Freud, as he grows old, sees himself surrounded by the members of the primitive horde, every one of whom is longing to get his teeth fixed in the progenitor's throat. But, behind them all stands little Sigmund, defending himself, and saying: " Me slap him 'cos he slap me ! "[1]

[1] Traumdeutung, p. 298.

CHAPTER FOUR

ANXIETY NEUROSIS

IN 1892, Brücke's "formidable blue eyes" were closed for ever. Meynert, the cerebral anatomist, who had been Freud's clinical teacher, died during the same year. I cannot regard it as a matter of chance that the first of Freud's joint publications with Breuer, the first indication that he had entered a new path, should have been published in 1893. Brücke and Meynert, Freud's scientific fathers, had both been champions of the organic view of disease; not until after their death could their " son " openly revolt, not until then could he impulsively turn away from anatomy and physiology.

The cathartic method of Breuer and Freud was the first in which an unconscious mental conflict was made the starting-point of analytical work. It is very remarkable that in the same year (1895) in which the Studies concerning Hysteria appeared, Freud should have published a paper upon "Anxiety Neurosis," in which he denied the significance of mental conflict in a domain where the working of mental conflict would seem to be most obvious, namely in the domain of anxiety.[1]

[1] Ueber die Berechtigung von der Neurasthenie einen bestimmten Symptomenkomplex als "Angstneurose" abzutrennen, Sammlung,

In this paper, Freud does not deal only with anxiety. He refers to a considerable number of sensations and other morbid phenomena which are to be regarded as " equivalents " of anxiety : palpitation, dyspnœa, sweating, tremor, vertigo, diarrhœa, formication, etc. Although the title of the essay was modest, conveying the implication that Freud was proposing to detach only a small group of symptoms from the general concept of functional nervous disorder, the reader comes in the end to the conclusion that all neurotic phenomena are contemplated by the author as equivalents of (it would be better to say, masks for) anxiety. The anxiety problem is, in fact, the core of the problem of neurosis. Anxiety is an invariable element in these cases, but is not always present to consciousness, for in many instances it has been " converted " into a bodily symptom. We have to become familiar with the difficult notion that anxiety is common in persons who are not aware of it.

Had Freud realised that, under the pretext of detaching a small group of symptoms from the general domain of neurosis, he was really proposing to subsume the whole field of functional nervous disorder under the concept of " anxiety and its equivalents," it is likely that he would have shrunk back in alarm. This much is certain, that in the very same year in which he taught (in the "Studies") that the neuroses arose from mental conflicts, he discovered, approaching the matter from another side, the " actual neuroses," which were not caused by mental conflict

vol. i, No. 5.—In Brill's translation of the Selected Papers (see Bibliography) this appears under the title, On the Right to Separate from Neurasthenia a Definite Symptom-Complex as " Anxiety Neurosis."

but by other noxious influences. In addition to a particular form of headache accompanied by gastric disorder, which was presumed to be the outcome of masturbation, he described anxiety states which he considered to be due to the practice of coitus interruptus. " In the phobias of the anxiety neuroses, the anxiety shows itself, on psychological analysis, to be no further reducible, . . . and it cannot be cured by psychotherapeutics."

During the days when I was one of Freud's intimates, Stekel would often ask Freud whether he could conceive of a pure case of anxiety neurosis in which the anxiety could arise out of the actual noxious effects of coitus interruptus without the intermediation of any unconscious ideas. Freud was in a dilemma. He said that he was now consulted only by persons suffering from the graver forms of anxiety neurosis, those in which hysteria existed as a complication. Nevertheless, he would not admit that pure types of his anxiety neurosis did not exist. Since Stekel was able again and again to describe anxiety states due to mental conflicts, Freud suggested to this importunate disciple the use of the name " anxiety hysteria " to denote such cases. Since then, Freud and his intimates (among whom Stekel is no longer numbered) have continued to recognise two types of nervous anxiety. In one set of cases the trouble has no roots in the unconscious, and is termed anxiety neurosis; but the cases in which unconscious mental conflict is operative are spoken of as anxiety hysteria. But anxiety neurosis, according to Freud and his immediate followers, is not amenable to psychoanalysis.

I believe the distinction to be unsound. With

ANXIETY NEUROSIS

Stekel,[1] I am convinced that anxiety is invariably due to conscious or unconscious ideas. Freud has taught us how we should question our patients. When a sufferer from anxiety consults me, I ask: " What are you afraid of ? " I refuse to be satisfied with the answer: " I don't know." Bernheim's Experiment B shows that we must not trust the patient in such cases even when the answer seems reasonable. The real cause is unconscious, and must be sought for until it is found.

Coitus interruptus is practised far too often for us to be able to regard it as a cause of anxiety states. When this objection was made, Freud's answer was that a " constitutional factor " must cooperate in the production of anxiety states. The tubercle bacillus was here, there, and everywhere; it did not give rise to tuberculosis except in predisposed persons.

Unfortunately, the idea of this constitutional factor predisposing to anxiety states is extremely nebulous. No doubt, hereditary taint plays its part in the causation of disease; but the idea that the sick and the hale were all bound in chains forty or fifty years ago is a gloomy one, and Freud's original aim was to free us from this tyranny by substituting the theory of repression. If there really are disorders that arise out of repressed ideas, anxiety can have no other cause than the ideas which give rise to it. In neurotic patients, these ideas are unconscious. The task of the psychoanalyst is to bring them into consciousness, and to render them harmless by the light of reason.

We have seen that Freud reached the turning-

---
[1] Wilhelm Stekel, Nervöse Angstzustände und ihre Behandlung.—For English translation, see Bibliography.

point in 1895. His new departure was leading him so far away from the teachings in which he had been brought up that he was aghast at his own discoveries. As far as his inner self was concerned, Brücke and Meynert were still alive, and under the admonishment of their eyes he lagged a long way behind Charcot and Möbius, who had both taught, before Freud, that all neurotic symptoms were due to ideas. Freud's paper on the " actual neuroses " (somatic neuroses) represents the inward negative which his mind opposed to the teaching of the *Studien* published the same year.

Precisely because of this mistake, Freud's work on the actual neuroses was generally acclaimed. It is true that in this paper we find the first indication of what was subsequently stigmatised as Freud's " one-sidedness "—the first references to the sexual factor in disease. I need hardly say that many writers before Freud had included conditions appertaining to the sexual life among the causes of neurasthenia. Where Freud was an innovator was in his contention that the sexual life played a predominant part in every case; and that other noxious influences, such as overwork, sorrow, mortified ambition, loss of money, and the like, need hardly be considered. This was the first sound of the trumpet with which the awakening giant proclaimed his sexual theory to the world. Ostensibly (though we, to-day, are better informed) Freud was illuminating no more than a small section of the vast domain of neurasthenia; and only of the diseases within this limited section did he seem to say that they were due to sexual factors. He found favour, therefore, for having at length given due place to the neglected sexual factors of disease. People were delighted at the direct trans-

ANXIETY NEUROSIS

formation of a noxious influence (masturbation, coitus interruptus) into a morbid entity. For those who were trained to think of disease in anatomical and other physical terms, the theory that unconscious ideas could cause disease was hard of digestion. The incredible notion that coitus interruptus could be a cause of anxiety was accepted. The doctrine of the actual neuroses (somatic neuroses), one of the few defects in the splendid edifice of Freudian research, found its way into the textbooks, and there it still remains. Students were told nothing of the great truths enunciated by Freud; but the untenable notion of the actual neuroses is now a part of official medical teaching. Freud's immediate followers continue to defend it—Ferenczi as recently as 1922. The ipse dixits of the master seem unchallengeable to his disciples until the master himself repudiates them. It would be well if Freud were to repudiate the theory of the actual neuroses (somatic neuroses) and thus to save his faithful pupils the labour of continuing to support this error.

Freud is not fond of discussing his earlier writings. When they are attacked, he will engage in savage rearguard skirmishes. For instance, he once maintained that the process of birth, the infant's forcible passage through the narrows of the pelvic outlet, was the primary cause of the emotion of anxiety. He still held this opinion in 1923. Freud, like his teacher Charcot, is a seer, and suffers accordingly. He looks at phenomena long and often, until they assume the aspect he wants them to assume.

I have seen any number of children immediately after birth, and have never been able to detect in them any signs of such affects—which, indeed, do not appear until a much later stage of mental development. Freud himself enquires how we are to explain the occurrence of anxiety in children delivered by cæsarian section. At first Freud maintained in all seriousness that those who had been, like Macduff, from their mother's womb untimely ripped, knew nothing of anxiety. Subsequently he put forward the notion of racial inheritance. The predisposition to anxiety had been instilled into our minds by the natal experiences of countless generations, so that an individual Macduff could not escape this heritage. The objector may enquire: "What about birds? They are not born after the mammalian fashion, but they suffer from anxiety." Freud's answer runs: "I am only concerned with human beings. I don't know how it is with animals."

That is what I call a rearguard skirmish.

Anxiety is characteristic of the whole animal kingdom. Anxiety in face of actual dangers is, in Freudian terminology, "objective anxiety" (Realangst). Anxiety for which there is no justification in danger actually present or reasonably anticipated is "neurotic anxiety." There is no such thing as unmotived anxiety. Every anxiety is objective or real anxiety, but the neurotic is not conscious of what he dreads. The motive for the anxiety is hidden in the unconscious.

I once saw a horse shy at sight of an airplane. This airplane was on a covered lorry which was moving backwards towards the horse. The shape of the plane showed weirdly through the covering, resembling that of a plesiosaurus or some other prehistoric monster. The horse had never seen anything of the kind before, and was terrified. Again,

ANXIETY NEUROSIS

I once watched a little boy, seven months old, to whom a teddy bear was offered as a plaything. The child drew back, obviously alarmed by the hairy creature, this being the first time that any anxiety had been manifested by the infant. I have no doubt that anxiety is racial, is phylogenetic, and that the experience upon which the feeling of anxiety depends lies deep in the unconscious.

The psychologist has to decide whether he is aiming at the formulation of philosophy (the goal of philosophy being to discuss the ultimate significance of all things); or whether, like other students of natural science, he is content to observe facts. Does he want to know what anxiety really is in its essence; or will he be satisfied to work with concepts regarding anxiety which are quite clear for practical purposes however obscure they may be metaphysically considered; just as the physicist works with " forces " ? The physicist measures forces and makes calculations about them without concerning himself as to the essential nature of force. He does not seek to look behind the phenomena. His metaphysical needs do not become active until he has grown old and weary of measurements and calculations, as has happened in the cases of Mach and Ostwald. Years ago, Freud used to say, quizzically, that he did not read the philosophers, for unfortunately he could not understand them.[1] But, now that he is getting on in years, he slips a volume of Schopenhauer into his pocket when he goes for a holiday. Like so many others whose life-work has been in the field of natural science, he turns towards metaphysics at long last.

[1] Cf. also Traumdeutung, p. 150.

In the terminology of Freud and his school, it is spoken of as "metapsychology." Now, natural science is a good thing, and metaphysics is another good thing. But to mingle the twain leads to confusion.

If a psychopathologist teaches us that the anxiety of neurotic patients always has a cause, even though no cause be manifest; if he insists that we shall always find an adequate cause if we look for it in the unconscious, and that the anxiety is therefore well grounded—this is descriptive natural science. Such a mechanism for the production of anxiety can be found by those who look for it, and can be demonstrated by them to others. The theory that coitus interruptus may be a direct cause of anxiety would also come within the domain of descriptive natural science, provided that this causal sequence (however incredible) could actually be shown to exist. But since the demonstration is not forthcoming, Freud, being loath to give up his idea, elaborates metaphysical mechanisms which are ingenious and profound, but belong to another sphere than that in which we work with our patients in order to help them.

Consider the following instance. A girl has a father-fixation. She is unaware of the fact, for moral considerations have led her to repress her incestuous impulses, so that they have become unconscious. She suffers from anxiety states. Freud believes that the repressed libido may find its way back into consciousness in the form of anxiety. How does this happen ? In virtue of what witchery does it occur ?

"The matter is by no means plain. . . . The

ANXIETY NEUROSIS

topical dynamic of the anxiety development is still obscure. We do not know what mental energies are given out in the process, or from what psychical symptoms they derive. I cannot promise you that I shall be able to answer these questions." [1]

Elsewhere, Freud speaks of anxiety as the negative of libido; and when he teaches that libido is always masculine, we may doubtless supplement this statement by saying that anxiety is its feminine counterpart. These assertions are, in fact, obscure, and of little account for practical purposes. An alternative view of the matter is perspicuous enough. The daughter is afraid of herself, afraid of the might of these impulses which are urging her towards something she loathes. From the subterranean conflict between morality and impulse, anxiety rises to the surface. The girl is afraid of herself. She feels that something terrible might happen, feels it plainly. But she is not intellectually aware what this terrible thing is, and therefore she does not know why she is afraid. She can be helped by psychoanalysis. But I need hardly say that, upon this plane of natural science, we do not know what anxiety is per se; and we do not know the essential nature of morality, conscience, impulse, and the unconscious. In his practice, the psychoanalyst can ignore such theoretical refinements. Indeed, he must not allow metaphysical considerations to interfere with his labours.

It seems to me indubitable that Freud's only reason for assuming the existence of a causal relationship between masturbation and coitus interruptus on the one hand, and anxiety or its equivalents on

[1] Vorlesungen, Taschenausgabe, p. 428.

the other, was the obvious fact that the former are often the temporal antecedents of the latter. But the real connexion is the following.

Masturbation is neither a vice nor a disease, but a normal form of human sexual activity. Per se, it is harmless. Had Stekel's only contributions to medical science been the enunciation of these propositions and their vigorous advocacy,[1] he would deserve to have a statue erected in his honour by the liberated youth of the world. Since masturbation is condemned by the canons of contemporary civilisation and by the principles of ordinary education, our young folk are forced to run atilt against windmills. In the struggle they grow pale, become timid, conscience-stricken, and anxious. What makes them ill is not masturbation, but the struggle against masturbation.

Still, the foregoing statements concerning masturbation are not exhaustive. In most cases, masturbation is merely a transitional practice, one which fills in the gap between the awakening of the genital sexual life and the conquest of the mate. If, for any reason, this conquest cannot be achieved, the practice of masturbation is apt to persist; and behind the act lurks a fantasy which is often so unethical and so repulsive to consciousness that it is thrust down into the unconscious. The repression of these perverse or criminal images and desires may certainly give rise to headache, or to some other form of neurosis; may arouse a consciousness of guilt, low spirits, melancholia, suicidal inclinations. In these cases, likewise, the remedy is not to be found in the prohibition of masturbation, but in unearthing the

[1] Stekel, Onanie und Homosexualität, third edition.

ANXIETY NEUROSIS

repressed fantasies by means of psychoanalysis. The gorgon's head must be brought into the open.

The owner-superintendent of an Austrian home for nervous diseases had read Stekel without fully understanding that author's drift. A young man who was one of his resident patients, and who later came to me for treatment, had been given the following prescription: "You must masturbate! At least twice a week!" This amazing neurologist knew nothing of the evil spirits that dwell in the unconscious. The lad was affected with an unconscious longing to kill his father and all his brothers and sisters in order that he might be left alone with his mother. The doctor's prescription meant that he was, in fancy, to commit murder, to wade through slaughter, at least twice a week. By following the advice, he had been brought to the verge of lunacy.

The working of the imagination is the quintessence of sexual intercourse, and classifications of the types of intercourse in which this feature is ignored lead us hopelessly astray. If two people love one another, any conceivable form of sexual intercourse they have a fancy for is normal and ennobling—if we must pass ethical judgments at all. On the other hand, what is termed "normal sexual intercourse" is a masturbatory act if the participants do not love one another. Inasmuch as human beings have an intense need of love, such intercourse is always accompanied by fantasies. The fact is familiar to every reader of Goethe's *Elective Affinities*. Each of the partners in such a coitus is picturing an imaginary happiness, and is annihilating the actual companion. In these cases it is assuredly better and more economical to masturbate. The imagination can work more freely when one is alone.

Per se, coitus interruptus is just as harmless as masturbation. But let us suppose that one of the parties to an interrupted coitus is out of tune with the other. Then, in connexion with the act, there will arise and will be repressed such thoughts as these: " Why am I bound to her ? She does not please me. If only I were free! If only we had no children! Perhaps she will die; perhaps my wife will die." In such cases, the moral authority in the mind will protest against the repressed ideas, and when the evil wishes make their way to the surface anxiety ensues.

Coitus interruptus is practised thousands upon thousands of times without ill consequences. Indeed, I am almost inclined to believe that it is quite harmless in the case of unmarried persons. Hamlet's wise saying must be remembered in this connexion: " There is nothing either good or bad, but thinking makes it so."

CHAPTER FIVE

DREAM INTERPRETATION

FREUD lost his father in 1896. He tells us that the death of the father is the most important occurrence in a man's life.[1] While the father still lives, the son is his child, and therefore remains a child. When the father dies, the son himself becomes a father, no matter whether he has children or not. From the father we take over the germ-plasm, the immortal part in us, whose mortal guardian we are for the brief span of life. As a rule, we do not enter into effective guardianship of this property until after the decease of the former guardian of the entail. As long as the father lives, we remain linked to the earlier generations, to the past, and therefore to childhood. An invisible umbilical cord connects us with the father until he disappears into the tomb. But at this turning-point in life the tie with the past is suddenly broken, and our gaze is henceforward directed towards the future, towards future generations—towards the sun. From of old, the sun has been the symbol of the father.

The cutting of the umbilical cord which connects us to the past, this final consolidation of individuality, is never achieved without internal struggles. A

[1] Traumdeutung, Introduction.

modicum of love (and, since feelings are bipolar, a modicum likewise of its counterpart, hate) is set free, and has to find attachment elsewhere. Friendships are formed or broken; marriages, often rash marriages, are apt to take place at this period. The mind is bewildered, so that strange outbreaks are prone to occur. Those who write biographies, and those who read them, should never forget the date of the father's death. Here is the key with which we can unlock hidden doors.

I have tried to show that the death of the spiritual fathers (Charcot, too, died in 1893) had a marked influence on Freud's creative activities. Even after 1893, however, he remained under the influence of Breuer, the old family friend; and he was still much influenced by the teachings of others. But after the death of Freud senior, Sigmund grew to his full stature and became Freud. In rapid succession were now written the books that were eventually to be published under the titles: *Die Traumdeutung* (1900); *Psychopathologie des Alltagslebens* (1901); and *Drei Abhandlungen zur Sexualtheorie* (1905). Freud was already forty when his father died.[1] Ostwald has a theory that great men find themselves early. Sigmund Freud, at any rate, was an exception.

---

[1] In the edifice of Freudian doctrine, an increasingly important place is given to the father. In Freud's latest work, Das Ich und das Es, 1923, he refers conscience and the ego-ideal or super-ego to the father complex.—The pianist M. R. recently told me the following story: "It must have been in the seventies when my father and I met Freud senior one day in the street. At the moment, I was arguing with my father about something. Freud senior laughingly reproved me: 'What, do you contradict your father? My Sigmund's little toe is cleverer than my head, but he would never dare to contradict me!'"

DREAM INTERPRETATION

Freud's *Interpretation of Dreams* has been fiercely attacked. The dullards who believe that they have a lien upon the human intelligence, and who always use it to darken counsel, are still shaking their heads over this book. Yet all who study dreams by the method discovered by Freud and elaborated by his pupils, are absolutely convinced that the Freudian theory of dream interpretation is sound.

The dream related by the dreamer is not the dream that has been dreamed. If we wish to learn the hidden significance of the dream, we must reach back from its ostensible meaning to the thoughts of which it is the mask. Like a cipher, the dream can only be understood with the aid of a key. Communications written in cipher are, at first sight, meaningless. So with dreams; but the deciphered dream invariably has a deep significance. The dream gives expression to impulses that are deeply hidden. Forbidden wishes, feelings of love and hate, criminal trends, delusions of grandeur, self-adulation, longing for death—all these manifest themselves in dreams, but their meaning is so artfully covered up that the dreamer is unable to grasp the significance of his own dream. The dream distortion is a good thing for the dreamer, for it relieves him of responsibility for his dream. Freud played the part of Prometheus. Not only did he bring the light which illumines the dark recesses of the dream, but he also forced us to assume responsibility for our dreams. So long as dreams were unmeaning froth ("songes-mensonges") there was no need to trouble about them. Undoubtedly, our responsibilities grow heavier when dreams are included within the domain of conscience; when we recognise that our dreams give expression to our evil impulses, to our protests against morality and civilisation; and when the bearing of the Delphic precept "Know thyself" undergoes so unexpected an extension. That is why Freud's discovery has been so unwelcome. The dead return—the dead thoughts of evil, the shapes that we would fain keep from the light of day, the thoughts that had been thrust down into the Tartarus of the unconscious. In our dreams, we murder our nearest and dearest. We revel in perversions at which we shudder in our waking hours. All our criminal instincts are unchained in the dream. We are venturesome, too, in dreams, for when we are locked in slumber we are not exposed to the dangers that would gather round us did we actually carry out all that we do imaginatively in dreams. No one knows what we dream. We do not even know it ourselves, for the dream distortion hides from us, as from others, the true meaning of our orgies. Dreams that might betray us too readily are forgotten; they cannot pass the censor.

There were thinkers before Freud who recognised the significance of dreams. Freud mentions as forerunner Josef Popper-Lynkeus (ob. 1921). Others quote passages showing that Nietzsche had grasped the meaning of the dream.[1] But there is a great difference between the flash of genius which discloses a truth in an aphorism, a truth that lapses a moment later into the ocean of oblivion; and the systematic conquest of a truth, so that it becomes one of the permanent acquisitions of science. When Freud was told that Nietzsche had foreshadowed many of the discoveries of psychoanalysis and much

[1] Cf., for instance, Menschliches, Allzumenschliches, I, 12 and 13.

DREAM INTERPRETATION

of the Freudian sexual theory, he answered that he knew little of Nietzsche, and that he must renounce the pleasure of studying Nietzsche's works, for he did not want "to be hampered by any preconceptions that might interfere with the elaboration of psychoanalytical impressions."[1] This was rather a strange thing to say. Nietzsche's writings are to-day part of the common heritage of culture. We meet his ideas at every turn—in the street, in the tea-shop, in conversations between analysts and their patients. Freud may refuse to make direct acquaintance with Nietzsche's thoughts, but he will still have these thoughts in his mind, and they will appear there in a garbled form. There are no water-tight doors by which he will be able to exclude the current of Nietzschean ideas. Indeed, Freud has changed his mind, and now takes Nietzsche as well as Schopenhauer with him on his travels.

"The dream is the royal road into the unconscious." Now that we understand the language of dreams—an advance made in 1900 after a pause of several millenniums—the doors to the unconscious have been opened, and it will be futile to struggle against entering the paths that lead into this underworld. Hitherto none but sincere Christians have known, in their humility, that they were miserable sinners. To-day, the man who prides himself upon his culture and refinement, the gentleman, the good citizen, is compelled to recognise his own criminal and anarchical impulses, and his responsibility therefor. The days of hushing-up are over; the reign of psychoanalysis begins. Incipit Zarathustra. If, in their inward selves, human beings are lower

[1] Sammlung, vol. iv, p. 12.

animals, it is well that they should be aware of the fact, and should not deceive themselves and others. The lower animals can be tamed more effectively when we know their sinister powers, and their "vices." For decades, the nations had lived together peacefully, and had come to regard war as impossible. Then, in a moment, war, in its incredible brutality was upon them. One would have thought that the horrors of mass murder would never have been forgotten. Yet what do we find? If any one who was at the front tries to talk of his experiences, people turn a deaf ear. Should he write a book on the subject, no publisher would look at it. "We don't want any war-books, thank you; the public is sick of the topic." People wish to forget these horrors. If our forefathers, those who had experienced war, had continually impressed upon their children what war really is, it is possible that the thought of these dread realities might have prevented the recent war. But our ancestors failed to do their duty, and we are heedlessly repeating their sin of omission. Since we are too cowardly to look into war's hideous countenance, since we will not keep this gorgon's head in our consciousness— because we repress it—it remains alive in the unconscious, to emerge, ultimately, and devour us. We make war because, in our innermost selves, we are murderers. Did we know that we are murderers, we should be murderers no longer, for murder is forbidden by the conventions of our civilisation. But we remain murderers because we refuse to recognise that we are murderers.

It is the same with all our passions. The munition manufacturer dreams of war; the henpecked husband dreams of free love; the woman whose husband is impotent dreams of athletes and operatic tenors. The munition manufacturer does not know that he has dreamed of wars which will bring him enormous profits. Nevertheless he feels guilty because of the dream which he does not clearly remember. He fosters mass murder, and his sense of guilt makes him pious, makes him a man of good works. We should prefer him to live a less exemplary life, for we have to pay for his benefactions with the lives of our children.

The wife who murders her husband in dreams makes up for it by lavishing so much attention on him that the poor fellow is driven almost crazy. The henpecked husband dreams of obscene adventures, and atones for his dreams in daily life by sanctimoniousness, by frowning upon the most innocent pleasures. Unconscious ideas work, though they are unconscious. Our guiltlessness is no more than apparent. In reality, we are all under the harrow.

The consciousness of guilt is so universal that it has given rise to the doctrine of original sin, and metaphysical explanations have been excogitated to account for it. Then came Freud, and said: You are choosing the wrong way of trying to free yourself from the burden of your sins. You are transferring the entries against you from the book Consciousness to the book Unconsciousness, and you fancy that when you have entered them in the latter you can disregard them henceforward. But your creditors are not satisfied. In your dreams, they remind you of your debts; and since you refuse to pay, you are committed to the debtor's prison. The credit entries in the book Consciousness ought to be balanced by heavy entries on the debit side. But you have falsified your accounts by erasing these debit entries from your ostensible balance sheet.

The interpretation of dreams increases our responsibility. Were this all it has done for us, we might fancy that it has made life harder. But the sense of guilt is of old date. Popper-Lynkeus calls it "the world's cry of anguish." For thousands of years the consciousness of guilt has laughed reason to scorn, though before the days of Freud no one knew what the sense of guilt really signified.

> Ein wenig besser würd' er leben,
> Hätt'st Du ihm nicht den Schein des Himmelslichts gegeben.
> Er nennt's Vernunft. . . .[1]

If the dream is a fulfilment of our secret wishes, we may let the dream have free play, without trying to destroy its wheel-work by some sort of infernal machine. We are not to blame for the dream. The criminal impulse exists within us, and finds harmless vent in the dream, injuring no one, and making its way into consciousness in so distorted a form that it does not burden our conscience—or at least does not load our conscience with the full weight of the transgression. Thus the dream frees us from the hidden wishes whose unattainability has been a heavy load.

Dream interpretation, in fact, is charged with "verborgnes Gift und von der Arzenei ist's kaum

---

[1] Faust, I, 283 et seq.
  He might live a little better,
  Hadst Thou not given him the semblance of heaven's light.
  He calls it Reason. . . .

DREAM INTERPRETATION

zu unterscheiden."[1] Of the milliards of dreams woven in our brains, only an infinitesimal portion, happily, is interpreted. Freud's own patients forced dream interpretation upon him; they were continually telling him their dreams, until at length the psychologist realised that the sufferers were trying to convey a message to him in the language of the dream; he had to study this new tongue, as the sages of fable studied the speech of the birds.

For ten years after 1900, when the first edition of *Die Traumdeutung* appeared, Echo was dumb. Thenceforward, many began to use the new instrument, and not always to the advantage of their fellow-men. Let no one who has the luck to be care-free try to lift the veil that hides the real meaning of his dreams! Dream interpretation as a social amusement has incalculable consequences. Leave the poor little pigs in their sty, if they are happy there, and grunt merrily over their trough. But when it behoves us to clean out a pig-sty, we must do it thoroughly. An incomplete psychoanalysis, a dream interpretation severed from its connexions with the general course of the life to which it belongs, is as dangerous as an operation which the surgeon has left half-finished. We may be warned by the suicide of the analysts who have studied the dreams of their patients, and have seen a caricature of their own unconscious mirrored in these dreams. Seized with horror, they have cut their own lives short. Otto Weininger, for example, practised a fragmentary self-analysis; and the glimpse into his unconscious drove him

---

[1] Faust, I, 1986.
. . . hidden poison, scarcely to be distinguished from a medicament.

to suicide. Three among the distinguished psychoanalysts I have personally known, Schrötter, Tausk, and Silberer, ended their own days. These were all members of the small psychoanalytical circle in Vienna. Others may follow in their steps. The practice of psychoanalysis should only be undertaken by persons whose minds are well poised and thoroughly healthy. Moreover, unless Freud's discovery is to become a curse, as cocaine has become a curse to drug-addicts, its use for therapeutic purposes must be restricted to those who labour and are heavy laden. Yet who among us is not heavy laden? Above all, the practising psychoanalyst must begin his work by being, himself, thoroughly analysed. The craft cannot be learned from books. Immunity against the dangers of psychoanalysis cannot be acquired except by one whose own unconscious has been elaborately swept and garnished.

Everyman is married. His wife no longer pleases him. First of all, she is ever at hand, and he can possess her without the smallest trouble. Secondly, she is an expensive luxury. Thirdly, he is tied to her for life. His friend's wife is much more attractive. None of the drawbacks just mentioned exist in her case. He dreams of his friend's wife, dreams that she comes to him, and that he delights in possessing her. But Everyman is a man of high principles, and would not readily betray his friend! Besides, he is not aware of his passion for his friend's wife. Originally, he was opposed to his friend's marriage, fearing that the friendship might suffer from the intrusion of a third person. Only a skilled interpreter can recognise the adulterous thought in his dream. Everyman had dreamed of a mountain slope, and of an excavation in it beside which he was standing. His first thought had been that this must be Napoleon's tomb in St. Helena. His friend's wife is called Helen.

There are the facts of the case.

We cannot pass judgment yet awhile. If the dream fulfils its function as a protective institution, the unconscious love may be fully discharged in this dream. Without burdening Everyman's moral consciousness, without notably impairing his conjugal peace, such dreams may continue for years to fulfil all the longings he cherishes in his unconscious for his friend's wife. There may have been a certain sense of antagonism towards his own wife, a spite against her, whose true causes have been hidden from all. The result of his unconscious longings may even be that he is extremely tender to his wife. —Obviously, there is no need to interpret Everyman's dream, and the interpretation might do him more harm than good.

On the other hand, it may happen that " die Liebe wuchs, genährt vom Traumverlangen ";[1] and that, after several years, this love flames up in the conscious. The entry of a long-repressed love into consciousness, sometimes occurs so suddenly and with such overwhelming force that the moral and reflective personality is hopelessly outmatched. The world is continually being astonished at the way in which people will sacrifice the fruit of many years' labour; will squander, not only money, but spiritual

[1] Love grew, nourished by dream desire.—This is from the German translation of Cyrano de Bergerac, Act III, Sc. 6. The original, " l'amour grandit, bercé dans mon âme inquiète," is less perfectly apposite to the author's thought !—E. and C. P.

values which they have long cherished—will sacrifice them under stress of a love passion whose object, as a rule, seems unworthy of the sacrifice. Schopenhauer tries to explain such behaviour, which seems utterly unreasonable, by ascribing it to the will-to-reproduction. The higher will of the species overpowers the will of the individual. This is metaphysics. But it is plain enough that the ready-made and unreasonable passion comes from a region where the laws of logic and morality do not run. In that region, during those early days when the passion was still weak, timid, and ashamed, it might have been brought under control if the dreams had been pondered and interpreted. A year ago, Everyman would have shrunk back in horror at sight of the gorgon's head. Conjugal duty, paternal duty, duty to his friend, position in society—the thought of these, and the desire for a peaceful existence, would have been stronger than the germinating love. Six months earlier, the influence of the love might well have outweighed moral considerations. But a safety-valve would have been found, so that Everyman would not have heedlessly forfeited his position. To-day it is too late. An explosion is inevitable.

The average life takes its course between these two extremes: that in which the unconscious with its dreams provides a vicarious satisfaction for forbidden wishes; and that in which the unconscious with its dreams adds fuel to the flames. Wishes and thoughts which we dare not yet entertain, or dare no longer entertain, are thrust into the dark recesses of the unconscious. They find their way back into the conscious in distorted forms, and that is why so many of our actions are distorted and unreasonable. Much of our daily life that is otherwise inexplicable, grows intelligible when the influences of unconscious mentation are taken into account. It may be hard to decide, in such cases as this imaginary but typical instance, when to " go down to the mothers in the underworld," and when to refrain from this.[1] A general rule is not easy to formulate. In their zeal for knowledge, the interpreters of dreams may be prone to take excessive risks. Knowledge entails obligations.

> Der menschen Frieden ist in Eure Hand gegeben.
> Bewahret ihn! Er sinkt mit Euch, mit Euch wird er sich heben.[2]

Freud's *Die Traumdeutung* is a very remarkable work. It incorporates the most outstanding of his discoveries, and yet it is impossible to describe it as a satisfactory book. In writing it, the author was subject to remarkable inhibitions. He had a will-to-confess, which to a great extent secured an active outlet, but in part operated as a curb. The author likes to use his own dreams as examples, and we therefore learn so much about his life that *Die Traumdeutung* develops into an extremely original autobiography. But, whilst we may tell our dreams unreservedly to the psychoanalyst, it is another matter to publish them to all the world. " Der Blick des Forschers fand nicht selten mehr, als

---

[1] The allusion is to the Second Part of Faust. Here Faust, who longs for the most beautiful woman in the world as his wife, is told to go down to the mothers in the underworld, for only through them can he win Helena.—E. and C. P.

[2] Schiller, Die Künstler.
> The peace of mankind is entrusted to your care.
> Safeguard it! It falls with you, with you it will rise.

er zu finden wünschte."[1] The consequence has been that a great many imperfectly revealed secrets are conveyed in these reports, and the book thus acquires a very peculiar stamp. In the case of many of Freud's dreams recorded in this book, the interpretation is no more than hinted at. I myself, or another who has worked under Freud and Stekel (the ablest dream-interpreter of our time), could give an exhaustive interpretation of many of these dreams. But this would be an unwarranted intrusion into the privacies of a personality—the personality of one who has already gone amazingly far along the road of self-revelation. The author does not invariably focus upon the true aim of his book, the elucidation of the dream language. Owing to the way in which he mingles personal revelations with a discovery of secular and universal importance, Freud fails to get into touch with his readers. It is difficult enough, in any case, to persuade people to accept a new idea which runs counter to all their traditional opinions. The task becomes almost impossible when, between the lines, there is to be read a personal statement running more or less as follows: "I have a great many faults, but I do not need to be much ashamed of them now, for at length I have made my great discovery."

In the later editions of the book, the personal note is less in evidence, for Freud has summoned collaborators to his aid. The size of the volume has been considerably swelled, mainly by the contributions of pupils who confirm the master's discoveries, and the additions strain the framework

[1] Lessing, Nathan der Weise, II, 7. The investigator's glance often discerned more than he wanted to discover.

of the original design. The book, considered as a work of art, has not thereby been improved. Freud has been unable to make up his mind to rewrite *Die Traumdeutung* throughout. Owing to self-analysis, it has become tabu to him—the father imago and its destruction. The upshot is that readers will to-day find it easier to learn about dream interpretation from other works than from Freud's original monograph; and it is generally agreed that the most masterly contribution to the subject is Stekel's *Die Sprache des Traumes*. Nevertheless, Freud is a writer of supreme ability, the ablest among all the authors of his school. When he likes, he can use brilliant imagery, incisive arguments, exquisite phraseology. In its pungency and terseness, his style recalls that of the writers of classical antiquity, and is not free from the faults of those writers, from their occasional obscurity and density. *Die Traumdeutung* is a mixture of incompatibles, and that is why Freud falls short in the very work which embodies the most fundamental of his discoveries. In the *Vorlesungen zur Einführung in die Psychoanalyse*, published in 1918, nearly half the volume is devoted to dreams, and the subject of dream interpretation is fully reconsidered. But in this restatement, practically no attention is paid to the independent researches of Freud's pupils.

For thousands of years, the ancient Egyptian writings remained unintelligible, until at length the discovery of the Rosetta stone, engraved with Greek and demotic transcripts of its hieroglyphic legend, enabled Champollion to decipher the ancient writing.

In like manner Freud has awakened to new life an art which, as we learn from much ancient testimony, was known to the sages of antiquity, and subsequently forgotten. Passages in Holy Writ and in many other works of old days show that the ancients had a detailed knowledge of the peculiar symbolism of dreams. We are all familiar with the story of Pharaoh's dream of the seven fat and the seven lean kine, and of Joseph's interpretation of the dream. To-day, we decipher from dreams, not the future, but the past and the hidden present. It is true that our wishes can readily fashion the future, and to this extent, therefore, we can read the future in our dreams. If our dreams give expression to our unconscious wishes, they must often represent the future in the making.

A patient of mine recently had the following dream. Three squads of gymnasts. In the first squad were children, doing easy exercises. In the second squad, more difficult exercises were in progress, but the gymnasts were not yet expert in these. The patient was in the third squad. Here the exercises were to be done with apparatus, on the horizontal bar, and so on. Since such exercises always make him giddy, he protested vigorously, and wanted to leave the squad.

The analysis of this patient was to be pursued for three weeks only. The dream was dreamed at the end of the second week. The squads were weeks, just as Pharaoh's kine were years. During the first week he had been quite content with our conversations. The second week had involved some unpleasant surprises. He contemplates the third week with dread. In the third week he will find it

DREAM INTERPRETATION

impossible to conceal from me any longer the workings of his inner self.—I leave unconsidered the sexual symbolism and the transference.

I was able to tell my patient that he was entertaining the thought of breaking off the treatment before the end of the three weeks, for which we had arranged to have the sittings. Thus can the future be foretold. Sometimes, too, as we learn from Joseph's proceedings, the future may be modified by foreknowledge derived from dreams.

Why should the dream choose a squad as a symbol? A week is a series of similar days. On one occasion, moreover, I had spoken rather sharply to my patient. It was during the second week, and I had blamed him for having struck his wife. He comes from Brünn, where the sound "ü" is pronounced "i" [Italian]. A dreamer will commit these local errors of speech, although in the waking state the same person will speak quite correctly.[1]

Those who find puns amusing are especially outraged by this feature of the dream. Dreamers make atrocious puns—puns which in the waking state only an imbecile would be guilty of! For my part, I learned dream interpretation in Stekel's school, where less importance is attached to such word-plays than by the strictly orthodox Freudians. But no one can deny that they occur. At an early date, Freud became aware of this trick of the unconscious. In the "Studies" (1895) he tells of a female patient who had a fantasy that he and Breuer had been hanged on two adjoining trees. The meaning was that each was the "pendant"

[1] The latter part of this explanation is only intelligible with reference to the German. "Squads" are "Riegen"; "to blame" is "rügen."

to the other!—In the nineties, one of Freud's earliest collaborators, I. Sadger, sent Freud an essay extolling Flechsig's works. Freud considered the essay bombastic, and since Sadger had previously written upon Ibsen, Freud dreamed of a " norekdal " style, the adjective being a condensation of " kolossal " [preposterous], " Nora," and " Ekdal."

Those who regard such word-plays as stupid or unmeaning will do well to recall that the dream is not angling for their applause. If the meaning is adequately distorted, the purpose of the dream has been attained. The joke perpetrated by the unconscious may be so amazingly bad that we can hardly believe in the possibility of its having been made. In that case, the dream distortion has achieved a triumph!

A female patient who had read Stekel dreamed that she was flying to Apulia. This province forms the " heel " of the Italian " boot." Now, in the Viennese dialect the heel is called " Steckel."— Another patient saw in a dream the chief square in Eger, where there are two ancient houses known as the " Stöckel " [Stekel].—Another dreamed of Kaa, the great python in Kipling's *Jungle Book*. Kaa represents strength [kraft]. But K [in the German alphabet pronounced " kah "] is also an initial letter. Most of the Jewish surnames beginning with K were originally Kohn. The woman with whom the dreamer was in love had been called Kohn, but had changed her name to Kraft. Only the initial letter has remained.

A dream symbol arises from the confluence of several trends of thought, which are jointly represented by some specific word or image. Thus every

DREAM INTERPRETATION

element in the dream is "over-determined." The dream condenses the latent dream thoughts. The latent dream is always a complete romance. Behind a dream that can be written in a few lines—behind even the single letter K, for instance—there may lurk the whole of the dreamer's life since earliest childhood. And it is here that the interpreter of dreams runs a grave risk, for it is so easy to open boundless vistas. Is it not true, nevertheless, that the whole man is implicit in the intonation of every phrase he utters, in his gait, in his demeanour? The graphologist gets marvellous results from the study of handwriting. Why should we not learn much from the study of dreams, which arise in the night during a period of complete self-absorption?

Metaphor is peculiarly characteristic of the dream. The most arid of mortals, those who in their waking life seem quite unable to visualise, will dream in charming and vivid pictures. They paint in slumber, just as they poetise in slumber. It is indisputable that the artistic masterpiece comes from the same workshop as the dream. Artists are those who have a keener ear than their fellows for the utterances of this portion of the mind. Popper-Lynkeus,[1] who in ordinary life was a man of mathematical mind, and one who gave himself out to be nothing more than this, at length astonished the world with a volume of fantasies. He published a collection of eighty-four tales which were most striking in the wealth of their imagery. The majority of these pieces were simply transcripts of dreams. They can all be interpreted, and only through interpretation

[1] This writer's real name was Joseph Popper. Lynkeus was a literary pseudonym

can their hidden meaning be disclosed. But why interpret? All love stories lead ultimately to the genital organs and their union. Some of the zealots of the Freudian School declare that a man must be shallow indeed if he fails to interpret everything in terms of penis and vagina. On this showing, the writers of the grosser types of music-hall ditty would be far more profound than Shakespeare in *Romeo and Juliet*—for there can be no doubt that they cross the t's and dot the i's more plainly than the British dramatist.

My experience has been that people soon grow weary of recounting their dreams. This sense of boredom arises from the ingrained conviction that dreams are utter nonsense. When, furthermore, the story of the dream is to be followed by a lengthy interpretation, there is an inclination to revolt, and an inclination to reject the whole theory of interpretation. We do not dream in order to be interpreted; we dream in order not to be interpreted. If, none the less, people are fond of telling their dreams to any one who has acquired a reputation as an interpreter, it is because they have a happy confidence that the distortion is adequate, and that nothing of importance will transpire. In actual fact, the interpreter cannot usually make much progress without the aid of the dreamer and his associations. Still, one who has already interpreted a few thousand dreams will usually unriddle more than the dreamer would like him to know; he unriddles, and keeps his own counsel. Let me repeat that knowledge entails obligations. Only for scientific or medical reasons, and only in a private interview, is it permissible to interpret a dream.

DREAM INTERPRETATION

Often enough, indeed, the trained interpreter will grow exasperated at an idiotic onslaught upon so well-established a discovery. Losing his balance for a moment, he will favour some peculiarly impudent dreamer with a fragment of interpretation. He would do better to hold his tongue. Truth is never a welcome guest!

A colleague of mine said to me once: "Dreams refer to the experiences of the previous day. It is impossible to say anything more of them than that. Yesterday I was reading about the South Sea Islands, and about the canoes hollowed out of tree-trunks, which are very easily overturned. Last night I dreamed of a boathouse by a lake, and of an overturned canoe in which there had been room for only one person, who must obviously have been drowned."

The dream is greatly condensed, but its meaning was not difficult to unravel. I knew that my colleague had an only child. An only child is the source of joy fraught with anxiety. If anything happens to this child, the parents will be childless. (Here came my friend's first nod of assent. The boy had gone on a school excursion and had come home late. The parents had been anxious.) It would be better to have a second child. (Further assent. He had discussed the matter at considerable length with his wife.) This way out of the difficulty would be quite easy if I were a South Sea Islander. God nourishes their children like the lilies of the field. But even this one boy already costs me more than I can afford. (Here the dream takes a new turn, in accordance with the law of bipolarity.) If the boy were dead, or if he had never been born, I

should have been more successful in my career. . . .
I break off the interpretation here. It would lead
us far afield, would lead us to the problem of birth,
to the fantasy of the return to the mother's womb,
and to an impotence complex (canoe = cannot).
It is impossible to expound all these considerations
to the readers of this book, and only those who
have had prolonged personal experience of psychoanalysis could fully understand them. Let me
therefore beg indulgence for a reserve which some
will call "discretion," and others "shirking the
issue."

The manager of a Swiss hotel, Herr Siegfried L.,
is universally called Fritz L., so that his real Christian
name has been almost forgotten. He becomes engaged to a girl from Reichenberg in northern Bohemia,
who is charmed with the name Fritz. Occasionally
she tells him about a Siegfried of her acquaintance,
and adds that this is a name she cannot bear. Her
betrothed does not venture to tell her his real
baptismal name. But at the registrar's office it will
inevitably come to light, and what will he do then?
This thought keeps him awake. He picks up a
book, selecting by chance [?] the campaigns of
Frederick the Great, the invasion of Bohemia, the
battle of Lobositz. At length he falls asleep and
dreams:

"In the hall of the hotel. The door opens.
Enter Frederick the Great with a crook-handled
stick in his hand, and huge, rolling eyes. Every
one makes a bolt for it, and the dreamer, too, sees
only from a great distance."

This dream, likewise, has, as its setting, a recent

DREAM INTERPRETATION

occurrence. The Queen of S. had come to stay in the hotel and had had an unfortunate reception. Of course, some sort of etiquette must be prescribed for such occasions! Unhappily, no one knew what was the proper thing to do. The result was that they had all run away, and had left Her Majesty standing alone in the hall.

But this dream, too, is extraordinarily condensed. The more superficial part of the meaning runs as follows: Of Siegfried, hardly a trace remains. Not only is he Fritz, but the Great Fritz. He is not merely the manager, but the undisputed owner of the hotel. He is the invader of Bohemia; he is irresistible in his seizure of the maiden from Bohemia. At the same time, however, the dream is tinged with anxiety. With heroic valour is associated heroic dread.

Behind the anxiety concerning the baptismal name his betrothed dislikes, another anxiety lies hid. A dread that he will prove sexually incompetent is cleverly masked by this alarm about the inferiority of his name.

Last of all, I will give two examples to show how dream interpretation is turned to account in psycho-analysis. One of my female patients dreamed: "My sister and I were wearing red dresses. Mine was slit up at one side. My sister's was not. I felt very unhappy about it."

Interpretation. This girl had been so unlucky as to have a sexual misadventure in childhood. It had happened when she was only ten years old. She was most anxious to conceal this "disgrace," and would not confess it to me for some time. The interpretation of the foregoing dream overcame her resistance, and she told me all about the affair. This enabled me to relieve her of much of the distress which the terrible experience had entailed.

In reality, the dream was much longer, and its interpretation far more complicated. I have simplified it for demonstrative purposes, though my conscience pricks me for doing violence to the manifold beauty of nature.

Another patient dreamed: "I meet Professor Freud: he is most cordial; more cordial than I like. My wife is standing in the background. Freud is wearing a false beard, plaited out of white paper; it hides part of his face. We walk on together; my wife has disappeared."

Our patients often tell us that they have dreamed of Freud. The implication is that they have made a mistake in consulting the apprentice when they might have consulted the master-craftsman. "It is a pity that Freud's fees are so high; his cordiality is excessive." We shall learn the remarkable way in which the dream Freud is, none the less, helpful. "My wife stands in the background. . . . My wife has disappeared." Those familiar with dream interpretation will know what this signifies. During the progress of the interpretation, the patient adds that his Freud was a strange little mannikin with a dried up, yellow face. The patient shudders as he speaks. The mannikin is not Freud, after all; he is Death. At the core of this neurosis was a detestation of the wife.

The death symbolism of dreams is a vast field, and it is one in which Stekel has been the most successful of explorers. "Almost every dream is a

DREAM INTERPRETATION

puzzle picture under which we may write the question: 'Where is the figure of Death?'"[1]

In one respect Freud has gone astray. His original doctrine was that every dream is a wish fulfilment. In 1920, he modified this assertion, and admitted that some dreams are reminiscences of unpleasant experiences. Not even yet has he recognised what his pupils Stekel, Silberer, Jung, and Maeder have proved by countless instances, that the dream is also the representative of morality, who raises his warning voice during slumber. For instance, a woman may dream that she is walking across a flowery mead towards a bog, and she is afraid that she will sink into its depths.

In the latest of his books, *Das Ich und das Es*, Freud recognises that there is an unconscious conscience. The inference is that there must be dreams of conscience. It would surely be as well, after decades of silence, to draw such inferences explicitly and in detail. Why continually speak of the infra-ego, while dismissing the super-ego in a line or two. Are we to be ashamed because the divine as well as the bestial dwells in our unconscious?

When, at this date, we survey the history of Freud's campaigns against his renegade disciples, and when, in *Das Ich und das Es* we read, "not only the lowest elements of the ego, but also the highest, may be unconscious," we cannot but ask, "Why has this admission come so tardily?" Nor can we fail to regret that the statement was not made more emphatic.

In the following passage from the same book we

[1] Die Sprache des Traumes.

seem to be reading the terms of a treaty of peace after a ten years' war :

"Should any one wish to maintain the paradox that the normal human being is not only far more immoral than he believes, but also far more moral than he is aware, then psychoanalysis, upon whose discoveries the former half of the contention is based, would not dissent from the latter half of the contention.

"The paradox is only apparent. Its simple meaning is that, in respect alike of good and evil, the nature of man transcends, enormously transcends, what he believes of himself—that is to say, what is revealed to his ego by conscious perception."

CHAPTER SIX

REPRESSION AND TRANSFERENCE

THE aim of Freud's journey to Nancy was to acquire a thorough knowledge of hypnotic technique. This seemed to him indispensable after the study of Breuer's case. But when he left Nancy, he broke with hypnotism for ever.

The most pitiful pretender may be a successful hypnotist. A black beard, a bold eye, a pair of check trousers, can do more in this field than penetrating intelligence and high spiritual worth. Freud had never been greatly drawn towards hypnotic methods. His impetuous journey to Nancy showed, indeed, that he did not feel sure of himself. But since, wherever we go, we rediscover ourselves, Freud acclaimed in Bernheim's Experiment B the possibility of bidding farewell to hypnotism. As Charcot's pupil he knew that hysterical symptoms can be induced by ideas imparted during the hypnotic state. Bernheim's Experiment A confirmed Charcot in this respect. Pierre Janet, older than Freud but his fellow-pupil under Charcot, had already begun to describe the unconscious, and other French authors were following in Janet's footsteps. The cause of hysterical symptoms was to be found in the unconscious. Cases of double consciousness had been elaborately described, and it was necessary to assume that the mind has a bipartite character, for there was no other way of explaining these cases. Indubitably there must be a mental domain outside the field of consciousness. Bernheim's Experiment B showed that, through persuasion, through insistent reiteration, we could force an entry into this obscure region.

This is the point at which Freud branched off into an independent research. He abandoned the use of hypnotism. He was weary of failures, weary of having to ignore the forces of his own powerful personality in order to practise an art that was unworthy of him. He told his patients that they could remember, that they would remember, that they must remember. As early as 1895, he could report successes with patients treated in the waking state. At that time he would still often lay his hand on the patient's forehead, as a stimulus to recollection. I do not think he does this nowadays. He certainly should not do so if he is true to his own theory, for this is a step on the way towards the induction of hypnosis.

In many cases, however, despite persuasion, laying on of hands, commands, the desired recollection would not come. Hours would pass without the patient saying a word. At length Freud came to the conclusion that he would make more rapid progress if he allowed his patients to say whatever came into their heads. No matter whether it was important or unimportant, sense or gibberish. Freud's primordial discovery was born of the physician's need. A study of the ideas and impressions that rise freely into the patient's mind, a study of the chains of thoughts, will in every case, and speedily, furnish a clue leading us into the recesses of the

REPRESSION AND TRANSFERENCE 87

unconscious. I call this the primordial discovery, for it furnished the key with which Freud was able to unlock so many of the dark chambers of the mind.

Patients often overwhelm us with a flux of words, with a torrent of information which we shall vainly endeavour to stem. Especially do they do this in the early days, before they have come to realise that we are in league with the devil! Nothing can stop the flow, and all the analyst can do is sit quietly and listen with quizzical attention. No one knows better than the psychoanalyst that speech was invented to conceal thought! We do not listen so much to what the patient says as to what he does not say, to what he says twice over, to what he emphasises. We take special note of gaps in his revelation, knowing that there we shall find his complexes—guided by the general technique of psychoanalysis, which by now is fully elaborated. The analyst allows the analysand to go on talking, confident that, in the end, the important and the true will rise unaided to the surface. I presume that Freud's primordial discovery must have been made in this way. He had to listen, so he listened to the end. But at the end there cropped out the hidden things which the flux of words was intended to hide.

For a long time I believed, and indeed still believe, that this use of the free flow of thought was peculiar to Freud. In 1920, a resident in Budapesth drew attention to an essay by Ludwig Börne entitled, *Die Kunst, in drei Tagen ein Originalschriftsteller zu werden*.[1] The essay concludes with the words: " Take a few sheets of paper and write down for three days in succession, without falsification

---

[1] The Art of becoming an original Writer in three Days.

or hypocrisy, everything that comes into your head. Write what you think of yourself, of your wife, of the war with the Turks, of Goethe . . . of the day of judgment, of those set in authority over you—and when the three days are over, you will be amazed at the new and strange thoughts that have welled up out of your mind."

Freud, who has always been fond of reading Börne, agrees that this essay may have played a significant part in the early history of the use of the free flow of ideas for psychoanalytical purposes.

We cannot suppose that Freud originally designed to become an interpreter of dreams. But his patients, whom he allowed to talk freely upon any subject they pleased, related their dreams inter alia, and did so often enough to arouse Freud's interest in the topic. He began to study the scientific literature of dreams. It is quite impossible to say how much he derived from these forerunners, and how much was the contribution of his individual genius. Not until he had finished his own book on dreams did he become acquainted with the views of Nietzsche and with those of Popper-Lynkeus. The Bible shows us that the ancients were aware of the symbolism of dreams; that the dreams which occur in any one night have the same significance (Pharaoh's dreams); that forgotten dreams can be brought back into consciousness (Nebuchadnezzar's forgotten dream). Artemidorus, the classical author of a work on dream interpretation, had come into Freud's ken. Frequent references are made to Scherner's *Das Leben des Traumes* (1861); Freud regards the book as obscure and turgid. I doubt if sufficient attention has been paid to the close connexion

REPRESSION AND TRANSFERENCE

between some of the doctrines in Freud's *Die Traumdeutung* and the teachings of Freud's direct precursor Scherner. Stekel, on the other hand, does full justice to Artemidorus and Scherner in *Die Sprache des Traumes*.[1]

From a number of scattered and casual intimations, Freud has, in masterly fashion, built up a scientific edifice. He has defended it magnificently against a world of foes. I still seem to hear the hyena-like laughter with which a meeting of doctors hailed the contention of one of Freud's pupils that, in a dream, a bird signified, or might signify, the penis. The invincible solidity of his theory of the dream gave Freud the power to rebut attacks upon other parts of his doctrine which were less firmly grounded. It is regrettable that this great man is so unwilling to accept improvements and additions to the theory of dream interpretation when they are suggested by other observers. Moreover, as I have already pointed out, he is reluctant to abandon contentions which criticism has shown to be erroneous. It would seem that a conservative tenacity must be inseparable from greatness. But whereas Freud has continually modified and improved other parts of his teaching, he has paid remarkably little attention to the theory of dream interpretation since the publication of the first edition of his book on this subject. *Traumdeutung* is tabu to him, and we know the reason.

With a royal contempt for philosophical con-

[1] Artemidorus reports that when Alexander the Great was almost inclined to abandon the siege of Tyre, the conqueror dreamed of a dancing satyr. The experts in dream interpretation congratulated him, saying that the dream signified σά Τύρος—Tyre is yours.

siderations, Freud terms that part of the mind's content which is unknown to consciousness "the unconscious." Learning from Experiment B and from his own experiences of neurotic patients that there is a resistance to the re-emergence of unconscious ideas, he called this resistance "the resistance," and described what had been pushed out of consciousness as "repressed." I doubt if most people realise to-day what a stroke of genius it was to coin these three terms, the unconscious, repression, the resistance. Because the words and the corresponding ideas are simple, it is easy to make the mistake of supposing that the discovery of them was simple.

A great many practitioners will still say : "What is the use of these interminable analyses ? In the first quarter of an hour I can find out all that the patient has to say." In reality, the patient (unwittingly) offers an obstinate and multiform resistance to the questioning physician. Psychoanalysis, with the aid of a difficult technique, must laboriously bring the unconscious ideas to light. A youth under my care was suffering from severe dyspnœa, anxiety states, and many other troubles. Twice he had become unconscious when witnessing dramatic performances of Tolstoy's *The Living Corpse*. He suffered almost as severely when he saw Grillparzer's *Die Ahnfrau* played, and again when he saw the opera *Aïda*. He had a dreadful longing to throw himself out of the window, was afraid to cross bridges, trembled at sight of a policeman ; and so on. He told me that, some years earlier, his sister had died of a mysterious disease.

I saw this patient almost every day for several months, and interpreted more than a hundred of

REPRESSION AND TRANSFERENCE

his dreams. For a long time my endeavours to overcome the resistance were futile, though I devoted my best energies to the task. The resistance was disclosed, not only by the dreams, but by many of the symptoms with which analysts are familiar. He would come too late for his appointment, or would fail to come at all. He would overwhelm me with more material than I could find time to deal with. Becoming piqued, he would consult another analyst; or would suddenly make up his mind that I was a humbug. He would be very rude to me, in the hope that I would give him his congé. He would oppose my explanations and hints for guidance with a resolute negative. For a whole hour he would preserve an obstinate silence, as if he were suffering from lockjaw. He would tell me that his business affairs were not prospering, and that consequently he would be unable to go on paying my fees. All these were merely symptoms of the resistance, which might put an end to the psychoanalytical investigation. The duplication of his personality was obvious. One of the two personalities, desiring to get well, wanted to tell me everything. The other personality was parasitic, like a devil that will not be exorcised. The evil spirit is in comfortable quarters, and defies the exorcist. Manifestly, the patient set a certain value upon the illness, and was unwilling to part with it.

But the unconscious complex was tracked to its lair. In the end the resistance was broken down. I need not trouble the reader with the toilsome details, and will be content to record the amazing result. His sister had one night got into his bed, and during some sort of sexual intimacy she had fallen into a cataleptic trance which had lasted for several hours and had naturally aroused intense anxiety in the brother. What on earth would happen if, when morning came, his sister was found in his bed? Fortunately, she came to herself in good time, and nothing was discovered.

When she died a few years later, the patient suspected that death had not really taken place. No one else in the family had any reason for such a suspicion, but he knew of her cataleptic tendency. He kept his own counsel and let them bury her. He fancied himself to be her murderer. By identification he became "a living corpse." That was why he could not bear to see the opera *Aïda*, in which the heroine was buried alive; and that is why he could not bear to see Grillparzer's play in which a brother kills his sister. What about bridges? They lead to the other shore—to the land of the other world. The policeman arrests murderers. . . .

Fifty symptoms or more were explained and uprooted by this belated revelation. Four months' work were requisite for the discovery.

The solutions are not always so dramatic as in this case. Invariably, however, the mysterious forces of the unconscious resist the discovery of solutions. Sometimes the analyst can discover them readily enough, but the discovery remains void of effect, because the patient refuses to accept the analyst's solution. He must, himself, realise what he has repressed and what has made him ill. Many people believe that we indoctrinate our patients with these solutions. We should be able to make our fortunes as imaginative writers if we could spontaneously hit upon such fantasies! It is enough for the analyst

REPRESSION AND TRANSFERENCE 93

to have experienced the significance of these flashes of recognition. They are primordial phenomena. A lady analyst of my acquaintance says: " When the patient discovers a solution, I should like to give him a good hug! "

But if the patient resists the disclosure of his unconscious ideas, why does he not simply stay away? What a fool he must be to come day after day, and to pay the analyst fees, that something may be discovered when all the time he is resisting the discovery! The answer is that the resistance is quite as unconscious as are the morbific ideas. The resistance is part of the illness, and is manifested only by its effects. Moreover, it is quite common for the patient to break off the treatment. A skilful analyst will read in the unconscious the imminence of such an eventuality. He will know the patient's intention before the patient is himself aware of it. If the analyst bluntly tells the patient that he is thinking of such a thing, the patient will deny the intention, in all good faith. Take, in witness, the following fragment from a dream: " I dreamed you said to me: ' There is absolutely nothing the matter with you.' Then you turned your back on me."

In this dream we have the favourite motif in which one persons shows another the broad of his back. The dreamer intends to bid me a final farewell. Of course, if I tell him that there is nothing the matter with him, the analysis will come to an end.

How does it come to pass that, in general, patients are quite willing that we should try to break down their resistance? This happens because a tie has been established between doctor and patient. To put the matter in crude terms, the patient falls in love with the doctor. If we wish to express ourselves with more refinement, and more accurately, we shall say that the patient transfers to the doctor feelings that were originally directed towards others. The phenomenon of transference is akin to the phenomenon of resistance. They are a pair of counterparts, constructed in accordance with the principle of bipolarity.

At first Freud found it difficult to explain the phenomenon of transference. To say that the patient had fallen in love with the doctor was a disagreeable way of phrasing the matter; it sounded vulgar. Nevertheless, not only in the positive phase, but also in the negative phase (in which aversion, jealousy, and passionate hatred make their appearance), the phenomena of the transference were so similar to those witnessed in a person who is "in love" that the expression was hard to avoid. Freud's first account of the discovery of the transference is contained in the *Bruchstück einer Hysterieanalyse*, published in 1905. This is the classical description of a psychoanalysis; and to-day it produces on us the impression aroused by Stephenson's "Rocket" when we compare it with a modern express locomotive. Since then, Freud has again and again returned to the subject of the transference. His opinion to-day may be summarised in the following terms.

We tell the patient that he is to remember. In a profound sense, he always knows what we want him to remember, for, though he can repress it from consciousness, he cannot really expel it from his mind. The symptoms from which he suffers, the dyspnœa, the dread of bridges,[1] etc., are symbolical memories. He is continually reliving his dreadful experience. "He is suffering from reminiscences." The patient has hitherto been lonely in this process of reliving. Now, in the physician, he has won the friend to whom he has to pour out his soul. He confesses, partly in words, and partly by transferring upon the physician that which he has once lived through. In his unconscious, he terms the physician his father, his brother, his friend. Nay more, the unconscious ignores differences of sex. The physician is his mother, his sister, his inamorata. He loves the analyst, or hates him, according to the nature of the repressed experiences for which the analyst acts as a substitute. The resistance is only at work to prevent the putting of the memory into words; it has no power over the transference.

We might think that it would be simpler to recall the original experiences, instead of thus erroneously reliving them in the physician's company. But there is a compulsion towards transference, an urge which is known as repetition compulsion. We are under the dominion of a sinister law, which Plato and Nietzsche speak of as the law of "the eternal recurrence of the similar."

"Thus we know persons for whom every human relationship ends in the same way. We know benefactors whose fate it is to be abandoned by their protégés. In the end, however much these protégés may differ, the inevitable quarrel ensues, so that

---

[1] The German term is "Brückenangst." Ernest Jones tells us that, though about 150 different "phobias" are spoken of in English, no term has yet become current to denote the fear of crossing bridges. On the analogy of agoraphobia, it would be "gephuraphobia."—E. and C. P.

the benefactor seems foredoomed to taste all the bitterness of ingratitude. We know persons whose friends in the long run invariably play them false. We know others whose fate it is again and again to appoint another to a position of authority over themselves, or it may be in public life; after a time they always put an end to this authority, only to replace it by a new one. We know lovers for whom every tender relationship with a woman passes through the same phases and ends in the same fashion. . . . Especially impressive are the cases in which the recurrent experiences seem purely passive, in which the person appears to exercise no active influence at all, but to suffer from the perpetual recurrence of the same destiny. Think of the story of the woman who was thrice married, each time to a man who speedily fell ill and had to be nursed by her till he died." [1]

In this way the phenomenon of the transference can be explained by the working of a mysterious law to which we are subordinated by fate. We are told that over the gateway by which we enter life there is written: " Thou shalt renounce, shalt renounce ! " Likewise inscribed over that portal are the words: " Thou shalt transfer, perpetually transfer ! " We see, then, that psychoanalysis " does not create the transference, but merely discovers it " —discovers a vital phenomenon which is ordinarily overlooked. Again and again we have to show the patient that he is transferring affects upon us. It is not from us that he demands love. He demands it from others, and while the analysis is in progress he imaginatively substitutes us for these others.

[1] Freud, Jenseits des Lustprinzips.

REPRESSION AND TRANSFERENCE

It is not to us that he is grateful, nor is it against us that he bears a grudge. If we are successful in this reiterated discovery of the transference, a recognised transference is as good a remedial measure as a memory recalled in words. We cure the patient in so far as we can receive his transference and disclose it to him.

"The doctrine of repression is the cornerstone of the psychoanalytical building," wrote Freud in 1914. Speaking of the "facts of the transference and of the resistance," he goes on to say: "Every trend in research which recognises these two facts and takes its start from them is entitled to the name of psychoanalysis, even though it may lead to other results than mine." [1]

Subsequently Freud demanded of the analyst that he should push his enquiries back into the patient's earliest childhood. "We can regard as correct psychoanalysis only those analytical enquiries which have succeeded in enabling the adult to pierce the veil which hides from him the memory of his own early childhood—when he was from two to about five years old." [2]

Less scientific is the view of Freud's more immediate pupils (a view which has never been repudiated by Freud), that every member of the Viennese Psychoanalytical Society and of the daughter societies elsewhere, is entitled to describe himself as a psychoanalyst.[3]

[1] Sammlung, vol. iv, p. 13.   [2] Ibid., vol. v, p. 201.
[3] Conversely, a member of the Viennese Society once contested my right to term myself a psychoanalyst, seeing that I was not a member of the Society.

CHAPTER SEVEN.

SLIPS, MISTAKES, AND BLUNDERS

The year 1898 was that in which Freud conceived the ideas which secured publication in the years 1901 and 1904, under the title *Zur psychopathologie des Alltagslebens*. The book had a great success, precisely because its full bearing was not at first understood. It is one of the best of Freud's writings, full of wit and charm. In the later editions, the author invited all his pupils to share the hospitality of its pages. I have said that the exercise of similar hospitality proved disastrous to *Die Traumdeutung* considered as a work of art, but the framework of the *Psychopathologie* is sufficiently elastic to house the merry company.

Freud's choice of motto for the volume was a stroke of genius :

> Nun ist Die Luft von solchem Spuk so voll,
> Dass niemand weiss, wie er ihn meiden soll.[1]

The book is so widely known that I can deal with it summarily. There is no such thing as chance. Our will is not free. The conscious thinks, but the unconscious directs. We make mistakes, slips of

---

[1] The air is now so full of these ghostly visitants,
That no one knows how to avoid them. (Faust, Part II.)

the tongue, we pick up the wrong thing, we forget, because the unconscious has a will of its own which differs from our conscious will; and because the unconscious does what it pleases with us when our strictly logical attention lapses for a moment. This inner will, which is so often an opposing will, can be known by its works, by manifold trifles of everyday occurrence. A great deal that is accounted humorous arises out of these everyday slips [" parapraxis " is the technical translation of the German term " Fehlleistung " originally used by Freud]; and anything that is really humorous always contains a serious kernel. Here is a specimen, from a lecture given by a Dutch analyst of the Zurich School: " We cannot *under*estimate the value of Freud's services ! "

Freud's view of these " Fehlleistungen," these slips of tongue or pen and other blunders, naturally encountered opposition in certain quarters. Lazy people—and most people are lazy where thought is concerned—charged him with undue generalisation. He had lumped all mistakes and blunders under one head. Really there were two kinds. Those of the one kind were, as Freud had rightly pointed out, due to a disturbance of the will through the operation of a counter-will. Those of the other kind were the outcome of pure chance; they were foam on the surface of things; they were matters of no account whatever; they could not be explained, and they needed no explanation. Such a contention irresistibly reminds us of the naive utterance of a child which, when its companions would fain enlighten it as to how babies come into being, answers: " Perhaps your parents did something of that sort, but I'm quite sure mine didn't ! "

When Freud noted the success of the *Psychopathologie*, he had good reason to quote Mephistopheles, and to say ; " Den Teufel spürt das Völkchen nie ; und wenn er sie beim Kragen hätte ! "[1] As soon as any one admits the existence of the unconscious, and agrees that there is a road leading down into this domain, he must make the best of the discoveries that ensue.

In the course of this book I allude to several of Freud's own slips. Here is one which no one else, I think, has yet pointed out. In *Die Traumdeutung*, the author refers to the inscription on the Viennese memorial to Emperor Joseph. He quotes :

> Saluti patriæ vixit
> Non diu sed totus.

But there is a misquotation here. The inscription runs :

> Saluti publicæ vixit
> Non diu sed totus.

For the sake of those of my readers whose Latinity is not of the best, I had better explain that " publica " may signify " publica puella," a prostitute. (Of course the inscription tells us that the emperor lived wholly for the public good in the familiar sense of the term public.) One of the German terms for prostitute is "*Freud*enmädchen," the equivalent of the French " fille de joie," or of the Chaucerian-English " gay girl." Now, as early as 1896, *Josef* Breuer had begun to dissociate himself

---

[1] Not if he had them by the neck, I vow,
  Would e'er these people scent the Devil !
    Mephistopheles speaks : Faust, Part I, Auerbach's Keller.
      (Bayard Taylor's translation.)

SLIPS, MISTAKES, AND BLUNDERS 101

from Freud's researches because the stress Freud laid upon the sexual life was repugnant to him. The significance of the "accidental" misquotation begins to dawn on us. We have also to consider the slip which led Freud to write "patriæ" instead of "publicæ" in the light of the fact that, as Freud himself tells us, his book *Die Traumdeutung* was the expression of his reaction to the death of his father (pater). Furthermore, Freud's teaching signifies a liberation of love from ancient bonds, and many of his contemporaries look askance at the discoverer of psychoanalysis for this reason. Saluti publicæ vivis! (Thou shalt live for the public wellbeing!) But Freud is a quiet citizen who would like to live and die at peace. In France, the champions of the enlightenment did not live to see the revolution; and Martin Luther died before the Thirty Years' War.

Relevant to this discussion of blunders is the following statement of Freud's.[1] In the nineties, or perhaps earlier, Freud became an intimate friend of Wilhelm Fliess, the Berlinese physician and biologist. Fliess is an able thinker, and is in more than one respect a kindred spirit to Freud. He adopted the notion of bisexuality, which is an old one, perhaps as old as the practice of dream interpretation; he vigorously defended it, and endeavoured to harmonise it with the teachings of modern science. The theory is that in every male there are also feminine elements, and conversely. Freud, whose foible it is to discover for himself everything that contributes to the development of his teachings, was at a standstill with his sexual theory until he

[1] *Traumdeutung*, p. 300; *Psychopathologie*, p. 170

availed himself of the doctrine of bisexuality to account for sexual perversions. When, in 1901, he at length made this step, he reported it to Fliess as an independent discovery. Fliess answered with astonishment: "But I told you about this idea two and a half years ago, and you laughed me to scorn!" Here we have a more recent instance of cryptomnesia, analogous to the submerged memory of having read Börne's recipe for becoming an author in three days (supra, p. 87). Freud had entirely forgotten his talk with Fliess about bisexuality. We know from what happened in the matter of cocaine that he takes it amiss when others are beforehand with him in a discovery. In his latest book, *Das Ich und das Es*, there occurs the following noteworthy passage: "If psychoanalysis has not yet duly appreciated certain matters, this has never been because it overlooked them or underrated their importance, but simply because it was following a certain course which had not yet led to them."

We learn in *Die Traumdeutung* that even before 1900 Freud had broken with several of his former friends. Fliess was to compensate him for all these losses. Fliess meant more to him than any one had meant before, and he was determined to cleave to Fliess for evermore.[1] Any one with psychoanalytical experience will have his suspicions aroused by this sort of glorification. We gather [2] that Freud must already have divulged various things which Fliess had told him in confidence. Consider, for instance, the following dream. "Fl. turns to me and asks how many of his affairs I have spoken about to P.

---

[1] Traumdeutung, p. 300.   [2] Ibid., pp. 257 and 297.

SLIPS, MISTAKES, AND BLUNDERS

This gives me queer feelings." In another part of the same dream we learn that Freud's daimon had determined to consign this enthusiastic friendship to Hades. "I meet him in the street, where he is conversing with my deceased friend P., and I go with them somewhere where they seem to be sitting opposite one another at a little table." It would hardly be possible to find a better example of death symbolism.

The actual cause of the rupture of this friendship, which occurred in 1904, was as follows. In 1903, Otto Weininger's celebrated book *Geschlecht und Charakter* had been published. In that work, the talented young author used the key of bisexuality to open the portals of his kingdom. Fliess was engaged in preparing an important work, which was published in 1906. His main idea was that bisexuality —the bisexuality of the cell—was supreme controller of living matter. Finding that Weininger had anticipated his discovery, he wrote to ask Freud whether the latter knew the author of *Geschlecht und Charakter*. The question was a natural one, for Fliess had never spoken of his theory of bisexuality to any one except Freud. Freud was, in fact, to blame, though at first he denied all responsibility. One of Weininger's friends, a young man of science, had been a patient of Freud's, and to him Freud had blabbed. We may grant that he had no bad intentions—in the conscious. But what about the unconscious? And what about the dream of 1899? Subsequently, Freud admitted with splendid frankness that he had forgotten the talk about bisexuality with Weininger's friend, had forgotten it because its consequences had been so unpleasant. He admitted, too, the probability that in the unconscious he might have harboured a grudge against his friend Fliess because of the latter's great discovery.

Such an example of " parapraxis " was beyond the range of Fliess' understanding, and the friendship was shattered. The eternal recurrence of the similar! In the conscious, his friendship with Fliess had seemed to Freud to be built on imperishable foundations. In the unconscious, the foundations had crumbled years before the final breach took place. Who can read the tale without feeling the tragedy of inexorable destiny?

CHAPTER EIGHT

EROS

In the year 1898, Freud made a third great discovery. He showed that our sexual life begins at birth, and not, as had generally been supposed, at puberty. This contention aroused intense and universal indignation in the camp of the enemies of truth. In later years, Freud has frequently declared that the fact that children have a sexual life is so obvious that we ought rather to be ashamed of ourselves for our failure to notice it than proud because we have found it out. There are a good many children in the world, and a good many grown-ups to watch the children. Why was it that no one, before Freud, noticed that infants have erections and that they masturbate; that children have an urgent desire to get into bed with father and mother; that at a very early age they display an interest in their own genital organs and in those of their playmates; that they are affected by the mental conflicts of love, suffering from jealousy, from the longings and torments of love, suffering intensely, though their sufferings are in this respect less vocal than those of adults?

Of course these things were seen before Freud pointed them out, but no one would admit that they were sexual manifestations. The nature of our science is determined by the nature of our general outlook. Children are little angels, and one of the most conspicuous distinctions between an angel and a human being is that an angel has no sexual impulse. There is, of course, a difficulty in the way of regarding children as angels, for angels have no excreta; but people put up with that little peculiarity in children. Still, they find it atrocious that any one should describe " innocent " children as utterly immoral libertines. That is how they summarised Freud's discovery, for in the view of our traditional educationists " innocent " and " sexual " are incompatible terms.

Even adults, respectable adults, were to repudiate sexuality as far as possible. It was permissible to speak of hunger and of social need, but sexual need must be kept to oneself. Any one who obviously displayed the latter was apt to become a popular butt, like the " old maid." If the display of sexual desire was made by children of school age, such contaminated specimens must be excluded from the flock, to the accompaniment of a chorus of moral disapprobation.

Fifteen years ago I wrote a book entitled *Die sexuelle Not* (Sexual Need), and dedicated it " To my honoured Teacher, Sigmund Freud." The editor of the Bernese " Bund " wrote to my publisher saying that the title of the book was both ludicrous and repulsive, and that, were it for this reason alone, he would be unable to publish a review of *Die sexuelle Not*. (The then editor of the " Bund " was a writer of considerable note, J. V. Widmann.) To-day, the phrase " sexual need " has become proverbial. At school, in the press, and in general discussion, people are less shamefaced about these matters than they were fifteen years ago. Others besides Freud and his pupils are fighting on behalf of liberation. A great wave is carrying us all forward. Poets, novelists, and men of science are the forerunners.

We have already learned that Freud's attention was directed at an early date to the nervous diseases of childhood. When quite a young practitioner he was interested in a form of paralysis in little children which might be due, he thought, to an injury received during intra-uterine life; or perhaps, in some cases, to a mental conflict in the mother. We see whither his thoughts were tending. From 1887, onwards, he was able to study the mental life of little children close at hand, in his own offspring. I think, however, that we may assume that Freud, like most persons of note, retained exceptionally clear memories of his early childhood, and that these memories may have helped to confirm the conviction that his theories were sound—a conviction in which he has never wavered.

As early as 1896, we find an account of sexuality in little children in an essay prefixed to a study published in that year by Stekel.[1] But I regard 1898 as the cardinal year of the discovery, for Freud writes in *Psychopathologie des Alltagslebens* (p. 60): " In my forty-third year, when I began to become interested in what I could remember of my childhood. . . ." Nevertheless, such ideas do not spring fully equipped from the brain. As late as 1900 we read in *Die Traumdeutung* (p. 94) that " childhood knows nothing, as yet, of sexual desire." In later

[1] Koitus im Kindesalter, "Wiener medizinische Blätter," April 18, 1896. For Freud's contribution, see Sammlung, i, 10.

editions of the book, this sentence is left untouched. Now, indeed, there is a footnote which mitigates its significance; but that note had not been added in the second edition, the one published in 1909! Herein we see an additional indication that *Die Traumdeutung* is tabu for Freud.

The lusty infant is sexual through and through. It knows nothing of utility, nothing of reality; and it recognises no obstacles to its desires. It is drunken without wine. To suck at its mother's breast fills it with ecstasy. The healthy infant, when awake, is perpetually in movement, and all its movements are pleasurable; it kicks and crows, has no dread of falling, ignores the risk of knocking itself against the hard objects in its environment. Its trusty guardians have to safeguard it against the disasters that would otherwise be entailed by its own heedlessness.

The infant sucks its own fingers and toes, for the action is pleasurable. In like manner, everything it can get hold of is thrust into its mouth. Things too big for that are thrown away, and it takes delight in destroying them. The passing of fæces is pleasurable; rolling in fæces is pleasurable; smells which to us are offensive are attractive to the infant. If not prevented, it will besoil itself and everything within reach.[1] Such is the nature of our "little angel"—and yet in all the world there is no more fascinating spectacle than the unending enjoyments of the infant.

The first serious privation the infant has to suffer is the loss of the maternal breast. A great many

[1] Freud speaks of this as the oral and anal phase of sexuality.

children, indeed, never enjoy this universal privilege of the mammalia—have never known the delight of sucking sweet milk from a warm hemisphere with a characteristic odour, the soft cushion into which the little snub nose burrows. Weaning, and especially a late weaning, is a terror to mothers and nurses. Soon after this the child is constrained to satisfy its bodily needs in utensils, instead of passing excreta at random, and has to renounce the pleasures that were derivable from contact with the warm and damp excreta. Rocking and kicking movements have to be controlled, for the child must now learn to walk. Collisions with furniture teach it respect for reality and for the dangers of reality. Thus, from the first, training comes into conflict with the promptings of desire, and the reality principle establishes its dominion over the pleasure principle.[1]

The child is born with an imitative impulse, or develops this impulse at a very early age. It imitates whatever pleases it. All children imitate the sounds they hear, and among other sounds they imitate those they themselves make in passing fæces and in breaking wind. It is by imitation that they learn to walk and to talk. Love must collaborate here. The child learns only from those it loves— learns from them because it wishes to become like them (identification). Through love, too, it learns things that are anything but pleasurable : obedience, moderation, abstinence, and renouncement.

In the year 1905, Freud gave a concise exposition of his views concerning sexuality in a little book

---

[1] Freud, Formulierungen über die zwei Prinzipien des psychischen Geschehens, Sammlung, iii, 5.

which has become classical, *Drei Abhandlungen zur Sexualtheorie*. Freud himself compared his theory with that of Plato's *Symposium*. The comparison was subsequently elaborated by his pupils and admirers.

The *Drei Abhandlungen* is Freud's best book. It contains the essence of Freud, that which will go down to posterity. Important though dream interpretation and the theory of resistance are, what the world sees in Freud is mainly the investigator of sexual problems. Psychoanalysis is by most people regarded chiefly as a method for the bold and revolutionary study of the sexual life. The new book was received with acclamations from the few who were competent to understand it. The theory was so tersely and luminously formulated, and was stated with a force that seemed so unanswerable, that it had an irresistible success.

The description of the sexuality of the child is the central feature of the book. Freud holds that in early childhood the sexual organs have not yet come to play a predominant part. The child draws its enjoyments from all sources, from all fields of sensation. The lips are the first and most important instruments of pleasure. The next important source of pleasure is the exercise of the muscular apparatus. When the infant falls asleep after being suckled, it is enjoying the ecstasy of a well-filled stomach. We may doubt whether any of the joys of later life, even those of love and of gratified ambition, are so intense.

In these early days, the child knows nothing, psychologically, of differences between the sexes. It does not even distinguish between its own body and the animate or inanimate objects of the outer world. The infant's own thumb, a comforter, its mother's nose—all are alike.

Freud teaches that all infants masturbate, but discontinue the practice ere long. Before the fourth year of life, most children resume masturbation for a time, to forget it once more. But the repression of the memory of this second period of masturbation simultaneously involves the repression of most of the memories of early childhood. This accounts for the phenomenon of "infantile amnesia," for the amazing fact that our memories are a blank as regards a period of life during which, to all seeming, memory was extremely active. But as regards early childhood, the sea of forgetfulness has swallowed everything except for a few islands. For the third time, children masturbate at puberty, and the memory of having masturbated at this age usually persists into adult life, although ordinary respectable folk are prone to deny having masturbated even at puberty.

In 1908, Freud published a paper entitled *Analyse der Phobie eines fünfjährigen Knaben*.[1] The phobia of this little boy of five has become classical. Freud recently reported that little Hans, who has now become big Hans, has no remembrance of his trouble of childhood, or of its treatment. Everything has been forgotten. He is a healthy and vigorous young man.

It is a law of our mental development that we should forget most of what happens to us during the early years of childhood. Analyses are rarely pushed back as far as this, and for that reason I feel incompetent to pass an opinion on the validity of Freud's

[1] Sammlung, iii, 1.

doctrine concerning the three phases of masturbation. I do not see how we can decide whether a repression of the reminiscences of childhood occurs in association with the repression of the memory of masturbation. Stekel opines that the child at this age lives in paradise, in a paradise so beautiful that it has to be forgotten if the life of subsequent years is to be at all tolerable. Such an outlook seems to me to be poetry rather than science.

Let us return to the facts of direct observation. Infantile sexuality is, on the one hand, a self-gratification that is independent of the outer world; and, on the other, the investment (cathexis) of the whole body with desire and gratification—skin, mucous membranes, muscles, intestines, sense organs. The former is "autoerotism"[1] and the latter is "pansexualism." These tendencies of the child are described by Freud as "polymorphically perverse," but the term is open to objection. If children are universally autoerotic and pansexual, if these manifestations are dependent upon general biological causes, the word "perverse" is a misnomer. We can guess at Freud's reason for using it. The *Drei Abhandlungen*, though restrained in tone, is really a polemic against sanctimonious humbugs. It is possible that Freud wanted to explode the very notion of the "perverse."

Even the adult does not completely lose his pansexualist trend. But in grown-ups, sexual pleasure is mainly concentrated in the genital organs, and for this reason the infantile form of sexuality becomes in the adult what Freud has termed "initial pleasure" (in contradistinction to the "terminal pleasure" of

[1] This word was coined by Havelock Ellis.

detumescence). A kiss is initial pleasure. So is the eating of a good meal. A walk with one's beloved, a little affectionate horseplay—these are constituents of initial pleasure.

In some of my other writings,[1] I have distinguished between two forms of pleasure. There are certain pleasures, like that which we experience in a hot bath, which remain unchanged from start to finish. The bath is equally agreeable, and the pleasure lasts as long as we please. This pleasure is timeless, amorphous, and unchanging; it may be termed feminine. Pleasures of the other type are crescent; they rise to a sudden climax and end abruptly. In their climax they are akin to pain, and in their end they are akin to death. Freud's distinction between initial pleasure and terminal pleasure corresponds to my own distinction between amorphous and passive pleasure, on the one hand, and formed and active pleasure, on the other. My classification leads back from Freud to Plato, whose sexual theory is built upon the distinction between being and becoming. According to Plato, Eros the god of the unresting urge, was the firstborn of the deep-bosomed and unchanging Gaia (the Earth): the masculine issuing from the feminine.

Many perversions are the outcome of a sort of frugality, which is content with initial pleasure and renounces terminal pleasure. We may regard in this light: sadism, and its counterpart true fetichism; inspectionism and exhibitionism; palpationism. In all of these, the sexual impulse undergoes premature arrest, is arrested at a stage of pleasure where arrest

[1] For instance in Alles um Liebe, and elsewhere.

is normal in childhood. Even homosexuality becomes more comprehensible in the light of the child's indifference towards distinctions of sex. After some hesitation, Freud has decided in favour of explaining inversion (he prefers this term to the hybrid word homosexuality) through bisexuality.[1]

If perversions and (as will be shown) all neuroses represent an arrest at an infantile stage or a regression to such a stage, we have still to answer the question, Why do neurotics and the sexually perverse suffer from infantilism? To answer this question, Freud formulates his libido theory, which occupies the last third of the *Drei Abhandlungen*. He watches over this theory jealously, will not tolerate the smallest deviation from it, and fences it round with a palisade. It is to be left exactly as he has perfected it with marvellous perspicuity after twenty years' continuous labour. But the theory of the libido has to bear the brunt of the hostile criticism of Freudianism. It was on account of differences concerning this theory that breaches occurred between Freud and three of the most noted among his scientific collaborators: Jung, Adler, and Stekel. We may, indeed, put down the breach with Breuer to the same account.

At one time, when Freud had brought an analysis to a successful conclusion, he used to show the patient an engraving after a painting by Ingres, "Oedipus solves the riddle of the Sphinx." The first description of the Oedipus motif as the basis of

[1] It should be noted that "homosexuality" is not perfectly synonymous with the term "inversion" as used by Freud. Concerning all these sexual perversions, consult Stekel: Störungen des Trieb- und Affektlebens; vol ii, Onanie und Homosexualität; vol. v, Psychosexueller Infantilismus; vol. vii, Der Fetischismus.

mental conflicts is found in the original edition of *Die Traumdeutung* (pp. 185 et seq.) and therefore dates from 1900. Oedipus, son of Laius, king of Thebes, killed his father and married his mother Jocasta. Every son, so Freud teaches, is jealous of his father and loves his mother. Every daughter, adds Jung, inverting the parable, loves her father and is jealous of her mother—as in the case of Electra. The theory of the Oedipus complex has supplied the energy which has driven Freud's triumphal car round the world. It was the proud privilege of the Viennese and of the Germans in general to mock at Freud for twenty years, or to ignore him. Elsewhere, he was acclaimed by those who were as if struck by the lightning of truth—and not by physicians alone, but by educationists, by serious-minded clerics, by sociologists, and, at length, by all who have a modicum of self-knowledge.

The signs of the Oedipus complex are so plain that it seems difficult to-day to understand why the world had to wait until 1900 before a bold psychologist could discover this light for souls that have strayed from the path. Even more incomprehensible was the resistance of the dullards to the revelation, once it had been vouchsafed. Who of us is there who does not know sons embroiled with their fathers and over-tender towards their mothers ? Consider, again, many a grown-up daughter of your acquaintance who is proud at being taken for her father's wife. How plainly is love for the father disclosed by the jealous hatred of the daughter for the stepmother when the widowed father remarries. Careful researches have shown that actual incest, sexual intercourse between persons within the prohibited degrees, is by no means rare. But psychical incest is universal. We are not aware of having experienced this incestuous passion, because we have repressed it from consciousness, have repressed it after severe struggles, which have likewise been forgotten. The idea of incest has become so repugnant to our minds that the mere formulation of the doctrine of the Oedipus complex arouses indignation. Yet from whom is the child to gain its experience of tenderness if not from the parents? As the child grows older, restrictions are imposed by the canons of our civilisation, and these feelings of affection must be detached from the parents and must find other objects. One who fails to effect this detachment will have the under hand in the struggle of life, and will sail back before the wind into the realm of childhood. The Oedipus complex is, therefore, the nuclear complex of the neuroses; and every one of the conflicts of life revives in the neurotic " the intolerable pain of the old wounds." The soldier on a stricken field, wounded to death, and gasping out his life with the cry, " Mother, Mother," teaches us this. " With the progress of psychoanalysis, the importance of the Oedipus complex has become ever more firmly established. The recognition of its reality is the shibboleth whereby we may distinguish the supporters of psychoanalysis from its adversaries."[1]

Among the various perversions which are normal to the amatory life of the child, incest would thus appear to be the most terrible. Parents who are too affectionate, expose their children to the danger of experiencing an Oedipus fixation. An only child will be hard put to it to escape neurosis. A child

[1] Drei Abhandlungen, 1922 edition, p. 89.

often suffers severely when a little brother or sister is born, for it no longer occupies the first place in the parents' affection. The family, with its demands and allurements, is apt to be the forcing-house of neurosis. On the other hand, we may often see that orphans are very liable to suffer from neurosis; so are children brought up away from home; so are illegitimate children. Excess of tenderness is harmful; but a lack of sufficient tenderness may be even worse. The outcast sees that others are treated with affection, and grows sick with longing. A German specialist in the diseases of childhood recently declared that children in foundling hospitals and similar places, though well cared for in other respects, often fall ill, and even die, simply from lack of being mothered. He called the illness " Kinderheimkrankheit "—institutional disease.

Nearly twenty years ago, when I first became a member of the Freudian circle, the Oedipus complex was a recent discovery, and occupied a leading place in our minds. We were full of the wonder of it, and we formed a little round table for the discussion of views that were still peculiar to ourselves. The echo from the outer world was not to come for some time yet. We knew that it would come ultimately, though we none of us foresaw the horrors in the form of Oedipus novels and Oedipus dramas which the future held in store. Freud was unlucky enough, when he unravelled the Oedipus complex, to present second-rate writers with a key enabling them, though quite without inspiration, to unlock the recesses of the mind. The misfortune is all the more undeserved inasmuch as Freud himself teaches that the work of the imaginative writer wells up from the unconscious, and is not derived from knowledge acquired from books.

Thus we received Freud's gift, and ploughed with his heifer, each after his own kind. Otto Rank compiled a comprehensive work *Das Inzestmotiv in Dichtung und Sage*, a book of seven hundred pages, which was not published until 1912. I give the titles of some of the chapters: Oedipus, Hamlet, Don Carlos; the Stepmother Theme, Don Carlos, Phædra; the Struggle between Father and Son, The Robbers, The Tantalids; Quarrels in the Younger Generation, Cain, Die Ahnfrau, Atreus and Thyestes. These selections will give some notion of the multifarious contents.

The physicians of the round table conducted analyses. Following Freud's example, they referred all neuroses to the Oedipus complex in one or other of its two forms, the father complex and the mother complex. " Du siehst mit diesem Trank im Leibe bald Helena in jedem Weibe." [1]

The analysts of that day have been charged with being excessively monotonous. The analyses lasted a very long time, and they all led to the same conclusion. The critics were amused. " Would it not be better," they said, " to make it plain at the very first consultation that the patient has committed incest with his mother and has tried to poison his father ? " But surely it was our duty to work the soil thoroughly with this new tool ! Not a grain of the new truth must fall on barren ground.

Freud subsequently described another motif, which

---

[1] Faust, I, 2603-4.
As soon as you have drunk this philtre, every woman will seem to you a Helen.

plays its part in individual development before the Oedipus complex arises. The little boy (and doubtless the little girl as well) sees in the great, strict, powerful father—wearing sombre clothing, speaking with a deep voice, and appearing in the nursery only at long intervals—an ideal. The father is godlike, the object of an unconditional respect; the child wishes and endeavours to be like the father. Thus the boy loves the father before he comes to have any reason for hating the father. We see our little ones play at being father, see them knit their brows and speak commandingly in something which is as near as they can get to a bass voice. The root of the religious sentiment is to be found in this attitude towards the father. When the reasoning faculty begins to develop, the actual father becomes inadequate as an ideal, and his omnipotence is therefore projected into the skies. The only way of introducing the idea of God into the mind of a child is to talk of a father in heaven.

When, in the next phase of development, the little boy comes to look upon his father as a rival, his tendency is to incorporate into his idea of himself the lofty qualities which he has imagined his father to possess. The psychological situation thus becomes obscure and complicated. At first the boy identifies himself with his father from affection; then he identifies himself with the father in order that he may be able to take the father's place with the mother.

Furthermore, the mother, first loved as the one who gives suck, now becomes the one whom the child holds responsible for its first experience of painful deprivation—that of weaning. Again, the mother is the first person to take in hand the education of the child, and education involves the renunciation of a great many pleasures; this tends to arouse feelings of hatred towards the mother. The Oedipus complex, which was simple, becomes extremely intricate.

These relationships are most obscure, and Stekel goes so far as to declare that hatred is older than love. But the easiest way of throwing light on the matter is to suppose that here, as elsewhere, the bipolarity of the feelings plays its part. Towards both its parents, a child feels hatred as well as love, and in every child these four sentiments are variously mingled according as individual inheritance and individual experience may vary.

It grows ever plainer that identification is one of the main characteristics of love. Identification is also one of the main characteristics of hatred. There are dreams of a return to the mother's womb. The opponents of psychoanalysis make fun of these dreams, but to ourselves they are an ever-renewed occasion for wonder. Imaginatively, the dreamer reenters the mother, thinks of himself as arising out of her, becomes of one flesh with her. There are also dreams of return to the father, and their discoverer speaks of these as " spermatozoa dreams." The name is badly chosen, for it makes too strong an appeal to the sense of the ridiculous.

It is Freud's way, after he has made an amazing assertion, to call a halt to himself, that he may consider how the critics will take it. He mitigates the hostility of his readers by confessing that he is himself very much surprised, and that he has objections to make. Among Freud's pupils, there is often a lack of such self-criticism. In this dark domain, the analysts of the second generation tread overconfidently, in a way which arouses the onlooker's mistrust. I, too, call a halt.

"This is monstrous!" exclaim the child-lovers. "What you say has a grain of truth in it, but you exaggerate grossly. You caricature. You make changelings and monsters of our children."

There is good reason for the protest. In normal children all these relationships and complexes are but lightly sketched; they are overcome without producing manifest injury; and they play no part in subsequent life. In other instances, however, the complexes of childhood, which have been apparently outgrown, become active once more. This happens when the life sustains such shocks that the soul, in alarm, seeks refuge in the unconscious—in the forgotten days of early childhood. In some, again, the sexual life of childhood is of such a character that it cannot fail to eventuate in neurosis.

Where a good many analysts display bias is in this, that they ignore the actual shocks, and are wholly concerned with disinterring the complexes of childhood. An untoward love affair, or any other grave deprivation, may induce a neurosis; and, when this happens, the neurosis will always exhibit some of the elementary characteristics of the amatory life of the child. It is our task to throw light upon the proximate determining cause of the neurosis, upon the actual deprivation. Freud's more immediate followers are apt to turn aside from this task. Their interest is concentrated on the Oedipus complex; of late, also, on the castration complex (see below); for a time, they were keenly interested in the narcissism of childhood. They make exhaustive analyses to learn what happened thirty years ago and more; but they do not learn, and they do not want to learn, what happened yesterday or the day before. That is why they often fail to secure good results. If a man is impotent because, in the unconscious, he detests his wife, we shall not help him much by convincing him that, long years ago, he was in love with his mother. He believes that he is devoted to his wife; he loads her with presents; he fancies he could not live without her. The analyst's " cruel " duty is to drag him out of his " heaven."

When Freud was blamed for disregarding the extant, the actual, he replied that the critics were asking him to do what he and Breuer had done in former days, and had given up.[1] But in 1895, when he was still working with Breuer, Freud did not yet know that the actual solutions can, in many instances, be supplied to the patient only by making a detour leading through the experience of childhood. The extant morbific conflict is not disclosed until the materials dating from childhood have been exhumed from the unconscious. Often enough, the nature of the actual conflict speedily becomes apparent, but this conflict continues to exercise a noxious influence until it has been detached from its anchorage in the primary complexes.

Before Freud appeared on the stage, the scientific explanation of neurosis was that it was all due to heredity and degeneration. The influence of heredity is undeniable, but the admission of this fact does not help us to cure our patient. He has his heritage, and we cannot alter it. But we have to bear in mind

[1] Sammlung, vol. iv, pp. 4 and 73.

that qualities which have been acquired early in life get such a grip on the character that they may easily simulate the results of inheritance. For example, there is no proof whatever that religious trends are inborn. Religion and the conscience are instilled into the child mind at so early a date, and they are so intimately amalgamated with the most primal father complex, that they seem to be congenital.

There are good grounds for Freud's contention that all deviations from the mental norm are due to disturbances in the evolution of the sexual life of childhood. That is the explanation, not only of qualities which are defects from the social point of view, such as those which manifest themselves in the form of the neuroses and the perversions, but also of the artistic faculty and of genius in all its varieties. The fundamental cause of neurosis is supposed to be a premature and unduly vigorous development of the impulsive life (precocity). We may doubt whether debility of the impulsive life can ever induce neurosis. The weakness of the impulsive life displayed by neurotics is, in most cases at any rate, merely the sequel of a premature and excessive manifestation of instinctive activity. Such precocity is often artificially induced, especially in great towns, and when the teachers are themselves hysterically inclined. Unwise or vicious manifestations of tenderness on the part of elders will foment the budding impulses. When the parents are hysterical, the child they rear can hardly escape neurosis, and the observer is apt to say that the illness is hereditary. It would be more correct to speak of it as contagious. No doubt, precocity of the instinctive life can be inherited, but we shall be wise to pay a great deal more attention to environment than to inheritance.

The poor little wretch with unduly active impulses will speedily come into conflict with environment. Such a child will always be wanting to do things that are forbidden, and things that are beyond a child's powers. Here we encounter the inferiority complex. The sense of impotence is morbific.

Freud's collaborators offered two ideas to round off the circle of Freudian doctrine. After considerable hesitation, he accepted the idea of bisexuality. Alfred Adler's contribution was the idea of inferiority struggling against overmastering forces. Freud could not digest this notion, and it has, therefore, continued to play the part of a foreign body in the wheelwork of the Freudian mechanisms. We shall see that much of what Freud has written since 1905 must be regarded as the expression of a defensive campaign against Adler and Adler's leading idea.

We have learned that, to begin with, Freud was hostile to the notion of bisexuality. Even to-day, I fancy, his mind is not free from a secret antagonism towards the notion. In 1907, Sadger maintained that all hysterical symptoms, and, indeed, all fantasies and dreams, were bisexual—that they all had a homosexual as well as a heterosexual root in the unconscious. The following year, Freud conceded a point, agreeing that the statement applied to a good many symptoms; but he refused to admit the universal validity of the principle.[1] At this period he would still, at times, make fun of bisexuality, and warn us against accepting it with too much

---

[1] Sammlung, vol. ii, No. 5.

enthusiasm. In a note added to the later editions of the *Drei Abhandlungen* (p. 82), Freud speaks of the terms " masculine and feminine " as lacking in clarity, and declares that if psychoanalysts use them, it must only be in the signification of active and passive. This is an attempt to explode the notion of bisexuality. On the same page he declares that the libido is always masculine. If that only means that it is active, he is not telling us very much. The libido is an impulse, and every impulse is active ; it impels.

It is true that on the next page (p. 83) we find the passage : " Since I have become acquainted with the outlook of bisexuality, I have come to regard this factor as predominant here. I consider that the actually observed sexual manifestation of man and woman is hardly comprehensible unless we take bisexuality into account." But to this is appended the before-mentioned note that, for psychoanalysts, masculine and feminine can signify nothing more than active and passive. One cannot but ask, " Why so much fuss, then ! "

I am myself disinclined to lay great stress upon this notion of bisexuality. I agree, however, that on the platform where we cooperate with our patients, the idea of bisexuality is a good working hypothesis. The pregenital form of sexuality, that characterised by autoerotism and pansexualism, knows nothing as yet of the distinction between the sexes. In its origin, therefore, sexuality is not bisexual. Freud teaches that the sexual impulses can be transmuted into the highest achievements of mankind. To denote this process, he uses a word which is also found in Nietzsche's writings, and speaks of " sublimation " of the libido. Now this sublimation, likewise, knows nothing, or knows very little, of sex distinctions. But if the sexual impulse is not bisexual either in its initial or in its terminal stage, we cannot regard bisexuality as one of its essential characteristics. I look upon bisexuality as nothing more than one expression of the higher law of bipolarity, which will be fully considered in due course.

When I was in Asia, in the huge continent where much has remained unchanged since the days of Abraham, and when I contrasted the infinity of Asia both in respect of time and space with our hustled Europe, the continent of petty subdivisions, I had a strong impression that Asia was feminine.

Night is feminine when compared with day, in which the sun rises and sets.

Ecstasy is feminine, and the dream is masculine.

Such comparisons and such contrasts lie ready to our hand; they are an ornament to the work of the poets, but they are dangerous in science. Everything is bipolar. Sometimes we stand near one pole, and at other times near the other. These criticisms concern the theoretical validity of the notion of bisexuality. As a working hypothesis, I use it myself every day, like other analysts.

Freud's illustrious forerunner, the divine Plato, ignored the distinction between the sexes. For him, in the last analysis, love was love of the beautiful. Freud tells us that sexual impulses can be sublimated. This means that they can be desexualised for spiritual ends, for the ends we denote by the names of art, science, and religion; and, on a somewhat less lofty plane, for such ends as craftsmanship, professional work, politics, all that we know as culture. There can be no talk of sexual distinctions within such sublimations. In them, there is neither sexuality nor bisexuality. No modern reader of Plato's *Symposium* or of his *Phædrus* can fail to be struck by the way in which the author refers only to love felt for young men, as if there were no heterosexual love, or as if the latter were a debased sentiment and unworthy of a philosopher's attention. When, to-day, we contemplate the libido in the light thrown on it by Freud, when we study its beginnings in the autoerotic child and contemplate its end in the lofty altitudes of sublimation, we achieve the rebirth of the classical thought that Eros has no sex. The animal nature within us makes us force him beneath the yoke of the sexual, but his divine nature makes him aspire heavenward and strive to free himself from the sexual. Provisionally, and obscurely, let me formulate the following proposition: The libido frees itself from sexuality by way of bisexuality (see below, p. 256). I believe that Freud is drawing nearer to this conception, and I am still looking forward to the book in which he will transcend us all by classical limpidity, and will give us imagery as beautiful as that of the Platonic simile of the two-in-hand:

" Of the nature of the soul, though her true form be ever a theme of large and more than mortal discourse, let me speak briefly, and in a figure. And let the figure be composite—a pair of winged horses and a charioteer. Now the winged horses and the charioteers of the gods are all of them noble and of noble descent, but those of other races are mixed; the human charioteer drives his in a pair; and one of them is noble and of noble breed, and the other is ignoble and of ignoble breed; and the driving of them of necessity gives a great deal of trouble to him." [1]

As late as 1914, Freud dismissed this idea of the two-in-hand contemptuously, writing of the Zurich School of psychoanalysts : " They have been able to hear one or two of the cultural overtones in the symphony of world happenings, but they are deaf to the elemental melody of the instinctive life." In 1923 he writes in a different strain : " Now that we can venture to analyse the ego, we shall be able to answer those whose moral sense has been outraged by our doctrines, those who insist that there must be a higher nature in man. ' Certainly,' we shall reply, ' and this is the higher nature, this ego-ideal or super-ego, which represents our parental relationship. As little children, we knew this higher nature, admired it, and dreaded it ; subsequently, we incorporated it into ourselves.' "

I think that even Plato would have been satisfied by this admission. Through procreation and birth, we are indebted to our parents for the fleshly elements in our composition ; and through the impression that, in the very beginning of our days, they make on our budding minds, we are indebted to them for the spiritual elements. Thus Plato's two horses are not coeval, but they both derive from the same source ; they both come from our parents. I have already had occasion to point out how difficult it is to distinguish between inherited qualities, and qualities that are early acquired.

[1] Plato, Phædrus, 246.—The English version in the text is quoted from Benjamin Jowett, The Dialogues of Plato, translated into English, Clarendon Press, Oxford, third edition, 1892, vol. i, p. 452.

CHAPTER NINE

FREUD'S PERSONAL CHARACTERISTICS

THE first time I saw Freud, he was lecturing, the lecture being one of a series delivered on Saturday evenings from seven till nine. He was hard on fifty years of age, but still looked young and vigorous. The audience was scanty, barely sufficing to fill the first three rows. He has not given any lectures for several years now. Should he again wish to do so, he would have to take a very large hall.

His black hair, slightly grizzled, was smooth and was parted on the left side. His beard was small, and was trimmed to a point. Many celebrities have large and piercing eyes, but Freud is an exception. Freud's eyes are dark brown and lustrous; they have a scrutinising expression as they look up at one. He is slender, of medium height, brisk in his movements; but his figure was already bowed when I first knew him. He had the student's stoop.

He spoke without notes for nearly two hours, and his hearers were enthralled. A later course than that of which I have been speaking was taken down in shorthand and subsequently published.[1] His method of exposition was that of the German humanist, lightened by a conversational tone which

---

[1] 1915–1917. Vorlesungen, etc., see Bibliography.

he had probably acquired in Paris. No pomposity and no mannerisms. There was a certain contrast between matter and style. Amiably, almost enticingly, he dealt with the representatives of traditional psychology, reminding us of the way in which Hauff's Satan genially appeals to his victim Hasentreffer with the words : " Come along over here ; it doesn't hurt a bit ! " On one occasion, when he was speaking of Wundt, Freud referred to the incident in Ariosto's *Orlando Furioso*, when a giant, in the heat of battle, has his head smitten off. But the giant is too busy to notice it, and goes on fighting. Wundt refused to admit the existence of the unconscious, although the interpretation of dreams had proved its reality. " We cannot help thinking," said Freud, " that the old psychology has been killed by my dream doctrine ; but the old psychology is quite unaware of the fact, and goes on teaching as usual."

Freud was fond of using the Socratic method. He would break off his formal exposition to ask questions or invite criticism. When objections were forthcoming, he would deal with them wittily and forcibly.

After the lecture, which was delivered in the old psychiatric clinic of the General Hospital, we used to accompany Freud in triumph through the courtyards as far as the Alser Strasse. There, he usually took a cab to his home, where he would play a game of cards. On the way from the lecture hall to the street we always made ourselves as conspicuous as possible. Freud was generally in a cheerful mood. The *Drei Abhandlungen* and the *Bruchstück einer Hysterieanalyse* had recently been published. We knew these books by heart, including all the footnotes ; we fully understood their significance, and we were as proud of ourselves as the pupils of Aristotle in the days before that philosopher's works had become widely known.

Freud once said that all his teaching was at everyone's disposal. This implied, not only that he showered upon us the gifts of his genius, but that it was a matter of indifference to him if others used these gifts without acknowledgment. At that time I could not understand his utterance. Was he then so rich? Or did he think himself perfectly secure, did he feel that he could apply to himself what the ancients applied to Homer when they said: "People are more likely to steal Hercules' club than to rob Homer of a single verse"? In actual fact, I was able to observe in subsequent years that many of Freud's pupils would publish works without adequately acknowledging that the ideas in them were Freud's. In instance I may mention *Die Bedeutung des Vaters für das Schicksal des Einzelnen*, by C. G. Jung; and *Das Problem des Hamlet und der Oedipuskomplex*, by Ernest Jones. Freud delighted in these studies. He had driven an adit deep into the mental life, and he needed collaborators who would line the walls of the tunnel with glazed bricks.

Others are, then, entitled to use Freud's ideas. He is so much opposed to his pupils coining independent ideas that he prefers to give them a superfluity from his own mint. One of these faithful disciples who has been in Freud's good graces for decades has a stereotyped answer to the question why Freud's pupils do not develop the master's teaching: "He has led the way everywhere; there is nothing left for us to discover." The orthodox

Freudians have all succumbed to this hypnotic influence.

In the year 1903 Freud founded a circle. Its members used to meet every Wednesday evening. It ultimately developed into the Viennese Psychoanalytical Society and gave birth to the daughter societies elsewhere. Its first members were Wilhelm Stekel, Alfred Adler, Max Kahane, and Rudolf Reitler. Kahane and Reitler are both dead. Neither of them made any notable contributions to psychoanalysis.

Kahane had been an intimate of Freud's early days. He translated Charcot's and Janet's lectures into German. About fifteen years before his death a breach occurred between him and Freud.

Since 1912, Stekel has been regarded by Freud with disfavour, but in earlier years his journalistic gifts had enabled him to do much towards making Freud's theories widely known in Vienna and throughout Germany. His panegyrics were continually appearing in the daily press. No doubt Freud would eventually have made good without the aid of such propaganda, but Stekel's services were none the less considerable at a time when courage was needed by those who proclaimed themselves psychoanalysts.

Adler quitted the Freudian circle in 1911, owing to differences of opinion on scientific matters. To-day, therefore, none of those who were wont to attend the Wednesday meetings are to be found in the orthodox Freudian group.

The circle founded in 1903 was soon joined by Paul Federn, Eduard Hitschmann, M. Steiner, and Isidor Sadger. Besides these regular attendants, there were a number of occasional visitors such as

PERSONAL CHARACTERISTICS   133

Friedjung, the specialist in diseases of childhood, Max Graf and David J. Bach the musical critics, and Hugo Heller, the bookseller. When I joined the circle, Otto Rank was already a member of it. He was then a very young man, without university training, who had attracted Freud's notice by his book *Der Künstler*. To-day he is a doctor of philosophy and Freud's Eckermann.[1] Rank has had quite exceptional opportunities for conversations with Freud, and it is to be hoped that he has kept careful notes.

We foregathered in Freud's waiting room, and sat round a long table. The door leading into the study was open, and through the doorway we had a glimpse of walls lined with well-filled bookshelves. Freud is a collector of antiques. In the waiting room there was a large Etruscan vase. On his desk are numerous statuettes, Egyptian for the most part. Everything in the house seemed important to us. The couch, and the arm-chair behind it, were the arena of Freud's Nibelungen labours. For us each article was laden with symbolism from the neurotic brains which had transferred their cobwebs to them.

Freud took the chair. We had all supped before coming, but at Freud's we were refreshed with black coffee and cigars. The chairman smoked like a furnace. Proceedings usually began with the reading of a paper, which did not necessarily bear strictly on psychoanalysis. Discussion followed, and all were expected to participate. The order in which we spoke during the discussion was decided by lot; Rank, who acted as secretary, arranged the drawing of the lots. The impression in my mind to-day is that Freud always

---

[1] An Englishman would have written " Freud's Boswell." Eckermann was Goethe's Boswell.—E. and C. P.

spoke last. It is quite possible, however, that this is an illusion of memory, and that I merely ceased to attend after Freud had spoken. Roma locuta causa finita!

The evenings were sometimes rather dull. Freud's design in the promotion of these gatherings was to have his own thoughts passed through the filter of other trained intelligences. It did not matter if the intelligences were mediocre. Indeed, he had little desire that these associates should be persons of strong individuality, that they should be critical and ambitious collaborators. The realm of psychoanalysis was his idea and his will, and he welcomed anyone who accepted his views. What he wanted was to look into a kaleidoscope lined with mirrors that would multiply the images he introduced into it.

Especially enjoyable were the evenings on which Freud presented his own work in the nascent state. Here is a list of four of the most notable papers of the kind: (1) A Memory of Leonardo da Vinci's Childhood; (2) Delusion and Dream in W. Jensen's Gradiva; (3) Analysis of the Phobia of a five-year-old Boy; (4) A Case of obsessional Neurosis.

In this circle of intimates, Freud's method was far more audacious than it was in a public lecture. He would begin by enunciating his main contentions categorically, so that they were apt to repel; then he would provide such a wealth of argument in support of them that his hearers could hardly fail to be convinced of their truth. Those who know Freud only through the written word will be far more ready to differ from him than were those who listened to the magic of his speech. Not that he is an orator, for he rarely raises his voice. Nevertheless, he is a Sieg-

PERSONAL CHARACTERISTICS

mund.[1] He fascinates; overthrows his adversaries. Personally, I find his later writings less admirable than I found the earlier ones. But I am perfectly willing to admit that they are no less excellent, and that the reason why they please me less is that I have to read them in cold print, whereas before I used to learn from Freud's living speech.

As early as 1906, Freud secured extensive recognition in other lands. From Hungary came the support of S. Ferenczi of Budapesth. He has proved an extremely able psychoanalyst, and is one of Freud's personal intimates. What especially impressed us was the respect for Freud and his theories displayed by the psychiatrists of Zurich. Bleuler, the head of the psychiatric clinic in that city, became an enthusiast for psychoanalysis; so did C. G. Jung and some of the other assistants at the clinic (Maeder, Riklin, Abraham, and Eitington). Even a pastor of Zurich, Oskar Pfister, espoused our cause. This international attention consoled us for the silence of Vienna. Freud ceased to trouble about local recognition, and entered into lively correspondence with the Swiss psychoanalysts. Thus the first clinic for the use of the new explosives was founded in Switzerland. In the spring of 1908, the international supporters of the Freudian doctrine met in Salzburg for the first Psychoanalytical Congress. Among those who attended were adherents from Geneva, London, and the United States.

I have never seen a more remarkable triumph

[1] In the spelling of Freud's first name the " e " of " Siegmund " has been dropped. Wittels restores it here. Siegmund was the victorious hero of the ancient saga. There is also a word-play. " Siegmund " is conceived as meaning " victorious-mouth."—E. and C. P.

than that secured by Freud at this congress. The Swiss, who are cautious folk, had a good many objections to raise; but Freud carried the critics off their feet by the impetus and the clearness of his utterances. It seemed to him that through the growth of the Zurich School his teachings would be given a footing in the domain of general science, and he had no foreboding of future disappointments. Freud's Viennese pupils, too, made a good showing at the congress. Sadger was able to report the first case in which a homosexual had been cured by psycho-analysis. Stekel delivered an address on anxiety states.

The ties that were formed with the Swiss psychiatrists were peculiarly fruitful in that at Zurich a start was made in the treatment of mental disorders by the new method. "The content of the psychosis" was now seriously considered, whereas previously it had been regarded as altogether unmeaning, and as, therefore, outside the domain of science. Freud had had no access to psychiatric material. At Burghölzli, near Zurich, it was now possible, with the aid of psychoanalysis, to win an entirely new understanding as to the nature of schizophrenia, paranoia, and melancholia. Nevertheless, the founder of psychoanalysis, in his essay *Trauer und Melancholia*,[1] and in the remarkable papers on The Paranoia of Schreber, the President of the Senate,[2] was able to open new vistas in the province of mental disorders—vistas which others had never glimpsed, despite access to far more extensive material.

In the autumn of 1909, Freud, accompanied by Jung, went to the United States, to lecture on psychoanalysis at the University of Worcester. Ferenczi

---

[1] Sammlung, iv, 20.   [2] Ibid., iii, 3 and 4.

travelled with them. When the party returned, we all had the impression that Freud had been somewhat disappointed by his American journey. The founder of psychoanalysis (which was growing more complicated day by day) was uneasy. He foresaw the coming storm, the " Freud craze " which rages to-day, not only in the States, but in all English-speaking lands. He also realised that those who became affected with this craze would preserve little more of his life's work than the name and the most elementary connexions. Freud has been repeatedly urged to revisit the States. He could now go there as a man with a world-wide reputation, but he persistently refuses. An intimate of his assures me that Freud's reason for declining is that the American diet did not agree with his digestion, which is permanently the worse for his trip to the States. I do not believe that the real explanation is of so trivial an order. I fancy that Freud dislikes being hopelessly misunderstood, and that he is too sincere to endure fulsome praise from persons who completely misunderstand him.

I do not actually know what Freud, Jung, and Ferenczi talked about on the homeward voyage, but I think there is good reason to suppose that they discussed the need for a strict organisation of the psychoanalytical movement. Henceforward, Freud no longer treated psychoanalysis as a branch of pure science. The politics of psychoanalysis had begun. The three travellers took vows of mutual fidelity, agreeing to join forces in the defence of the doctrine against all danger. One of these dangers was that with which every scientific doctrine is threatened as soon as it becomes popular—the danger of vulgarisation and misunderstanding. Another risk seemed especially imminent to Jung, who was afraid of the trend of some of Freud's Viennese disciples, was afraid of the Viennese far-fetched interpretations. When Jung spoke of the Viennese disciples, he would be thinking primarily of Adler and Stekel, but secondarily of Sadger and the rest. It is probable that the Swiss were not entirely free from race prejudice. Freud, though he must have known the whole-souled devotion of his Viennese disciples, was at this time markedly drawn to Jung. His face beamed whenever he spoke of Jung: " This is my beloved son, in whom I am well pleased ! "

At this period it was my privilege during the greater part of a year to watch Freud at work, for I was present when he was analysing a case of dementia præcox. It was because the patient was a dement, because her perceptions were so greatly dulled, that Freud could allow me to be there. But for the very same reason, I did not profit as much by this great opportunity as might have been expected. The treatment was not particularly successful. What I did gain was the advantage of studying the penetration with which Freud scanned the mind of the patient in the persistent hope that he would be able to lighten her darkness.

In the spring of 1910 the second Psychoanalytical Congress took place. My memories of this Nuremberg congress are less congenial than those of the Salzburg congress. The results of the recent excogitations of Freud, Jung, and Ferenczi now became manifest. Ferenczi proposed the foundation of an International Psychoanalytical Association. Jung was to be its perpetual president, with absolute power

PERSONAL CHARACTERISTICS 139

to appoint and depose analysts. All the scientific writings of the members of the Association were to be submitted to him for approval before publication. The responsibility for the further development of psychoanalysis was to be taken out of the hands of Freud, the founder, and was to be entrusted to those of Jung.

It can readily be imagined that the unsuspecting Viennese ("We had no anticipation of such an onslaught") were utterly dismayed by these proposals. I doubt if powers so absolute have ever been entrusted to any one except the heads of certain Roman Catholic orders. A young and rapidly developing branch of science was to be placed under the rule of a youthful recruit. It ultimately transpired that Jung felt ill at ease in the psychoanalytical family. Subsequently, Freud attempted to explain his course of action on this occasion.[1] Nothing can explain away the fact that the politics of psychoanalysis began with an attempt at a coup de main, which was, however, frustrated by the prompt and energetic opposition of the Viennese.

Freud behaved like the Old Man of the primitive horde—was simultaneously ruthless and simple-minded. When he perceived that his Viennese pupils were up in arms, and that they were determined to resist Ferenczi's proposal with all their might (this determination was especially conspicuous in the cases of Adler and Stekel, whose interests were more closely touched than those of any of the others), he postponed the vote until the next sitting. The three years' struggle within the psychoanalytical camp had begun, the unedifying struggle that was to end in three great

[1] Sammlung, iv, 1.

secessions. In its essence, it was a struggle for power much more than a dispute about scientific principles. Three, at least, of the protagonists—Freud, Jung, and Adler—had the lust of dominion. Stekel, I fancy, would have been willing to live and let live.

On the afternoon of this memorable day, the Viennese analysts had a private meeting in the Grand Hotel at Nuremberg to discuss the outrageous situation. Of a sudden, Freud, who had not been invited to attend, put in an appearance. Never before had I seen him so greatly excited. He said: "Most of you are Jews, and therefore you are incompetent to win friends for the new teaching. Jews must be content with the modest role of preparing the ground. It is absolutely essential that I should form ties in the world of general science. I am getting on in years, and am weary of being perpetually attacked. We are all in danger." Seizing his coat by the lapels, he said: "They won't even leave me a coat to my back. The Swiss will save us—will save me, and all of you as well."

The Viennese held out. In the end, an International Association with various local groups was founded, and Jung was appointed president of the International Association for two years. Adler and Stekel started a periodical which was to expound their scientific outlook.[1] Freud signed the editorials. This had not been part of Adler's and Stekel's original design.

Already at the Nuremberg congress one of the Swiss analysts took occasion to say that it was a mistake to lay so much stress upon sexuality, for this served merely to provoke opposition. The

[1] "Zentralblatt für Psychoanalyse," 1910–1913.

movement would advance more smoothly if psychoanalysts were a little less blunt in their phraseology. Freud answered acrimoniously. It has ever been his way to dwell with inexorable frankness upon his conviction that sexuality, naked and unashamed, must be made the foundation of the theory of the neuroses. He would have sustained fewer attacks if he had been willing to mince matters now and again. But hear his own words: " From the very first, in psychoanalysis, it has seemed better to speak of these love impulses as sexual impulses. Most ' cultured ' persons have taken offence at this nomenclature, and wreak vengeance on psychoanalysis by stigmatising it as ' pansexualism.' Those who feel that sexuality is something that shames and debases human nature are, of course, at liberty to employ the more distinguished terms ' Eros ' and ' erotic.' I could have employed these terms myself, and had I always used them I should have saved myself a great deal of friction. But I do not like to make concessions to weakness. I never know where they will end. We may yield, first, where words are concerned, and pass by degrees to the sacrifice of more important matters. I do not see what we shall gain by being ashamed of sexuality. The Greek word Eros, which is to spare our blushes, is merely the equivalent of the word love. He who can afford to wait, need make no concessions."[1]

Freud had come back from Salzburg in a thoroughly cheerful mood. After Nuremberg he was less easy in his mind, for his conscience pricked him on account of the way in which he had treated his Viennese

---

[1] Massenpsychologie und Ich-Analyse, 1921.—The style of this book is fascinating in its brilliancy.

disciples. It is true that these latter could not be described as a happy family. They fell foul of one another at their Wednesday gatherings, and fiercely contested one another's claims to have done the best service on behalf of psychoanalysis. At this juncture, Freud, saying that his waiting room was too small, had the sittings removed to one of the halls of the Viennese Medical Society. Here the atmosphere was chill and uncongenial—the personal touch was lacking. New members joined our circle. One of these, the late Viktor Tausk, was an extremely argumentative person. During the summer of that year I resigned from the Psychoanalytical Society.

The body continues to meet every Wednesday. It has long since acquired quarters of its own, issues two periodicals, has given birth to a number of daughter societies, has established a psychoanalytical clinic in Vienna, and has inaugurated a psychoanalytical publishing house. I am told that there is still a good deal of bickering at the meetings of the Society, and it is reported that Freud recently remarked: " The study of psychoanalysis seems to awaken people's worst instincts ! " I venture to demur. The trouble arises from the suppression of free criticism within the Society. Suppression makes people snappish.

The members have metapsychological leanings, and I am afraid they are inclined to stray into scholastic paths. A simple student of natural science finds it hard to follow them here. Indeed, the game would hardly be worth the candle. Freud is treated as a demigod, or even as a god. No criticism of his utterances is permitted. Sadger tells us that Freud's *Drei Abhandlungen zur Sexualtheorie* is the psychoanalyst's Bible. This is no mere figure of speech. The faithful disciples regard one another's books as of no account. They recognise no authority but Freud's; they rarely read or quote one another. When they quote it is from the Master, that they may give the pure milk of the word. The medical element has passed into the background. The philosophers hold sway.

Monroe Meyer, an American, came to Vienna to study psychoanalysis under Freud. He published the following dream, presumably his own: " I am in the act of eating a beefsteak. I put too large a piece into my mouth, and am in danger of being choked. I thrust my fingers into my mouth, and pull out the piece of meat." This dream recurred six times during the night. There were intermediate fragments of dream, in which the dreamer was laughed at by two waiters because he could not swallow the piece of steak. Then he found himself attending a lecture. Some of his colleagues among the audience were talking across him, " using a primitive language, perhaps Hungarian." He complained to the lecturer that this chatter among the audience made it impossible for him to hear the lecture, and he begged the lecturer to intervene. Thereupon the two students who had been talking began to pinch him and to strike him.

Here are the associations with daily happenings. The dreamer was having analytical sittings with Freud six times every week, but it had now been arranged that he was to have five sittings only. The sixfold repetition of the dream expresses the desire to go on having six sittings. Meyer's interpretation runs: " The dream represents a pregnancy and parturition fantasy, and depicts a feminine attitude towards the father accompanied by jealousy of the mother."

Stekel comments as follows: " I will not dispute my colleague's interpretation, but the intermediate fragments of the dream point in another direction. It seems to me that the beefsteak represents the indigestible analysis. My unfortunate colleague is compelled six times every week to swallow a wisdom which threatens to stifle him. The dream is the way in which his internal resistance to the analysis secures expression. . . . Psychoanalysis is to him a foreign language, and he feels himself misused by the master's two advanced assistants (waiters)." [1]

Stekel's interpretation, which seems convincing, should serve as a warning. Persons without medical qualification treat patients in the name of Freud. This is monstrous, for the most profound of philosophers is incompetent, if without medical training, to distinguish cancer or tuberculosis from nervous disease. In the hands of scholastics and talmudists, psychoanalysis becomes so incomprehensible that it is lost to natural science. The domain will soon have to be reconquered.[2]

[1] " Medizinische Klinik," 1923, No. 11.

[2] There is a remarkably close resemblance between the schisms of the psychoanalytical schools and those of the Christian sectaries. It is well known that civil wars raged among the Christians over a single letter of the alphabet—the homoousian and the homoiousian controversy. In like manner, there is a fierce struggle between those who write " psychoanalysis " and those who write " psychanalysis." Philological considerations would certainly lead us to prefer the shorter form. The founder considers that the use of the " o " makes the word more euphonious, and its use is incumbent on all the faithful. Stekel writes " psychanalysis." Bleuler and Pfister, who dropped the " o " for a time, have both been won back to " psychoanalysis."

CHAPTER TEN

ALFRED ADLER

ADLER was one of the ablest of Freud's pupils.[1] He had but one notable weakness; he could not analyse. He found it difficult to discover the phenomena of the unconscious mental life. It was, in many cases, easy to amend his dream interpretations; in his study of his patients he could seldom find his way into regions which Freud and most of Freud's other pupils could enter without difficulty. I do not think that Adler lacked talent. His inability was the expression of a lack of desire.

Adler's mind was dominated by a single idea, one which seemed to him of supreme importance, one whose development has continued to monopolise his attention. This idea was derived from Nietzsche, who spoke of the will-to-power. What do human beings desire? What do all living creatures desire? Power! What distresses them more than anything else? Weakness! Inferiority! One who is conscious of inferiority, driven by his lust of power, will passionately endeavour to excel, in order to relieve the intolerable sense of inferiority. By building up a psychical superstructure, Demosthenes the stammerer

---

[1] The following are Adler's principal writings: Ueber den nervösen Charakter; Das Problem der Homosexualität; Praxis und Theorie der Individualpsychologie.

becomes an orator; the myope becomes a painter; the paralytic becomes a Stilicho or a Torstensson. If the victory is secured, the inferiority is compensated, and more than compensated, by the psychical superstructure. Superiority has grown out of inferiority. The two generals I have named, both paralytics, were renowned, and dreaded, for the speed of their marches.

Sometimes, however, one who suffers from a sense of inferiority despairs of victory. In that case he will take refuge in illness; just as one who wishes to have nothing more to do with the world becomes a monk, takes refuge in a cloister. Such a flight into illness usually brings with it the advantage that the neurotic patient is able to tyrannise over his environment. He forces the members of his immediate circle to pay him attention, show him sympathy, spend money on him. Wrapped in his illness, he becomes a person of far more importance than he ever was in the days of health.

Adler (himself a short and stumpy man!) hurled this group of systematised ideas into the intricate network of the Freudian mechanisms. I can still picture him at the round table, his eternal Virginia [1] between his lips, talking always in the Viennese dialect, and perpetually returning to his idea of "the inferiority of the organs." It was obvious that he harboured some deep design. He expressed himself cautiously: "Our science is still in its initial stages." ... "In the present state of our knowledge we cannot go quite so far as . . ." "At any rate, I should not myself presume . . ."

[1] In Austria, a particular sort of long, thin cigar is known as a "Virginia."—E. and C. P.

ALFRED ADLER

Thus he prowled, as a cat prowls around a bowl of cream. A struggle was going on within him. It was not a struggle for knowledge, seeing that he had his ideas ready finished in his mind. It was a struggle for the courage to bear testimony when he knew that this could not fail to lead to a breach between himself and Freud. It is no small matter to break with such a man as Freud. One cannot expect to encounter his like again.

According to Adler, the child wants to be a man, and the woman also wants to be a man, because the man is stronger than the woman or the child. Not every man, however, is a real man, and men who feel themselves to be weak would like to become strong. In all weak creatures, therefore, the will-to-power expresses itself in the same fashion, in a way which Adler has rather unhappily named the "masculine protest." The term is unsatisfactory because the protest has nothing to do with the male sex, being just as vigorous in women and children as in men.

Adler considers that all persons must be allowed the greatest possible freedom of action, that they may be spared the need for the masculine protest. Those who hold sway must wear a velvet glove on the iron hand, to conceal the hardness which hurts. These are excellent maxims. The reader will readily understand why Alder was strongly antagonistic to an essay of mine in which I opposed the idea that women should study medicine. Women wanted to become men; let them follow their bent, said Adler. My convictions that women could only be happy as women, as the objects of masculine desire, and that the normal man desired in women gentleness and the feminine form of tenderness, seemed to Adler mere philistinism.

Freud did his utmost to incorporate Adler's master thought into his own teaching. He was ready to acknowledge the existence of ego impulses side by side with the sexual impulses which generate what are usually termed Freudian mechanisms. The ego impulses were to be mainly looked upon as aggressive impulses.

Regarding Adler as ambitious (and probably with good reason), Freud treated him with marked distinction. This offended other members of the circle without being enough to satisfy Adler. After the rumpus in Nuremberg, Freud appointed Adler chief of the Viennese Psychoanalytical Society. But it became ever more obvious that Adler had no interest in the Freudian edifice with its main pillars of repression, resistance, and transference. Freud put the matter as mildly as possible when he said that Adler took far too summary a view of the data of psychoanalysis. In actual fact, Adler repudiated these data. From a subsequent controversial essay of Freud's I may quote an admirable passage, in which the affronted titan displays his marvellous dialectical powers at their best :

" From the first, Adler had no understanding for the theory of repression. In one of our Viennese discussions, he expressed himself as follows : ' If I ask where repression comes from, I am told that it is the outcome of civilisation. But if I ask where civilisation comes from, I am told that it is the outcome of repression. You see that it is nothing more than playing with words.' A very small fraction of the shrewdness Adler has devoted to defending his idea of the neurotic constitution, would have sufficed to show him the way out of this vicious circle. Surely it is reasonable enough to suppose that civilisation is built upon the repressions effected by earlier generations; and that each new generation is required to maintain this civilisation by recapitulating the same repressions. A child once asked: 'Where do eggs come from?' The answer was: 'From hens.' Thereupon the child asked: 'Where do hens come from?' This time the answer ran: 'From eggs.' The child thought its elders were making fun of it, and burst into tears. But there had been no word-play on the part of the elders, who had answered the child's questions quite truthfully. Adler's utterances concerning the dream, 'the shibboleth of psychoanalysis,' are just as futile as the child's tears."[1]

But this was a later judgment. Down to the spring of 1911, Freud did his utmost, and perhaps attempted more than was in his power, in the hope of persuading the most exacting among his creditors to be considerate and patient. I describe Adler as a "creditor" because it is impossible to deny that the sense of inferiority plays a great part, and often the decisive part, both in neurotic patients and in children. Moreover, he was continually pressing his claim with the question, "What about the sense of inferiority?" The conflict between will (the will-to-power) and can (inferiority) is obvious enough. What lies behind it? Adler maintains that it is a primary phenomenon for him. The will-to-power is elemental. Freud, who did not agree, was not then in a position to formulate satisfactorily what he subsequently came to speak of as narcissism and as

[1] The History of the Psychoanalytic Movement, pp. 47–48 (differently worded in that translation).—E. and C. P.

the castration complex. He wanted to gain time, but Adler grew more and more impatient.

I have said more than once that Freud is rarely or never pleased when his collaborators develop independent ideas. This seems to throw a rather unfavourable light on the master's character, and the harshness of our judgment is not sufficiently mitigated by the trite formula that we must not apply the same standards to the great ones of the earth and to lesser mortals. A peculiarity of the Freudian method of searching out the secrets of the human mind is that the observer must be left quite undisturbed. Freud is, indeed, a masterly dialectician, and is fully competent to deal with his adversaries. But he finds it a nuisance when lights other than his own are thrown athwart his path, or when others try to push him forward or to divert him from his chosen course. Whenever necessary he erects outworks to cut off inconvenient cross-lights. But when he has to do this, he feels that he is being made to waste his time, and that in due course he would have provided the necessary lights and would have placed them in the right quarter. Such sentiments in a man of genius account for the irritability which has so often led to the rupture of the personal and scientific ties between Freud and his intimates.

In the spring of 1911, Freud asked Adler to give a connected exposition of his ideas. Adler agreed, and was allotted three of the Wednesday evenings. He was hopeful, for he expected that this formal interchange of views would bring about an enduring peace with Freud. He wanted to convince his teacher. The result belied his hopes. On the fourth evening, the general discussion began. The Freudian adepts made a mass attack on Adler, an attack almost unexampled for its ferocity even in the fiercely contested field of psychoanalytical controversy. I was no longer a member of the circle. Stekel told me that the onslaught produced on his mind the impression of being a concerted one. Freud had a sheaf of notes before him, and with gloomy mien seemed prepared to annihilate his adversary.

The climax of the counter-attack came on the fifth evening, when a member of the Society proposed that Adler should be invited to leave that body, now that he had set himself in irreconcilable opposition to its chief. This was the not altogether creditable way in which Freud finally alienated the most notable among his disciples. Hitherto, Adler had been the favourite—but the Tarpeian Rock is adjacent to the Capitol. Adler's resignation was accompanied by that of nine of his adherents. It should be noted that political influences played a part in these joint resignations. Adler and his nine friends were all socialists.

Adler is not content with counterposing ego impulses and sexual impulses; he goes further, and denies the elemental character of sexuality. His way of putting the matter implies that the signs of the working of the sexual impulse that are manifest in human relationships are symbolical merely. We speak of love, but we mean power. The very act of sexual intercourse is, according to Adler, to be regarded as an expression of the will-to-power. Adler's presumptuous, his incredible, aim is to hurl Eros from the throne.

I have watched Adler at work. He hardly troubles himself to study the patient's unconscious ideas by the method of free associations or by the process of dream interpretation. He is convinced that the neuroses, however multiform their manifestations, have but one object—they are all the expression of an ill-conceived attempt on the patient's part to exalt himself above his fellows. Adler is continually trying to impress this notion on the patient's mind. "You bring your troubles upon yourself in pursuit of self-importance." To a patient whose love for the mother was so obvious that Adler could not deny its existence, he said : "All you want is to show that you are a thoroughly bad lot. You do not even respect your own mother."—Once, when he was treating a young girl who refused food and had become terribly emaciated, he said to me : " Just look at her ! See how she crouches there like a lioness, how she clings to her illness simply because she wants to play the tyrant in her home circle. What a pitiful waste of energy ! " Now with irony, now with kindness, now with severity, he tries to make his patients use their own reason to convict them of absurdity. He says: "Many of those who come to consult me have been undergoing psychoanalytical treatment for years. They know the subject from A to Z : the Oedipus complex, and all the rest of it. But what they have never yet realised is that they find the sense of inferiority intolerable ; and that for this reason they have taken refuge in illness, instead of putting up a fight, and overcoming their feeling of inferiority in some sensible way." On one occasion, when he was in the vein, he summarised his views in popular phraseology, thus : " Do you know how to find the key to all the neuroses ? The real question in the neurotic's mind is : 'How am I going to become top dog?' They are ill in order to spite some one."

Thus it is that this gifted man seems to ignore all the famous achievements of psychoanalysis. He is content with the cheap laurels which can be plucked by "common sense"—the common sense of those who see things as they have always been seen, and refuse a profound understanding that clashes with the trivial understanding of the eternal yesterday. Of course, there is an element of truth in Adler's views. But Adler can only see the uppermost strata of the truth. He refuses to follow Freud when the latter delves beneath the surface. It was a commonplace of neurology, long before the days of Adler, that hysterical patients use their illness as a means of enforcing respect. At this very day, the exponents of official medical science treat hysterical ailments by disregarding them, the aim being to deprive the illness of its motive. What Adler speaks of as the sense of inferiority is almost identical with what Janet speaks of as "Le sentiment d'incomplétude." Adler has seized on this traditional view, and in his book *The Neurotic Constitution*, he expounds it brilliantly, and in a new setting. He incorporates a number of details which had previously been overlooked. Were it not for his monomania, he would have been a notable investigator.

Every analyst is familiar with cases in which, for a considerable time, the progress of the analyses is arrested at the stage where Adler sees the very foundation of the neurosis. The analysis is always a struggle between doctor and patient. In this struggle the patient tries to avoid disclosing his symptoms and their roots, for he is afraid of being forced into the position of one who fights a rearguard action. Among pathogenic experiences, we often find humiliations by various kinds of corporal punishment, and also humiliations due to the patient's own performances having been excelled by brothers and sisters or by schoolfellows. One of my patients made a point of refusing to accept the solutions I propounded, although what I said was convincing to his reason. His expedient was to produce these same solutions a few days later, to enunciate them independently, as if they had been original (cryptomnesia, or submerged memory). I let him have his own way. Several times he admitted that there was nothing so distasteful to him as being forced to accept from me an accurate dream interpretation or some other solution. This aroused an extremely distressing sense of inferiority. The patient's trouble was that he could not endure anyone to exercise authority over him. He always wanted to pose as being the better informed; he had an obsessional urge to pass adverse judgments upon the masterpieces of art; and he described his associates as little better than idiots. Yet, all the time, he suffered from an overwhelming sense of inferiority. Castration complex and narcissism notwithstanding, the analyst finds it hard to treat such a patient—to begin with, at any rate—by any other method than Adler's.

Since his breach with Freud, Adler has done remarkably good work in the field of educational science. He teaches that those who have to deal with difficult children must try to discover the nature of the inferiority complex by which these children are affected. The sufferers must be guided in directions where they will become able to substitute a feeling of superiority for the feeling of inferiority. Adler speaks of his method as "individual psychology," and its main field is the pedagogical. An affectionate deference for the child's individuality justifies the name Adler gives his method.

There are some who believe that Freud might have been able to retain Adler's talents in the service of psychoanalysis. They think that the humiliating expulsion from the Society forced Adler into courses where the significance of sexuality is so utterly ignored. At the outset, they contend, Adler would have been willing to affiliate his doctrine concerning organ inferiority to Freud's doctrine of the erogenic zones.—Freud, as is well known, describes certain zones, such as the mucous membrane of the lips, that of the anus, etc., as subject to a libidinous investment or charge (cathexis). Adler contends that the libidinous investment occurs when the zones are " inferior."

This amalgamation of the notions of " erogenic " and " inferior " is untenable. Some erogenic zones do arise through inferiority. For instance, disturbances of the process of evacuation of the rectum may favour the formation of an erogenic anal zone. There are, however, certain erogenic zones in connexion with which no association of inferiority is demonstrable or even conceivable. Freud emphasises the fact that, among neurotics, those who are markedly afflicted with inferiorities are certainly not in the majority. Good-looking women, and those who are greatly desired, seem especially prone to become the victims of neurosis. On the other hand, " the great majority of ugly, malformed, crippled, and otherwise miserable specimens do not show any disposition to react by the development of neurosis." [1]

[1] The History of the Psychoanalytic Movement, p. 47 (differently worded in that translation).

It is never easy to say what would have happened, if only things had been different. All we can know is what actually has happened. We cannot even be certain why things happened as they did. In this particular instance, if we bear in mind that Adler had resolved from the very first to apply his doctrine of the sense of inferiority to the whole domain of the neurotic constitution (regardless of the fact that this involved straining the theory to an extreme), we can recognise the likelihood that, even had Freud not taken strong measures, Adler would a few years later have found himself just where he is to-day. He would have developed his "individual psychology," the psychology which places the dangerous and "obscene" sexual theory under an interdict, and may therefore be said to represent a psychology "for mature youth." Anyhow, the step whereby Freud put an end to his relationship with Adler had its heroic side, and we cannot refuse it the respect we pay to resolves that are both bold and painful.

The breach occurred just at the time when Freud believed that he had become competent to explain the neurotic's sense of inferiority in accordance with the general terms of the sexual theory. Long ere this he had discovered that the sexual intimidation to which we are exposed in early youth is the fundamental cause of neurosis. The religious authorities threaten children with the fires of hell; the secular authorities often threaten them with amputation of the genital organs; both the religious and the secular tyrants rage like berserkers against youngsters whenever masturbation is in question. Under the influence of Adler's views, Freud had given psychoanalysis a new trend, so that what is spoken of as the castration complex has come to be regarded as the essential root of the feeling of inferiority.

Unfortunately Freud, before he decided to overwhelm and replace Adler's " masculine protest " by other concepts, had availed himself of the so-called ego impulses as a temporary expedient. By degrees this temporary edifice has been demolished by its own builder. But when we compare the classical achievements of Freud prior to 1911 with those of Freud after that critical year, we detect in the latter something crude and unsatisfactory, which I am inclined to ascribe to the influence of the indigestible Adler. For what do we know of the ego? During most of his life Freud was an antimetaphysician. Surely he must have known that in our own Vienna the physicist Mach declared that the ego was beyond saving! Even if the ego be a real entity, why should Freud father the aggressive impulses on the ego, and find a different origin for the sexual impulses? And what are we to do about the moral impulses? Owing to the reliance placed upon this theory of the ego impulses, Freud has had to devote twelve years to a campaign against his own lack of clarity and against the contradictions that have resulted from it. In each successive publication, the problem was stated in new terms; and on each occasion it was made manifest once more that Freud felt ill at ease in the realm of the ego impulses. He has repeatedly declared that he is quite ready to abandon this part of his theory as soon as he can find a better.[1]

Temporary structures, run up in haste as a refuge against criticism, have their inconveniences. They

---

[1] Vorlesungen, Taschenausgabe, p. 445; and Sammlung, vol iv, 1922, pp. 82 et seq.

spoil the view. Adler was not conciliated by this one. On the other hand, Jung's universalisation of the concept of the libido was unacceptable to Freud, who was loath to abandon the idea of the ego impulses. None of these theories are essential to the practice of psychoanalysis. In *Störungen des Trieb- und Affektlebens*, Stekel has shown that this practice can be carried on effectively by persons who do not cumber their minds with the questionable doctrine of the ego impulses or with the theory of the libido.

Freud knows that all which is popularly termed the ego is the outcome of experience. We do not come into the world with an ego. The ego is something which develops, and down to the end of life it remains in a state of flux. Little children speak of themselves in the third person, and develop this person according to the perceptions they make in the outer world. A huge bundle of such perceptions is aggregated by the child to form the idea of its own ego, this happening when the child is able to love the structure termed the ego, the structure imaginatively built from without into the soul (narcissism is this love of the ego). Let me quote from my book *Die sexuelle Not*: " When I was still a little boy, I awoke one morning with the overmastering conviction that I was an 'I.' I knew that to outward appearance I was like other children, but I was confident that I was fundamentally different from them, and enormously more important. I stood in front of the mirror, looked at my image attentively, and addressed it many times by my name. My purpose manifestly was to build a bridge from this image in the outer world to myself, a bridge along which I could penetrate into my unfathomable ego. I do not remember whether I kissed my own image in the mirror, but I have seen other children kiss such images. They come to an accommodation with their ego and show it that they love it."

But if the ego be a construction, an artifact, an unreal product of the imagination, our impulses, on the other hand, are so essentially real that outside of them there is no reality; they alone " work." [1] Whatever the ego may be, the impulses play with it as if it were a toy—as God plays with sun and moon and stars. That is why the notion of the ego impulses and the classification of impulses in terms of their relationship to so empty a notion, is an error which cannot be excused on any ground of convenience. The psychological cause of this error was Alfred Adler, and philosophical levity acted as godfather. Freud frankly owns to this levity:

" I agree that such ideas as that of an ego-libido, an ego-impulsive-energy, etc., are neither easy to grasp nor adequately equipped with content. . . . These ideas are not the essential foundation of the science [psychoanalysis] on which everything rests; the essential foundation, the only foundation, is observation. They are not the substratum but the pinnacles of the edifice, and they can be replaced or removed without injury to the rest of the building." [2]

These utterances of a brilliant amateur philosopher will not satisfy every one.

[1] In German, " reality " is " Wirklichkeit," derivatively meaning something whose essence is that it works (wirkt).—E. and C. P.
[2] Sammlung, vol. iv, 1922, p. 83.

CHAPTER ELEVEN

THE CASTRATION COMPLEX

CASTRATION has been extensively practised by stockfarmers, and this has kept a knowledge of the practice alive among western races, to which the castration of men has become unfamiliar. Those, indeed, who took part in the retreat of the German and Turkish army from Syria during 1918 learned that the Arabs made a practice of castrating their defeated enemies. The gentler-minded among the conquerors contented themselves with pedication. In both cases the aim was to humiliate the vanquished by emasculation, actual or symbolic. Since the days when Herodotus visited Asia Minor, moral outlooks in that part of the world have remained unchanged in this matter. But, until quite recently, we none of us realised how extensive a part the idea of castration [1] continues to play in the minds of civilised human beings—not in their conscious thoughts, but in the darkness of the unconscious, where elemental savagery persists.

I have known a number of neurotic patients who were peculiarly ready to adopt the use of the word

[1] The term " castration " in psychoanalytical literature includes the idea of amputation of the penis as well as that of removal of the testicles. Indeed, when writing of castration anxiety, etc., analysts refer to the former rather than to the latter. Nor is the idea of castration anxiety restricted to the male sex.—E. and C. P.

THE CASTRATION COMPLEX

castration as soon as they had heard me employ it. Their reminiscences then tended to assume some such form as the following: " My mother castrated me when I was a very little boy. But the one who especially castrated me was my paternal grandfather. . . ." Or they will report of a mistress who is no longer wholly congenial: " Yesterday Mitzi castrated me." One unfamiliar with Freud's expansion of the idea of castration, who should hear such phrases for the first time, would fancy that he must have found his way into a lunatic asylum!

It is to be presumed that all this is the outcome of a terrifying experience during childhood—of a threat to cut off the penis. The experience was so terrifying that it was repressed into the unconscious, but all the manifestations that Adler subsumes under the notions of inferiority and masculine protest are supposed to be sequels of such an experience. Of late years the orthodox Freudians have been busily engaged in reconstructing the theory of perversions and neuroses upon the basic conception of castration anxiety (Oedipus complex + castration). They would have us suppose, therefore, that the threat of castration is one frequently uttered by elders to the children under their care, and that it is of decisive importance in the causation of subsequent neurosis. Girls are presumed to refer their bodily and social inferiority to the lack of the penis, the organ their little brothers possess. Boys, on the other hand, contemplating the female sexual organs, are apt to dread being turned into girls, and this dread gives a substantial reality to their elders' threats. Penis envy in girls and penis anxiety in boys are postulated as the essential cause of neurosis.

Or, rather, since the Oedipus complex is not to forfeit its position as the nuclear complex, castration is the terrible punishment inflicted on Oedipus for his crime. When Oedipus blinds himself in the Greek tragedy, this is a substitute for emasculation. Ostensibly, the neurotic merely feels himself to be inferior; in reality, he feels himself to have been castrated.

Fantastic though all this may sound, many facts which support it force themselves on the analyst's attention. We must never forget that Freud's theories are not the outcome of speculation, but are based upon direct observation. (No doubt, interpretation and generalisation play their part.) Plait-cutters would seem to be persons whose impulse to mutilate has been transferred from the lower part of the body to the upper. I had a patient who was continually threatening to cut a tonsure in his elder brother's hair when the latter was asleep. This obviously signified the intention to turn his brother into a monk, or, if you like to phrase it thus, to castrate his brother. The brother, likewise a neurotic, seems to have realised something of the sort, for the younger lad's threats used to infuriate him, and he would cry: "If you do, I will strangle you!"

I knew a man suffering from dementia paranoides who was operated upon for appendicitis. After the operation, he heard "voices" telling him that there had been no trace of inflammation of the appendix, and that he had been humbugged. His elder brother, said the "voices," had had him anæsthetised and castrated. This was a young man of family, whose elder brother stood in his path. He regarded the

THE CASTRATION COMPLEX

brother as his supplanter; the brother had castrated him. When we recall that lunatics live consciously in a mental world which exists also for the healthy, but in them is unconscious, we shall easily see how this instance fits into the Freudian classification.

For hundreds of years a choir of castrates used to sing at St. Peter's in Rome. These singers were men whose virility had been sacrificed to the glory of God. The celibacy of Catholic priests is a barbaric custom having a similar significance. Ritual circumcision, as practised by Jews, Mohammedans, and others, is a mitigated sacrifice of virility in order to placate evil spirits. Thus castration and its derivatives still linger amid our civilisation. The description of ritual circumcision as a hygienic measure is nothing more than the rationalisation of an act really performed to placate demons.

Freud opines that antisemitism has an unconscious root in the Jewish practice of ritual circumcision. The unconscious confounds circumcision with castration, and therefore believes the Jews to be cruel. Those who castrate their own children are capable of committing any atrocity, and are therefore capable of committing ritual murder. The unconscious thus despises the Jews because they have been castrated, and at the same time dreads them because they castrate their children.

This contention of Freud's is amazing in its boldness. My own clinical experience does not justify me either in accepting it or in denying it. One of my patients (not a Jew) was a homosexual who from earliest childhood had had a fantasy of a gigantic penis without a foreskin. This might have been a symbol of the castrated father. The patient suffered from obsessions, and from a tormenting sense of inferiority.

Stekel considers Freud's explanation of morbid antisemitism to be erroneous. He believes that other unconscious determinants are operative.

Jung once suggested that the reason why American whites hate and despise negroes is because the black man with the vigorous impulsive life symbolises for the white man the blackness of his own soul. The antisemite's attitude towards the Jew may be a similar one.

The reader who wishes fuller information regarding the castration complex, should consult the chapter devoted to that subject in Sadger's *Die Lehre von den Geschlechtsverirrungen*, or should turn to Stärke's essay on the topic.[1] In addition to much of remarkable interest, he will find a good deal that is far from easy to accept. Nevertheless, we must remember that many of Freud's discoveries aroused almost universal dissent at the outset; and yet, in the end, others have been enabled to see what was at first obvious to Freud alone. What we have to ask is whether the unprejudiced analyst does or does not find the castration complex in the unconscious. Inasmuch as castration is so often practised in lower phases of civilisation, we certainly need not be surprised to find that it casts its shadow athwart the minds of neurotics. The question whether this shadow is always present—whether, like the Oedipus complex, it is an essential part of the mechanism of the neuroses, whether it is an invariable constituent of psychosexual infantilism—this is a question which I cannot venture to answer. As late as 1914, Freud was

[1] "Internationale Zeitschrift für aerztliche Psychoanalyse," 1922.

teaching that the castration complex is not to be detected in every case of neurosis.[1]

Stekel, who has access to a vast abundance of material and sifts it with marvellous skill, denies that the castration complex is of fundamental importance.—Boys in whom the sexual impulse awakens early are apt to envy the father the possession of his gigantic genital organs, and in their jealous fantasies they castrate the father. This analytical experience is in line with the notion of the primitive horde, as developed by Freud. The sons wish to destroy the father, who stands in their path. But when they cherish this wish they suffer from pricks of conscience. In the unconscious, the law of retaliation (an eye for an eye, and a tooth for a tooth) holds sway. The son, therefore, who has unconsciously wished to castrate the father, unconsciously dooms himself to castration.—We see that Stekel is far from denying the existence of the castration complex. But he refuses to accept it as a universally valid principle.

Freud understands by "castration complex" precisely what Adler understands by "masculine protest." According to Adler, every one of us wants to become top dog. When he cannot win his way to this position, he creeps, as it were, into the position of under dog, and suffers from a sense of inferiority. For Adler, therefore, the feeling of emasculation (when it exists) is merely a symbol of defeat in the struggle for power. According to Freud, behind such struggles lurks the will to castrate the antagonist. The little Oedipus wants to castrate his father in order to take the father's place with the mother. Subsequently,

[1] Sammlung, vol. iv, p. 100.

he wants to castrate his brothers, so that in the younger generation he may be the only competent male, the only effective owner of a harem. Ultimately, he wants to castrate all the men in the world, that he may be autocrat in the realm of love. Since the individual lacks the power to carry such wishes into effect, and since these wishes come into conflict with conscientious scruples, they are repressed. Then the little boy imaginatively castrates himself, as a punishment for his wishes. Thus operating in the unconscious, the complex exercises its influence upon consciousness in symbolic forms: giving rise to lust for power and to arrogance, on the one hand, and to the counterparts of these, over-scrupulousness, humility, the "sentiment d'incomplétude" (Janet), on the other. The views of Freud and Adler are completely antithetical. Freud regards the will-to-power as nothing more than a symbol for the longing to castrate. Adler looks upon the will-to-power as a primary phenomenon, and considers castration (like all that is sexual) to be merely a phenomenal form of the elemental will, or a symbol thereof.

On the face of the matter, most people will be inclined to agree with Adler, and will be estranged by Freud's theory. But we should be cautious in coming to a decision, and should bear in mind how often time has proved Freud to be right. There are more things in heaven and earth than are dreamed of in our wisdom of the schools.

One of Sadger's patients said: "Death is the climax of castration. I can find no other way of describing it." This is a dark saying, and might almost seem to have been spoken in mockery, but we find that the following considerations may be

THE CASTRATION COMPLEX

adduced in its support. He who dies, loses his ego; and yet the germ-plasm lives on in his children. On the other hand, one who has been castrated retains his short-lived ego, but his share of the germ-plasm, which had seemed predestined for immortality, perishes. The castrate dies eternal death; one who has been murdered dies a temporal death. Castration, therefore, is the only form of death which we can truly experience. We experience it because we outlive it. Dread of the loss of the germ-plasm may be regarded, in the sense of Schopenhauer's metaphysic of sexual love, as a transcendental anxiety which surpasses the personal dread of death. Sadger's patient should therefore have expressed his thought in the inverse way, saying: "Castration is the climax of death." In death, the thing that matters is the destruction of the germ-plasm. This thought enables us to understand why, in his latest publication (1923), Freud refers all forms of anxiety to castration anxiety, which is a transcendental dread of death. In the life of our familiar civilisation we have, indeed, little cause for explicit castration anxiety. Death threatens us in manifold forms; but in our daily life we are hardly ever threatened with castration—not, at any rate, in adult life.

The experience of savages may be different. Castration must have been discovered during the evolution of civilised man out of the ape-man by way of primitive man. Animals do not castrate one another. It was left for primitive man to discover the refinement which enables him to leave his enemy alive in a condition which is more than death. Primitive men fought over their women as stags fight for the possession of does, and cocks for the possession of hens. The first man who bit off or tore away his enemy's genital organs had discovered castration. Subsequent experience would show that the enemy to whom this had been done was no longer a rival in love, but was all the more useful as a slave. The realisation would come that it was better to castrate one's defeated enemy than to kill him.

For thousands of years, a dread of castration may, with good reason, have been active among the forefathers of civilised men. The neurotic is the victim of regression. What the adherents of the Freudian school have adduced in support of the idea of the castration complex is too scanty and too devoid of universality to sustain all the symbolism of inferiority. Freud is aware of this, and that is why he appeals to phylogenesis, to racial history. Prior to 1910, hardly any mention of phylogenesis can be found in Freudian teaching. When some of the Freudians, and especially Jung, began to lay stress on phylogenetic considerations, Freud became uneasy. He said that it was essential to make an exhaustive study of individual experience and individual inheritance before entering the nebulous domain of phylogenesis. The criticism was sound. Nevertheless, the castration complex cannot be saved without an extensive use of phylogenetic considerations. Virility secures its central expression in the penis. Its counterpart is the dread of castration, conjoined with the desire to castrate the rival. The dread and the desire may be an ancient heritage.

We must not confuse possibilities with proved facts. Unquestionably, without troubling about the castration complex, psychoanalysis can in most cases put the patient on the road towards cure.

THE CASTRATION COMPLEX

This complex, if it be discoverable at all, is apt to be so deeply buried that the patient is cured, or discontinues treatment, before we have disinterred it. Thus the question becomes one of purely theoretical interest; and it may more suitably be discussed in connexion with the general problem, why so much is to be referred to the sexual sphere. We reach the alleged "one-sidedness" of the Freudian doctrine, and it behoves us to pay special attention to this matter.

When people used to ask Freud why he laid exclusive stress upon sexual factors among the causes of the neuroses, and how he accounted for his peculiar views upon this matter, he would answer that he made no attempt to account for them. Sexual factors were continually forcing themselves on his attention. Like other students of natural science, he made it his business to describe what he saw. He would leave it to the philosophers to cudgel their brains in the endeavour to explain why a natural phenomenon occurs. He had no bias in the matter, and his doctrine was not one-sided. If there were bias or one-sidedness, it was in nature. His function was merely to discover and to describe. None the less, it is indubitable that Freud worked with preconceptions. He had intuitively recognised that Eros (who plays his part in every activity of all that creeps and all that flies) has a yet more notable significance in the case of man and man's mental life.

Man is preeminently distinguished from the lower animals by the enormous development of his libido. We are apt to differentiate man from other creatures in virtue of his upright gait, or his use of the hand, or his faculty of speech. An even more conspicuous differential characteristic is man's vigorous and persistent libido. In most of the lower animals, libido is only manifest during a brief rutting season. Man loves without intermission. He has emancipated love from the law of reproduction, for he loves a great deal more than is necessary to ensure reproduction, and more even than is serviceable to reproduction. In some of the lower animals we already notice that the reproductive impulse finds expression in artistic forms, such as nest-building, dancing, song, and, actually, the formation of States. It has been demonstrated that certain human institutions originate out of love. Speech is a development of song. Clothing was originally ornamental. The ardent males decked themselves to please the females. If any one should cling to the old delusion that all progress is the outcome of need, that necessity is invariably the mother of invention, we cannot do better than point to the pictures (some in black-and-white, and some coloured) on the walls of the cave-dwellings in southern France. These drawings, admirably finished and amazingly accurate, date from a period in which primitive man had not yet invented so simple a tool or weapon as the axe. Our ancestors possessed art before they possessed anything else.

In harmony with these discoveries is the fact that the growth of the ape-man into man must be presumed to have taken place during a period when nature was bountiful—in late tertiary times. This was before the Glacial Epoch; the climate of Central Europe was sub-tropical; elephants roamed through the luxuriant forests. Art, like love, flourishes in

THE CASTRATION COMPLEX

the soil of abundance and luxury. In the historic age we note that the fine arts have always thriven best in the periods when luxury prevailed.

All living things grow. As soon as the living creature has attained the limits of its individual growth, it undergoes a growth which transcends these limits, taking the form of reproduction. When the limits of reproduction (narrow limits, as far as the higher animals are concerned) have been reached, the urge towards growth still persists. Now that the material possibilities of growth have been exhausted, the creature grows mentally. The things that were originally intended to lure the female—beauty, song, artistry, strength—become ends in themselves. We can watch the process at work in a canary that sings in its cage, sings all the more heartily because the bird cannot gain the natural end of song—union with the female. The song becomes its own end, becomes art, becomes solace; the love-yearning is diverted from the unattainable hen bird, and the song is irradiated with all the splendour of the libido.

That which constrains the singing bird in the cage, constrains man likewise, impelling him towards a thousandfold manifestations of art and civilisation. A good many years ago, I attempted a detailed exposition of the way in which the primitive culture of mankind arose, during the late tertiary period, out of love and plenty.[1] The Ice Age partly anni-

[1] Cf. Otto Rank, Der Künstler, Vienna, 1907.—My own books on this topic are, Tragische Motive, Berlin, 1911; and Alles um Liebe, Berlin, 1912.—A few months after the publication of the last-named work, Ferenczi included my conception of the Ice Age as a modifier of civilisation in a paper published in the " Internationale Zeitschrift für aerztliche Psychoanalyse " under the title Entwicklungsstufen des Wirklichkeitssinnes. My name was not mentioned!

hilated and partly transformed this love civilisation, so that to-day many people regard civilisation as the offspring of need. At any rate, as far as the arts are concerned, it is plain enough that they are outgrowths of the love-yearning—that they are a reservoir alike for the artist and for the amateur of the arts.

The libido is yet more intimately connected with religion and ritual. Inasmuch as even atheists look upon religion as something exalted, whereas most people regard sexual desire as base (the former being the divine and the latter the animal in man!), impatience is apt to be aroused by the demonstration of the close connexion between sexuality and religion. An otherwise intelligent psychiatrist maintains that such phrases as " the bride of Christ " and " Christ, the beloved bridegroom " have nothing to do with sexuality, and have merely been coined because language has no more beautiful expressions for a sublime feeling. In like manner, the medieval councils of the church were able to persuade themselves that the Song of Solomon, with its glorification of the body of a girl, was not referring to a woman in the flesh, but to the holy city of Jerusalem. Nothing but this little artifice could have secured for the obnoxious poem its place among the canonical books.

Now that the perversions known as sadism and masochism have been described, it has become difficult to regard the self-castigation of monks and nuns and the burnings and rackings inflicted under the ægis of the Inquisition as anything else than sexual. Since, on the other hand, no one will deny the religious enthusiasm of inquisitors, Jesuits, and penitents, I should have thought it hard to ignore the intimate connexion between religious practices

THE CASTRATION COMPLEX 173

and sexuality. But repression, and the obstinate resistance of the unconscious, are potent enemies of truth.

The every-day occupations of mankind are less obviously tinged with sexuality, but even here the cloven hoof is continually peeping out. Property is sexualised through and through. It is not by chance that we use words derived from the same root when we speak of one man as having a " competence," and of another as being sexually " potent." We " breed " children; and we say that " money breeds money." We love our property as we love wife and child; the property remains when we die, and so do the children. A wife was the first object suitable to become property. A man had to win her from rivals, and to defend his possession of her against rivals; thus she became the first of his goods—long before he had any other goods. To-day we express the value of our property in terms of gold. The unconscious, however, has so profound a contempt for this yellow metal that, in dreams, gold is always a symbol for fæces; just as, in the legends, Satan's gold always changes into excrement. What money and property signify to our inner self, is likewise disclosed in dreams. Here, money always means love. To dream " he owes me money " means " he does not love me enough." The valuation of love in terms of money, and the falsification of love by money, are familiar experiences in waking life as well.

A man must be a veritable Comstock if he fails to note that the drunkard who caresses his bottle is inspired with the same sort of feelings as the lover who caresses his mistress. The miser runs his fingers through his gold, as a Romeo runs his fingers through the tresses of his beloved. In a word, the most important thing in life, the most fundamental of our experiences, is love. Who knows not this ? . . . The other things that we do are delightful to us only when we sexualise them. Unless we sexualise them, we do them solely when compelled and under more or less conscious protest (the pleasure principle versus the reality principle). In the folk-lore of every nation we learn of a paradise in which men lived for pleasure alone. Man was driven forth from this paradise by the Ice Age. We must never forget that hunger, which now holds us in thrall, did not yet exist for the men of the tertiary epoch, and was the creation of a subsequent time.

Each one of us has his days in paradise. The infant lives for nothing but pleasure, until the struggles of education begin. We are all born in Arcady. When the troubles of life become too keen, we turn back to the sources of memory and grow childlike. Confusing and multiform are the manifestations of neurosis, but common to them all is the flight into childhood. Away from money, from ambition, from fraud, from disillusionment, the neurotic returns into a day when there was no money, when there were no tax-gatherers, and no commercial crises. The only conflicts known to the age of childhood concern the desire for tenderness, and the desire to exercise power over immediate associates. That is why the neurotic translates all his experiences into the affective language of childhood. Money is love, or excrement. Every living hindrance (persons in authority, rivals of all kinds) is impersonated as the father who was our rival in our mother's affections. The whole of life, on the other hand, life which has to be conquered, is represented as the mother. In the folk-speech this is still perfectly plain. To the peasant, his mother is the earth, whose favour he woos.

I consider that we grow up under protest. Only under protest do we become dwellers in the world of reality. We should all prefer to remain children. Who can take this life of ours seriously? In it we are exiles. Nowhere are we at home except in paradise. We are born for love, but life castrates us. This is the castration complex.

CHAPTER TWELVE
CARL GUSTAV JUNG

FROM 1910 onwards, I had no intimate personal knowledge of the politics of psychoanalysis. I have been told that Jung looked askance at Adler and Stekel, Freud's most distinguished pupils, and that the two latter were sacrificed because of Freud's devotion to his Swiss recruit. I should have thought, rather, that the abrupt dismissal of Adler was brought about by the danger that the Zurich contingent would find Adler's non-sexual theory more to their taste than Freud's own views, which were not altogether " respectable " in the eyes of Swiss Protestants. Freud certainly had a way of treating his pupils like children with an alternation of rewards and punishments, and by keeping them out of bad company. Perhaps the Swiss were not to be allowed to see that there was some one who had a preferential explanation to that afforded by the libido; one whose doctrine of the neurotic constitution was so simple, and did not involve any appeal to sexual factors. " Why does a man become a pæderast ? "—" To put women in their place ! " " Why is a wife bedridden with paralysis ? "—" To put her husband in his place ! " . . . The Zurichers must be safeguarded against contagion.

But these Swiss recruits were to prove Freud's

CARL GUSTAV JUNG

greatest disappointment. I made Jung's acquaintance at the Salzburg congress. He was tall and upright of figure, like a young Siegfried. He had a bullet head with closely-cropped hair, was clean-shaven, and wore gold-rimmed spectacles. My feeling about Siegfrieds is like that of Hebbel's Hagen—they smack too much of the dragon! I have several times been struck by Freud's fondness for bullet heads. His devotion to Jung was, however, altogether exceptional. To this man, Freud was lavish with his intellectual gifts, so that Jung has been able to live ever since upon the master's brilliant suggestions.

Soon recognising Jung's inability "to endure another's authority," Freud threw over in Jung's favour the faithful Viennese collaborators, proposing to make them subordinate to this new adherent—as if it were possible to win over an egoist by granting all his demands. I am entitled to say that the ambiguous attitude of the Zurichers was patent to me as early as 1910. Some of the older members of the Psychoanalytical Association will perhaps recall that I said after the Nuremberg congress: "Freud does not think much of us, his Viennese pupils. If he knew the Swiss as well as he knows us, he would like them still less!"

The third Psychoanalytical Congress was held at Weimar, in September 1911. Jung took the chair. The congress appears to have run a smooth course. Adler had been dismissed. Freud had a great deal to say—presumably apropos of his splendid analysis of the paranoia of Schreber, the President of the Senate—concerning the sun; and concerning the eagle, the only creature able to look at the sun. Stekel aroused applause by the reminder that Freud had left in Vienna an eagle [Adler] who had dared to look at the sun.

A fourth Psychoanalytical Congress was held at Munich in 1913. Here Jung was again president, but for the last time. Now the proceedings were stormy. Jung's *Wandlungen und Symbole der Libido* had appeared [1]; and Jung's colleague Maeder read a paper upon the dream, [2] an exposition of an outlook he had long been considering. The dream, he held, gave expression to the divine in man as well as to the animal. The Oedipus complex and all the other discoveries of psychoanalysis in the sexual field were not what they seemed; they were only symbols. It will readily be understood that Freud was ill at ease. It was the second part of Jung's *Psychology of the Unconscious* which especially troubled him. Hardly had he cut off one of the Hydra's heads, the head that passed by the name of Alfred Adler, when two new heads (Jung and Maeder) sprouted in its place. Considerably annoyed, he declared at the congress that the work and inferences of the Swiss could "not be regarded as legitimate developments of psychoanalysis." Nevertheless, three-fifths of those present voted in favour of Jung's re-election as president of the International Association, the appointment being for another two years—during which Jung actually held this post. Since then, the Viennese School and the Zurich School have worked apart. The breach between them has continually widened, and the Viennese deny the right of the Zurichers to speak of themselves as analysts.

[1] "Jahrbüch für Psychoanalyse," 1911, 1912 (Englished as The Psychology of the Unconscious).
[2] Ueber das Traumproblem, Vienna, 1910.

Soon Freud was to lose Stekel as well. Then, like Wallenstein, he could say of himself:

> Den Schmuck der Zweige habt ihr abgehauen,
> Da steh ich, ein entlaubter Stamm! Doch innen
> Im Marke lebt die schaffende Gewalt,
> Die sprossend eine Welt aus sich geboren. . . .
> Gewohnt wohl sind sie unter mir zu siegen,
> Nicht gegen mich—wenn Haupt und Glieder sich trennen,
> Da wird sich zeigen, wo die Seele wohnte.[1]

In February 1914, he declared proudly, in words that remind us of Schiller's: " Men are strong so long as they represent a strong idea. They become powerless when they oppose it. Psychoanalysis will be able to bear this loss, and will gain new adherents in place of those who have been lost. I can only conclude with the wish that the fates may prepare an easy ascension for those who have found their sojourn in the underworld of psychoanalysis uncomfortable. May it be vouchsafed to the others to bring to a happy conclusion their labours in the depths." [2]

The classical and almost cheerful sentences which close a lengthy polemic report may produce a false impression. We cannot doubt that Freud had been greatly disappointed, and that, excellent sleeper

---

[1] You have hewn off the glory of the boughs,
And I stand here a naked tree-trunk! But within,
In the pith, there lives the creative force that can give birth
To a world of sprouting verdure . . .
They are wont to conquer under me,
Not against me—when head and limbs are severed,
We learn where the soul dwelt.

[2] The History of the Psychoanalytic Movement, p. 58.—The English version is slightly modified from A. A. Brill's translation.

though he is reputed to be, he must have had a good many broken nights over this affair.

In the early days of his psychoanalytical activities Jung's writings were those of one who had wholeheartedly accepted Freud's teachings. Freud supplied the ideas and Jung expounded them with remarkable skill. But Jung has a proud stomach. The moment must have come in which he said: "Am I to be only a satellite? Am I always to stand in the shadow of a great name?" Such secessions lead us far into the tragedy of Judas. (A differentiation occurs, inspired by dread lest there should be too complete an identification.) In his own domain, Freud was incomparable. He himself says, modestly enough, that the leap he had made fifteen years earlier was not one which could be made a second time. What he does not say is that his mission was unique, and that while he lived he must necessarily be its supreme leader. No other can take the reins as long as Freud is there. Ambitious disciples, therefore, those anxious to shine with an independent light, must look to right and to left in search of country over which the chief's gaze has not extended. That was why Adler conceived the idea of the "masculine protest," and that was why Jung came to advocate the "genetic" conception of the libido. It will be shown that Jung's outlook has considerable importance, both heuristically and philosophically. But Freud, with a firm grip on the reins, was unwilling to leave the road along which he had been driving for twenty years. The magnificent confidence with which he holds fast to his convictions would mark him out as a classicist, were it not that the daimons which rule in his depths had predestined him to be a romanticist.

Adler said that the will-to-power was the driving force among human beings. Sexuality (the libido) was no more than a partial manifestation of this will. Jung, on the other hand, contended that sexuality (the libido) had originally been all in all, but that a part of this primal energy had been desexualised during the progress of human civilisation, and that this part was now counterposed to the energy that had remained sexual, was distinct from and alien to the latter. In a sense, then, both Adler and Jung are monists, and their outlooks are but superficially divergent. In reality they both have in mind something which a greater than either of them, namely Schopenhauer, named Will.

Jung incorporated his views in a comprehensive work, the before-mentioned *Wandlungen und Symbole der Libido*, the two parts of which were published at an interval of a year and a half. This book was written by a man of mark, by one who is profoundly versed in the literature and the mythology of all ages and all lands. But it is a fatiguing book to read, owing to the way in which the flow of the thought is continually being broken by quotations. These quotations have so weighty a content that they strain the framework. In the first part of the book, Jung is still being towed in Freud's wake. In the second part, however, the libido is created genetically and is desexualised in the way already indicated. Jung, before he wrote this book, had successfully mastered an idea to which Freud had given expression in the first edition of *Die Traumdeutung*—the idea that the unconscious appertains to an old and derelict stage of thought; and that it is to this stage that dreams, and the fantasies of the neurotic, belong. The Swiss spoke of unconscious mentation as "archaic." All the workers in this school busy themselves to show that mental patients and neurotics reproduce in every detail the myths, cosmogonies, and primitive conceptions of the early ages of man. They endeavour to turn the discovery to practical account. They track out such archaic images in the minds of their patients, and expound these images to the latter. I find it hard to understand what benefit a patient can derive from being told: "There it is once more! This idea of yours represents the Aztec god Vitzliputzli!" Presumably the patient will be somewhat astonished, and perhaps rather crestfallen to learn that his thoughts have been straying along such outworn paths. But how can it help him (I paraphrase Ferenczi's apt criticism) to have one unknown, his own aberrant self, explained in terms of another unknown whose name is Vitzliputzli?

By way of the cult of the archaic, the Swiss come to the cult of the Calvinistic—they preach. Jung's conception of religion is obscure. If I understand him aright, there are two kinds of religion. One of these is merely the transformation of erotic impulses into religious activity. This religion, says Jung, is base and contemptible. "The unconscious recasting of the erotic into something religious, lays itself open to the reproach of a sentimental and ethically worthless pose." [1]

Besides this "worthless" religion, Jung recognises another form of religion, one in which the whole personality is tinged with religious emotion.

[1] Psychology of the Unconscious, p. 82

"Whoever, on the other hand, to his conscious sin just as consciously places religion in opposition, does something the greatness of which cannot be denied." [1]

It seems hardly credible that the man who penned this sentence could have had the advantage of a lively interchange of ideas with Freud throughout a period of nearly five years. One who can write in such a way seems to have no conception of the dynamic of the unconscious. As Ferenczi justly remarks in his criticism of the passage, it is utterly devoid of psychology. The statement is pure theology.

Jung asked himself what force could have compelled the primal sexuality to desexualise itself (in part) so that the part of the libido which has remained sexual is counterposed by another kind of libido—by Freud termed ego impulse—which, before the days of Jung, no one had been able to recognise as an offspring of the primal sexual libido. He considered it unthinkable that this failure of others to discern the force which antagonises sexuality could be the outcome of an external resistance, of a concrete obstacle. He inferred, therefore, that there must be an internal resistance, something within the human mind which works against sexuality, much as the divine works against the animal. Setting out from these two apodictic utterances, first that an external resistance was unthinkable, and secondly that an inner and elemental moral influence was at work, Jung was able to sail with a fair wind away from the land of evil psychoanalysis to the land of good (Swiss) psychoanalysis. From the Freudian doctrine, which

[1] Psychology of the Unconscious, p. 82.

aims at ridding the world of the Moloch of sexual hypocrisy, he could make his way back to Christianity and the old morality—which have beyond question done many good things in their time, but assuredly it is not the purpose either of psychoanalysis or of Sigmund Freud to support the ascetic morality of the old creed.

Jung is doubtless right in his contention that Christianity compelled civilised man to sublimate a considerable part of his sexuality. Religious practices comprise a fraction of such sublimation, but it is hard to define the point at which civilised sublimation ceases and hysteria begins. Consider, again, the three maxims: that work is a blessing; that work is the most precious thing in the world; and that by unceasing work we win, not only the heaven from which no traveller returns, but heaven on earth. All these maxims are the gifts of Christianity. But Christianity itself was a gift of poverty. Like Buddhism, it was engendered in the womb of an impoverished people. When the classical world adopted Christianity, poverty was the determining cause. Sensual joys are always discarded when the world is too poor to enjoy them. Delight in them is reborn (the Renaissance) when the world grows rich once more—as the western world was enriched by the discovery of America, by the opening of the sea route to the Indies, and by the overthrow of Europe's Mohammedan competitors by Genghis Khan and his Tartar hordes. Unfortunately, the transcendental arguments of the Christians against unbridled sensuality were unexpectedly reinforced by one of the gifts Columbus brought back from America—syphilis, which has poisoned our blood ever since.

In my view, therefore, the external force, which to Jung seems unthinkable, is plainly manifest behind Christianity. Everyone knows it—need has castrated us! The first great castration of sexuality was effected by the Ice Age. Psychoanalysis has revealed that in the unconscious we never cease protesting against this castration. Although the protest is often unconscious, it is absolutely real; and for my part I find it almost inconceivable that any one who has practised psychoanalysis can maintain that the manifestations of unconscious sexuality have a merely symbolical significance. The Oedipus complex is as real as anything in the world. A moment's reflection enables me to recall dozens of instances in which this reality was incontestable.

I will content myself with a few examples from my own recent practice. A man came from abroad for treatment in a Viennese sanatorium. His mother accompanied him on the journey. The mother was sixty; the patient was thirty-five, married, with two children. He was an agriculturist.

" Where is your wife ? "

" She makes me nervous. When I am ill—I suffer from debility, sleeplessness, and hypochondria—I get on better with my mother."

In the course of the analysis, the patient informed me that he had always been a " mother's darling," and that he had a preference for the society of elderly women. He remembered an old washerwoman, who, after she had done her day's work, used to wash her feet in the courtyard. To do this, she kilted her petticoats above the knee. The scene exercised a sort of magical lure upon the patient, who was then fifteen years old. He would crouch for hours at a window lest he should miss the chance of seeing the old woman at her toilet. When he was rewarded for his pains, he would become sexually excited, and would masturbate.

The same patient told me that he was sent to a university in a large town. The woman where he lodged had a pretty niece who was quite disposed to be responsive to any advances he might make. But as far as she was concerned, he was a laggard in love, not wishing—so he said—to harm an innocent girl. (A rationalisation of his relative impotence!) However, he flirted with her, and this excited him. He thereupon satisfied his desires in a liaison with the aunt, an elderly woman past the change of life.

Perhaps such records have little interest to psychoanalysts whose notebooks are full of similar ones. But the Zurich School denies the reality of the Oedipus complex, and I therefore propose to give additional examples.

A young man inclined to melancholia told me that when he was seven years old his widowed mother had made up her mind to marry again. He had spent many sleepless nights wondering what he could do to dissuade her. At length he decided to write to her (he was away at a boarding school) suggesting that she might be content with a baby's comforter which he had picked up in some nursery. Many people will say that the boy must have been an infamous little wretch. I am inclined, rather, to be touched by the pathetic resolve of this little Oedipus. The same man was only satisfactorily potent once in his life, and that was with—his wife's mother. When the old lady died suddenly, the man left his wife, who no longer had the smallest interest for him. Since then he has been a mysogynist, unfit for work, and melancholy.

Here is a third instance. A young blacksmith, twenty-six years old, boards with his mother and his stepfather, the mother's second marriage having taken place five years earlier. The two men quarrel every evening. Nevertheless, the patient cannot bear to think of leaving his present quarters. He remembers having slept in the same bed with his mother up to the age of twelve. Once his mother noticed that the boy had an erection, and exclaimed, in her wisdom: "You ought to be ashamed of yourself!"

I could give plenty of examples of the other element in the Oedipus complex, hostility to the father. Since, however, the complete Oedipus complex may assume any one of four forms, and since various mixed types exist, I had better restrain my pen. There are some analysts, like Stekel, who will not agree that the Oedipus complex is the central feature of neurosis; but no analyst can doubt the reality of this complex. How, then, are we to explain that the Zurichers, none the less, deny its reality. (Pfister, who follows Freud, is an exception.) We can only explain it by having recourse to psychoanalysis. Truths clear as daylight are repressed if they are distasteful. The Siegfried of Burghölzli regards the Oedipus complex as a dragon. Calvin and Freud cannot live together in the same heart. The Swiss have plumped for their national hero.

But Rousseau, too, is a national hero of Switzerland. In a work published in 1918, Jung deplores that town-dwellers and the industrial proletariat have lost touch with the soil, from which the peasant daily draws new energy and fresh moral strength. But the notion that the countryman is more moral than the townsman savours of mysticism. Were the great moralists, the great founders of religion, men of peasant stock? The peasant is apt to be spiteful, vindictive, miserly, quarrelsome, litigious, and brutal. Proportionally to the population, sexual offences are commoner in the country than in the town. Freud tells us that among nineteenth-century authors, Zola was preeminent for his knowledge of neuroses. Those who wish to study a truthful portrait of the peasant, may turn to the pages of *La Terre*. In political matters, the peasant is reactionary; and the territorial nobles, to whom political reaction is advantageous, esteem the peasantry for this very reason. Persons of pious disposition must always have something which they can regard as sacred. But it is surely rather stupid for those who have described " work " as sacred, to establish a hierarchy, and to declare that the work of the peasant is more sacred than that of the urban proletarian.

In 1921, Jung published a comprehensive study entitled *Psychologische Typen*. His aim in this book is to show how those who accept his methods can classify their patients according to type. After the analysis, the patient can be directed along the right path, each according to his particular type being shown the road by which he can best climb upwards. The analysand is not merely to be freed from his unconscious complexes, but is to be given good advice for his journey. By the Zurichers, this is termed " psychosynthesis." Now, the human mind is a complicated structure, its phenomenology is obscure, and its analysis is therefore difficult. But when we go further than analysis, and attempt a synthesis, we are obviously opening the door to all kinds of arbitrary procedures. One adviser may look upon Christianity as sublime, while another may regard its influence as pernicious. One may believe that we ought to return to the soil, in the sense of a return to primitive methods of agriculture; another may hold that the advance of mankind will best be promoted by the application of the most highly developed methods of modern technique in the backward province of agricultural production. It is likely that psychoanalysis will always be open to the objection that it still fails to probe the innermost recesses of the mind. Nevertheless, if properly employed (i.e. without preconceptions) it can only bring to light the actual contents of the mind. The revelation does not invariably contribute to the patient's comfort; but at any rate it is a truthful revelation, and has the ennobling qualities that attach to truth. In many cases, the doctor will find it necessary to be something more than an analyst; he will have to be an educator as well. Freud admitted as much in his address to the fifth Psychoanalytical Congress held at Budapesth, in September 1918. But it is a hazardous venture to dignify such educational efforts with the proud name of psychosynthesis, and thus to imply that they are as valuable as, and perhaps even more valuable than, psychoanalysis. The latter, at any rate, is a science; but psychosynthesis may easily degenerate into unmeaning babble. Inasmuch as psychoanalysis is difficult, whereas babbling is easy, there will always be more babblers than analysts. Freud complains that the Zurichers, in their study of the unconscious, merely scratch the surface of the ground; and that as soon as they have done this they overwhelm the unfortunate patient with a flood of good counsel. There are too many oriental prophets loose in Europe to-day; there are schools of wisdom, devotion, and uplift. Jung is the director of one of these schools—a good one of its kind, for Jung is talented and erudite. His treatments last a long time, one or two years; and he makes his patients promise to reconsult him at regular intervals. I think that the orthodox Freudians are justified in their hostility to this notion of a synthetical psychoanalysis, and in their complaint that the very name is a contradiction in terms.

Freud considers that analysis is the fundamental matter. He has repeatedly declared that, for him, therapeutical successes occupy a secondary place among his interests as the founder of psychoanalysis and as the explorer of the depths of the unconscious. To the patient, no doubt, the cure is of supreme importance; it is in the hope of a cure that he consults the analyst and pays the analyst's fees. Nevertheless, the scientific appraisement of medical successes is impracticable. Every doctor, and in especial, every neurologist, knows full well that a cure proves nothing. The variable factor of suggestion —which is an element in the psychoanalytical " transference "—is, usually, the decisive matter here. But the psychoanalyst, when probing the patient's forgotten experiences, makes it his rule to deprive the transference of its power by continually disclosing it at work.[1]

[1] Vide supra, pp. 93 et seq.

Quite recently, therefore, Freud has reiterated his view that the psychoanalyst must shun the temptation of playing prophet and saviour to his patient. The aim of the analysis should be " not to make the morbid reactions impossible, but to endow the patient's ego with the freedom of self-determination."[1]

So rigid, so cruel a restriction of the task of analysis may be theoretically conceivable. In practice, however, the analyst is compelled to work for a cure. It suffices that he shall be aware of the point at which science ceases and hocus-pocus begins—for the art of medicine (as distinguished from the science) cannot be completely freed from hocus-pocus.

In the first instance, Freud left the criticism of the Zurich innovations in the hands of his pupils— and Stekel, though himself already under the ban, was one of the critics.[2] But in the very month in which Freud broke with Jung and the other Swiss disciples, he wrote the closing passages of *Totem und Tabu*. This was in September 1913, at Rome, whither the admirer of Roman grandeur had withdrawn after the storm in Munich. Jung had attacked several of Freud's teachings, and Freud's sorest wound had been caused by the denial of the reality of the Oedipus complex. In *Totem und Tabu*, Freud wreaked a scientific vengeance upon Jung, following the latter into the domain of folk-psychology, and there annihilating Jung on his own vantage ground. In 1910 there had appeared the four volumes of J. G. Frazer's *Totemism and Exogamy*. By one of those happy chances which are apt to occur at the

---

[1] Das Ich und das Es, p. 64.
[2] Fortschritte der Traumdeutung, " Zentralblatt für Psychoanalyse," iv, 1914.

right moment in the lives of great men, Freud's attention was drawn to this book. In it, and elsewhere, Freud found abundant materials enabling him to explain primitive religion and primitive society in terms of the tangible reality of the Oedipus complex. Jung's materials were derived from ancient and almost incomprehensible sagas; Freud's materials were drawn from the study of South Sea islanders, whose life and doings are open to direct observation to-day. The savage's dread of incest is manifest, and primitive social institutions are full of barriers against incest. Now, why should there be such barriers unless there is a strong urge towards incest—an urge which is suppressed by savages as anti-social?

Totem und Tabu found admirers in circles far wider than those of the customary admirers of "Freudian mechanisms." Freud was demonstrating archaic manifestations which need not be hunted up in the musty legends of antiquity, but can be studied at first hand in the mental life of savages and neurotics. Freud had not secured such universal approval since the appearance of *Zur Psychopathologie des Alltagslebens*. His own satisfaction with the book was shown by its reissue unaltered when a second edition was called for seven years later. In this volume we find the first mention of the primitive horde, or rather, the first Freudian elaboration of the idea. The sons, weary of the father's tyranny, rebel and kill him. Freud took it as a matter of course that the children, being cannibals, would have eaten their murdered sire. Stekel says that Freud has the primitive-horde complex. He is the Old Man, afraid of his disciples. It must be admitted that the behaviour of Adler and Jung has to some extent justified the master's anxiety.[1]

Since the Zurichers denied the reality of sexual manifestations emanating from the unconscious, it was impossible to come to terms with them. They had turned their backs on the truth. Had they been content to affirm the existence of moral tendencies in the unconscious (the tendencies which Silberer speaks of as " anagogic "), their labours would have led to the permanent enrichment of psychoanalysis. For nearly ten years, Freud's stubbornness—no milder word can be employed here—made him decline to recognise that the Zurichers were furnishing an important contribution. His earlier investigations had disclosed the instinctive human being to be an unsocial egoist, and he clung to this conception. He could not bring himself to admit the reality of the anagogic until ten years of habituation to the secession of the Zurichers had been superadded to the ten years of his original researches. In the interim, as Freud himself phrases it, " psychoanalysis was continually being charged with paying no heed to the loftier, the moral, the super-egoistic elements in human beings." Freud regards this accusation as unjust. For my part I think there are good grounds for it, although I sympathise with Freud's feeling that he did not come into the world to supply ammunition for moralising doctrinaires. In his latest book, Freud has abandoned his former untenable position. Human beings have lived a social life for so many generations that the need to comply with social

[1] In all humility, I want to take this opportunity of pointing out that I myself anticipated Freud in the description of the Freudian phase of the primitive horde. This was in 1912. Cf. Alles um Liebe, p. 44.

demands has become instinctive (the impulse towards such compliance arising out of "the it," if we use Groddeck's quaint phraseology).[1] The "cultural overtones" are now an integral constituent of the mind; through the practice and the heritage of millennia, they have acquired the force of a categorical imperative. The sexual impulse serves to secure the survival of the species, and for that reason it must transcend the intellectual control of the individual. In like manner, social demands must transcend the intellectual control of the individual, for the human being does not merely will to live, but he wills also to live in society. Without social life, man is inconceivable. He is under the control of instinct, not only as a sexual being, but also as a civilised being.

We may, perhaps, point out that the moral impulses (conscience, ego-ideal, super-ego) in the unconscious are in the more superficial strata—if we are to talk of stratification at all. But at whatever levels, these moral impulses exist. There are profoundly religious persons who are not aware of being religious; in actual life they may play the part of Satanists, and may suffer intensely from an unconscious conflict because of their inward religious convictions. Kant says with truth that we can hardly imagine a criminal who is not inwardly aware that he is a wrongdoer.

Unconscious religious impulses are among the most deeply hidden of the complexes. The patient finds it harder to disclose them than the most dread secrets, harder to disclose them than criminal and perverse trends. It seems as if he were profoundly

[1] Groddeck, Das Buch vom Es.

humiliated by having to admit that he is endowed with religious inclinations.[1] Psychoanalysis always discloses impulses that repudiate civilisation sooner than it discloses impulses that affirm civilisation. That is why Freud took so long to recognise the existence of the latter. He claims the privileges of a cautious and unprejudiced investigator. The Swiss analysts approached the unconscious with a prior conviction that it must contain moral elements. Inasmuch as this conviction happened to be right, they discovered these moral elements sooner than Freud discovered them.

In reality, moreover, Freud was not unprejudiced. He worked with the prior conviction that the content of the unconscious was animal, and nothing more. Had he held another view, he could not have failed to find the super-ego in the unconscious much sooner than he actually found it. When the Zurichers fell away, and when, in their secession, they repudiated almost all the acquisitions of psychoanalysis, Freud was not in the mood to learn anything from these renegades. We have here a fresh demonstration of the fact that the thoughts of others do not help, but rather hinder, this marvellous man's thought-process. When others try to introduce their thoughts into his system, he denies them hospitality. He can only come back to such thoughts after a long detour, and by way of cryptomnesia.

The all-embracing law of bipolarity compels us to postulate the existence of criminal trends at the

---

[1] Stekel holds that fetichism is the patient's unconscious religion. Cf. Fetischismus, 1923—a work remarkable for its analytical insight as well as for its abundance of material.

same level in the unconscious as that at which we find moral trends. These conflicting trends are mutual counterparts. It is not easy to decide whether these criminal impulses, which are certainly of very frequent occurrence, are, at a still lower stage, referable to sexual wishes.[1] This much is certain, that criminality is definitely impulsive. So, in like manner, are such anarchistic protests as a longing for the unrestricted gratification of sexual desire.

[1] Stekel, Impulshandlungen, 1922.

CHAPTER THIRTEEN

NARCISSISM

IN the *Psychology of the Unconscious*, a book which was to be momentous in its influence upon the relationships between Freud and Jung, the latter extended the idea of the libido far beyond the domain of the sexual. When he did so, Jung believed that Freud himself, in a work published in 1911,[1] had amplified the concept of libido that had been expounded some years earlier in the *Drei Abhandlungen*. Through the instrumentality of Ferenczi, Freud definitely repudiated this allegation. Freud followed up the statement in person a year later. The vehemence of Ferenczi's repudiation is all the more remarkable, seeing that the Hungarian analyst pauses in the midst of his animadversions upon Jung to remark that he himself, before Jung, had wanted to expand the concept of the libido. Freud, he said, had been opposed to the notion, and he (Ferenczi), as a good disciple, had complied. In my own book, *Alles um Liebe*, I deduced the origin of civilisation from a concept of the libido which, for my then purposes, it was not necessary to desexualise. I treated of the libido as sexual, although to outward appearance it might assume

[1] Psychoanalytische Bemerkungen über einen autobiographisch beschriebenen Fall von Paranoia, *[" Jahrbuch für Psychoanalyse," vol. iii, 1911.—Republished in Sammlung, vol. iii, No. 3.

other forms. I am, in fact, of opinion that the monism which both Jung and I have introduced into the conception of human impulses is plainly manifest in Freud's first formulation of 1905. Inasmuch as Freud substantially admits this to-day, we must interpret his opposition to Ferenczi and Jung in their attempts to enlarge the concept of the libido as meaning nothing more than this: " Let me alone. I shall myself expand the concept of the libido when the time is ripe!"

But the time was already ripe in 1905. If the libido can be sublimated, if it can be turned away from a sexual object, if its energy can be utilised in other directions (ranging from the collection of postage stamps to the writing of the Ninth Symphony), it is difficult to see what activity of the human mind can take place without the intervention of the libido. Two things were obvious in 1905. First of all, the libido was a transmutable form of energy. Secondly, everything that civilised human beings undertake. even in domains that seem to have nothing to do with the sexual life, is in one way or another connected with the libido. " We cannot get on without the assumption that there is a transmutable form of energy," writes Freud in 1923. But in 1907 and 1908 I published essays in which I discussed the transmutation of affect, which I already regarded as one of the most important of Freud's discoveries.

Nevertheless Freud, who had pointed out such paths to us lesser mortals, continued for many years to maintain against us that there were quite distinct forms of impulse, ranking equally with the libido, and furnishing the energy for the characteristically " civilised " activities of human beings. Such cultural

NARCISSISM

activities were undertaken with more passion, were in a sense transfigured, when the libido was part of their driving force; but the libido could not be invoked as an adequate explanation of all the activities of man. Thus Freud clung to his dualism, and contemptuously rejected Jung's "genetic" theory of the libido. At that time, Freud was still free from metaphysical leanings. He would not go so far as to deny that the sexual impulse and the impulse to seek food might have had common roots far back in the history of the human race. But such a contention was of trifling importance. With mordant humour, Freud wrote: "This contention relates to things which are so remote from the problems of direct observation, and have so little content of real knowledge, that we waste our time equally in affirming them or in denying them. It may be said that such a primitive identity has no more bearing upon our analytical interests, than the primitive kinship of all the races of man has a bearing upon the legal proof of kinship demanded of one who would make good his claim to an inheritance." [1]

Thus did the master chase away from the steps of his throne the analysts who were in search of a philosophy. The libido was at work everywhere. If Freud's teaching was to be accepted, human character, even, was formed in accordance with the erogenic zones. The triad, cleanliness, miserliness, and pedantry, was connected with the working of the anal zone. Ambition was a urethral-erotic character trait. Doubtless there was another force, of which Freud could not say much more than that

[1] Sammlung, iv, Zur Einführung des Narzissmus, p. 83 of second edition, 1922.

it existed. He did not even know whether it was a single force or an aggregate of forces. But whenever he was censured for making sexuality the universal motive energy, he could answer: "Have I not broken with my favourite pupil precisely because he wished to refer everything to the working of the libido? I am fully aware that there are ego impulses as well as libido."

In his latest publications (1920–1923), however, Freud, somewhat ruefully, ascribes an all-embracing significance to Eros. The ego impulses are dismissed to the oblivion which has long been their due. From the epistemological point of view, as I showed on pp. 157 et seq., they have always been impracticable conceptions. As far as the actual work of psychoanalysis is concerned, they are superfluous. Undoubtedly Freud is right in his contention that epistemological questions are not of much importance upon the plane on which, as doctors, we work with our patients. In any case, even on this plane, phenomena have come to light which make the assumption of ego impulses needless. Freud and his followers subsume these phenomena under the name "narcissism." To-day, few analysts will deny that the fiction of the ego is created by narcissism.

The word narcissism was coined by Havelock Ellis.[1] The concept, Freud tells us, was the out-

[1] It is true that Freud writes (Drei Abhandlungen zur Sexualtheorie, 5th edition, p. 81): "The term narcissism was not coined by Naecke, but by Havelock Ellis." This statement is not perfectly correct. Ellis described the perversion, but Naecke supplied the name. We have the direct authority of Ellis for this assertion. He writes to us on March 16, 1924: "I described the perversion, as a variety of autoerotism, with cases, in 'The Alienist and Neurologist,' invoking the name of Narcissus. Naecke, with whom I was in close touch, reproduced my description, and added an 'ismus' to Narcissus. I think one should say that the term is due to Havelock Ellis *and* Naecke."—E. and C. P.

growth of certain ideas propounded by the psychoanalyst Abraham, who at one time lived in Zurich, but for more than fifteen years has been at work in Berlin. Abraham is a meritorious investigator, and I should be the last to deprive him of any credit which is his due. But Freud is cryptomnesic, not only in respect of matters which he regards as his own, but also in respect of ideas which he fathers upon his pupils when they really originated with himself. The conception of narcissism is so far-reaching, and it is so characteristically stamped with the Freudian imprint, that posterity will be loath to dissociate it from Freud's immediate personality.[1]

However this may be, narcissism was first studied, not in the neurotic patients who constituted Freud's clinical material, but in those suffering from mental disorder, who were available for examination in Zurich. One of the essential distinctions between mental disorder and neurosis is that in some forms of mental disorder the patient has lost all interest in the outer world. That is why an effective contact with lunatics is so difficult. They have undergone "introversion." Let me make this characteristic of mental disorder more intelligible by a comparison with the mental life of the sane. Lunatics behave like dreamers, in that they are quite alone in the world. But the sane dreamer can be awakened, whereas nothing can shake the lunatic out of his dream. The lover, again, behaves in many respects

[1] Concerning this question, Freud writes to me as follows: " I have never maintained that narcissism was not my own independent discovery. I have merely pointed out that earlier writers have hinted at it." It would seem, therefore, that I must have misunderstood what Freud said in his lectures (Vorlesungen, Taschenausgabe, p. 438.—Cf. English translation, Introductory Lectures, pp. 346–7.)

like a lunatic. He has but one interest in the universe. Dead to all other interests, he enormously overestimates the importance of the only one left to him. The hypochondriac may be chosen as a third instance. He cares for absolutely nothing outside his liver, or whatever other organ he may fancy to be the cause of his troubles.

These examples make it needless to give a detailed definition of narcissism. Where do all the desires of the lover converge? Upon the person of his beloved. In the case of the lunatic, who has lost all interest in objective happenings, where do the desires converge? Upon his own person. Freud writes: "The subject's ego is invested with libido." But since the ego does not really exist, it will be better to say that narcissism creates the ego, exalts and debases it, according to the amount of libido left available for this nebulous object—which in reality consists only of an aggregate of perceptions, promoted by the libido to become the concept of the ego.

No human being and no ego is conceivable without narcissism. It was discovered by the study of extreme instances, as in lunacy, the love passion, and hypochondria—which last, in its more accentuated forms, is lunacy. But every one is in love with himself. He possesses in his libido a transmutable energy, with the aid of which he has brought to pass the most splendid achievements of civilisation. Nevertheless, the first and most obvious application of the libido is towards one's own self—body and spirit. While a man prizes his beloved, and passionately overestimates her value, there is another object of libido which he overvalues even more grossly, more persistently, and with yet greater conviction.

He values himself at a higher rate than any outward object of sexual desire. There are few exceptions to this generalisation, and they belong to the domain of mental disorder. The most conspicuous example of excessive valuation of the self is seen in megalomania. But we are all megalomaniacs, and are only ashamed—of one another. We need but take the first steps in analysis, we need merely " scratch " the surface of the mind, and narcissism comes to light. Since all things are bipolar, there is always a factor of underestimation as a counterpart to the factor of overestimation. A certain degree of the sense of inferiority attaches to narcissism as its antipole.

When they hit upon the concept of narcissism, the Freudians opened a new window through which light could penetrate into the dark recesses of the mind. Since this occurred at a comparatively late stage in the development of psychoanalytical theory, all the other parts of the theory had to be reconsidered in the new light. The ego impulses had been an ill-considered defence against Alfred Adler. Narcissism, on the other hand, was a successful refutation of the Zurichers; a resexualisation of Eros, whom they had desexualised.

Freud had always taught that the neurosis and its symptoms really depicted the patient's sexual life. Every neurotic detaches part of his libido from the outer world, and directs its energy inward. The hypochondriac, whose trouble is on the borderline between neurosis and lunacy, invests his own body with libido where he fancies his body to be diseased; the affected organ is treated like an erogenic zone, has become the hypochondriac's genital organ. This explains the perfect seriousness and the invincible obstinacy with which a hypochondriac clings to his false estimates. Where we are dealing with love, again, we find that the individual is proof against experience, and that rational considerations have no influence on him. The hypochondriac is closely akin to the melancholiac—and, indeed, every narcissist is melancholy. Can any one who is in love with himself find satisfaction? The prototype of all narcissists is the youth in the Greek saga, who sadly contemplates his image in the pool.

We find that the most adequate cause for grief exists when a much-loved person has died. Some of the survivor's libido has then, willy-nilly, been set free, and must find other objects to invest. The grief only lasts until such other objects have been found. I knew a man who had been greatly devoted to his wife. When she died, he bought a motor car, and toured at top speed all over the country. As travelling companions, he had now one fair lady, and now another, and this aroused unfavourable comment from those who had regarded him as a devoted husband. But a year later he was overwhelmed with the most profound grief, which his well-wishers now regarded as a trifle exaggerated. During the first year after his bereavement, he had been trying to run away from his grief, and had endeavoured to effect a forcible transfer of the liberated libido, to bring about its attachment to new objects. He would only admit his grief when this attempt had failed.

Freud explains the difference between grief and melancholia as follows: The mourner, one whose trouble is grief, tries to transfer to other objects the love that has been set free by the loss of the beloved. The melancholiac, on the other hand, is, as it were, struck by lightning owing to his loss. As though the energy had been short-circuited, the liberated libido turns back from the lost object towards the ego. This phenomenon is not so often seen in cases of bereavement as when the loss has taken some other form. Frequently the loss which has induced melancholia is one which the patient is loath to acknowledge, and in many cases it is one which he has repressed from his own consciousness. His self-accusations, his feeling that life is no longer worth living, and his conviction that he is a lost being, are, according to Freud, nothing but narcissistic paraphrases of complaints against others. The melancholiac, having lost a beloved person, has incorporated the lost one's personality into his own ego.

One of my patients, a wealthy man, was persistent in his complaints that life had become intolerable, and that he was ruined. The reason for his distress was that, by the laws of his country, he was compelled to cede a few acres of land. It did not console him in the least to be told that there was still left to him a large estate, with several houses, a motor car, and so on, and so on. Now, six months before, this man had lost his only daughter—by marriage. She was the " piece of land " of which he had been deprived. But it is not considered good form to bewail the fact that one's daughter has made a good marriage. For a time he had not been able to find any way of rationalising his melancholy.

Inasmuch as the efficacy of psychoanalysis depends upon transference, and inasmuch as in cases of mental disorder the inwardly directed narcissistic libido is but little disposed to undergo transference upon the analyst, the result is that, in certain forms of dementia, melancholia, and hypochondria, and in cases of delusion of persecution, megalomania, delusion of reference, etc., at an early stage of the analysis we encounter (to use Freud's term) an insuperable obstacle. The distinction between such mental disorders, on the one hand, and hysteria and obsessional neurosis, on the other, seemed so important to the founder of psychoanalysis that he classed the two latter as " transference neuroses "; whereas the types of mental disorder just enumerated were denominated " narcissistic neuroses."

If only it were not necessary to classify ! The extreme types of narcissism are doubtless incurable. But we are all narcissistic to a degree; every one may exhibit a certain measure of hypochondria; not one of us is free from delusion of reference. As far as the neuroses are concerned, in every one of us at a given time the mood tends a little towards exaltation or towards depression. Seeing that melancholia is in many cases curable by bringing about a transference upon the analyst, the boundary line between narcissistic neuroses and transference neuroses is blurred. For most of those afflicted with severe psychoneuroses, the " end of the world " has taken place. This is what made so strong an impression on Freud in the case of Schreber, the President of the Senate. We must be careful not to take this phrase " the end of the world " too literally. The " destruction of the world " conceals what has really been destroyed. We may recall, in this connexion, Alfred Adler's brilliant remark that neurotics are fond of play-acting, and that their " end of the world" is a fiction whose foundations can be undermined by bringing about a transference. Freud makes an apt remark when he says that there are two different mechanisms whereby a person may become dead to the world. "There are the cases in which all the libidinal cathexis (investment) flows away towards the beloved object, and those in which it all flows back towards the ego." For two persons who are ardently in love with one another, the rest of the world is non-existent. Each has lost himself or herself in the other—" anti-narcissism."

The counterpart of narcissism (we have just touched upon the matter in this reference to ardent lovers) is "identification" with another person. The essence of love is identification. "Each becomes conscious only in and through the other." Great poets have always described the love sentiment in this way. To the bodily union in the love act, to the transference of the sexual products, there corresponds a spiritual union and a spiritual transference. Even the infant loves already by identification. He imitates everything. He learns by imitating those he loves. He identifies himself with the father and with the mother; identifies himself to a lesser degree with all the members of his environment; until ultimately, after the lapse of a few years, by this persistent swallowing of others, he has expanded his own ego to such dimensions that he can love it. At long last, he identifies himself with himself.

The concept of autoerotism was familiar in psychoanalysis long before that of narcissism. The idea was taken from the sexual life of the infant, all of whose sexual pleasures are derived from its own body and from all parts thereof. Narcissism can best be understood by regarding it as a spiritual amplification of bodily autoerotism. In 1914, Freud actually formulated the notion of " a primary libidinal cathexis of the ego, from which subsequently libido was directed towards outward objects." In the course of subsequent years, however, Freud came to realise more and more that the ego, if it exists at all, is at any rate not brought by the child into the world, but comes into existence later. Recently, he has described the ego as originating through identification. According to Freud's account of the matter in 1923, the libido is first outwardly directed. From objects, it is then withdrawn towards the ego. This withdrawal, towards the ego, of the libido which had been outwardly directed, is termed by Freud " secondary narcissism." But, in that case, I do not know what is left of primary narcissism. In my view, there is only one kind of narcissism, and the only ego is a narcissistic ego. Thus the ego would be no more than a postulate, which manifests itself as an ego in order to supply a tangible substratum for the narcissistic libido.

Some may find this exposition difficult to understand, so I will put the matter in a more popular way. I knew a lady of pleasure named Bella von M., whose quarters for the night were sometimes in one barrack and sometimes in another. This was long before the war and its upshot had destroyed the Austro-Hungarian synthesis of nations. When she had passed the night in the cavalry barrack, she would talk next morning with the Hungarian accent of the hussars. After a sojourn in the infantry barrack, she spoke German like a Bohemian. When she had been visiting the uhlans, her accent was

Polish. Thus she invariably identified herself with her latest intimate, and there might have seemed to be a risk of her ultimately becoming a typical example of " multiple personality." In her case, there was little scope for narcissism ; the direction of her libido was almost exclusively outward. In conformity with this, her ego was scantily developed. From day to day she was an ephemeron living in the shadow of her last lover's personality, the lover who was to be forgotten as soon as a new evening began. But when the previous night's lover had been forgotten, Bella von M., about whom there was nothing real—not even her name—could not go on living. If one has no narcissism, one has no ego, and that is terrible. For this reason she was constrained to hasten to the nearest barrack, in order to find an object for her libido.

A respectable girl does not behave in this way. She has an ego, " and loves it, and has good cause to love it."

There are many women who have no ego, and therefore no anchorage. Some women, on the other hand, have too much ego in the narcissistic sense, and are consequently incapable of genuine love. In 1907 I described this type of woman under the name of the " child-woman." [1] At that time I knew nothing of narcissism. I explained the child-woman as one who, owing to the premature development of beauty, had prematurely become the object of desire. Thus the beautiful child had failed to develop into a woman, and had remained a child, as she had been when she had first become the object of desire (for to be desired is the biological purpose of the woman).

[1] Die sexuelle Not.

Such a woman, therefore, remains simple, childishly beautiful, and childishly free from inhibitions. She flies from one man's hand to another, and early perishes. Venereal diseases and tuberculosis [1] lie in wait for her, and the men who are at first eager to woo her favour, come to regard her as a harlot because she can keep faith with no one. At that time the substratum of my thought in this matter was the concept of infantile autoerotism, but I developed from it a part of the idea which subsequently came to be called narcissism. I read the essay to Freud before it was published.

To-day, the attractive force which the child-woman exercises, and also the peculiar nature of her sexuality, are easier to understand than they were in 1907. I said then that the child-woman was the primitive woman. In 1914, writing of "the commonest and perhaps the most typical woman," Freud described the following love mechanism:

"Woman, especially when conspicuous for beauty, possesses a self-sufficiency which compensates her for the fact that convention forbids her the free choice of the object of love. Strictly speaking, such women love themselves alone, love themselves as intensely as a man loves them. Their love need does not take the form of loving another, but of being loved; and they like the man who satisfies this condition. The significance of such a type of women in the amatory life of men is very great. They exercise a powerful attraction upon men, not only for æsthetic reasons (inasmuch as they are usually beautiful), but also because of interesting psychological constellations. . . . But this great charm of the narcissistic

[1] "Phthisicus semper salax!"

woman has its seamy side. Much of the dissatisfaction of male lovers, their doubts concerning the reality of woman's love, and their complaints concerning the enigmatic nature of women, arise out of this incongruency in the objects of their affection."[1]

In this passage, Freud comes to a view which he had not yet adopted in 1907. When I read my paper on the child-woman at a meeting of the Psychoanalytical Society, Freud said that this type must be sharply distinguished from the civilised woman. The child-woman was nothing but a "drab." The study of narcissism has modified my own outlook since then, and I realise that the great hetaira can never love any one but herself. Her motto is ἔχω οὐκ ἔχομαι—I possess, but I am not possessed. Yet she continually needs fresh assurances that she is lovable; she needs beautiful dresses, ornaments, and her mirror; she needs that many men shall tell her that she is the most beautiful woman in the world. When such assurances are lacking, or when her competitors win successes, the hetaira is greatly discomposed; for, though she is narcissistic, her narcissism is not fixed, and is carried away on the ebb of each departing day. She must always be more and have more than anyone else. This wish of hers makes her resemble the man in one of Hauff's tales whom the devil had promised that he should always have twice as much in his pocket as the richest farmer in the village. On one occasion, this man was playing cards with the village Crœsus, and won all the cash the Crœsus had with him. The loser, wishing to continue the game, proposed to borrow some money from the winner, but the latter now found that he

[1] Sammlung, iv, 96.

had not even a penny left in his pocket. The devil's promise had been that he was always to have twice as much as Crœsus, and since Crœsus' pockets were empty, his own contained—twice nothing. Thus is it, too, with the ego of the great courtesan. Such an ego exists only as the reflex of wooing, or as success over a rival. This is what I term the narcissism of inferiority.

Inasmuch as a permanent fixation on the beloved can only come about through an overflow of the lover's personality into that of the beloved, a great love always presupposes a vigorous ego. That is why I consider the idea of the ego and the idea of narcissism to be identical. What we love and worship in another is our own ego, which we have exteriorised into the other's personality. We must think a great deal of ourselves if we are to be able strongly and enduringly to love our own ego when it has assumed the form of the beloved. This is quite beyond the competence of such as Bella von M. Child-women cannot develop an ego, and therefore they cannot love.

There is something else which I have failed to discover in Freud's writings, but which has been made clear to me by the study of Stekel's book on homosexuality. The immense success of women who are ardently desired and greatly loved depends upon homosexual impulses in men. The hetaira-cult of our days is no less homosexual than was that of classical Greece. What a man loves in the hetaira is the other men who have lain and will lie in her arms. Since the homosexual impulse is unconscious, it cannot manifest itself in the form of direct love for another man. We must not imagine that the men whose desires always turn towards especially beautiful women are men of a peculiarly virile type. They love such women because they know that beauty will attract the glances of other men towards these women. This leads us to Hebbel's Candaules motif, which has been discussed by Sadger in *Friedrich Hebbel, ein psychoanalytischer Versuch*, and by myself in *Tragische Motive*. I have also published a novel in which the Candaules motif forms the central feature,[1] but this was written at a time when I was myself still unaware of my hero's unconscious homosexuality.[2]

What I have been saying as to the homosexuality of men whose only love interest is in very beautiful women, forms so assured a part of our knowledge that I feel justified in inferring homosexuality when a patient tells me, usually with great pride, that he has never loved and possessed any but beautiful women. I then say to the patient: " What you want is that these women should please, not only yourself, but also another man, one with whom you are in love, though perhaps without knowing it."

In these instances, the analysis invariably discloses the existence of such a man; and it is a great advantage to the patient when the hidden homosexuality is brought into the focus of consciousness. We cannot strive against the invisible.

Just as Sadger was the first who made use of psychoanalysis for the cure of homosexuality, whereas Freud has not even to-day wholly abandoned the opinion that this trend is constitutional (Steinach's view), so likewise Sadger was the first to recognise

[1] Wittels, Der Juwelier von Bagdad.
[2] Cf. also Freud, Ueber die allgemeinste Erniedrigung des Liebeslebens, Sammlung, iv, 13 and 14.

that narcissism belongs to the same order of phenomena as homosexuality. The narcissist, in his search for the object of love, pauses where the object seems most like to himself. It is natural that this should tend to be a person of his own sex, one who possesses the same kind of genital organs as the self-enamoured narcissist. No doubt the psychological structure of homosexuality is extremely complicated. There are some homosexuals who have undergone fixation on the mother, and who can only secure release from that fixation by identifying themselves with the mother. They thus feel themselves to be women, and their desires turn towards man as a complement. This mechanism was described by Freud in 1921.[1] In such little matters, it is no longer possible to speak of priority in psychoanalysis. Thousands of investigators are at work, and simultaneous discoveries are frequent.

Thus identification has two distinct forms. In one of these, the object is swallowed, and therewith the narcissist is complete. In the second case, the ego flows away into the other person, and the love for the ego (narcissism) has to follow the ego like a shadow.—But the reader is aware that I incline to regard the ego as the shadow of narcissism.

Freud makes some very striking observations regarding the love felt for one's own child. This love, he says, is narcissism. Conventional inhibitions restrict us in the manifestation of love for ourselves, but no such restrictions are imposed on the love we feel for our children. The children are portions of ourselves, and yet we are permitted to love them without being charged with egoism. Still, people

[1] Massenpsychologie und Ich-Analyse, p. 73.

guess what is in the wind when parents are over-affectionate, and such parents are the butt of popular wit.

"There is a tendency for the narcissist to attach to the child all the cultural acquirements which the former has wrested from his narcissism, and to renew in the child the claim to long-relinquished privileges. The child is to have a better time of it than the parent, is not to be subjected to the restrictions which have hampered the parent's life . . . In the child's person, the narcissist arrogates to himself the title ' His Majesty the Baby.' The child is to fulfil the parent's unfulfilled dream wishes; is to become a great man and a hero, where the father has failed to become one; or (if a girl) is to have a prince for husband as a belated compensation to the mother. The weak point in the narcissistic system is the longing for the immortality of the ego, which is menaced by inexorable reality. This longing takes refuge in the personality of the child. The touching fondness of parents for their children, itself an essentially childlike sentiment, is only the parents' renascent narcissism, whose original nature is plainly manifest even when thus metamorphosed into the love of an external object." [1]

[1] The quotation in the text, from Sammlung, iv, p. 99, is merely a repetition. The following passage from Die Traumdeutung, first edition, p. 275, shows that Freud was already on the track of narcissism before 1900 : " It is easy to perceive that the suppressed megalomania of the father is in the latter's mind transferred upon the children. Indeed, there is good reason to believe that this is one of the ways in which the suppression of megalomania—a necessity of practical everyday life—is usually effected."

CHAPTER FOURTEEN

WILHELM STEKEL

THE breach with Stekel occurred between the Weimar congress and the Munich congress. During these years there must have been smouldering some of the hatred which was to culminate in the rupture. Still, I have no proof of this assertion, and I know that several times Freud has broken with old friends in similar fashion. At the beginning of the century, he cut adrift from Breuer and Fliess; towards 1912 he severed his relationships with Adler, Stekel, Kahane, and Jung. In the cases of Adler and Jung there were, no doubt, insuperable differences anent scientific matters; but as far as the quarrel with Stekel was concerned, the reasons were mainly personal. There were differences upon matters of theory as well, but no important principles were involved, and it would have been an advantage to the psychoanalytical cause if the two men could have continued to exchange ideas. In his writings, Freud tells the world plainly why he broke with Adler and Jung. As regards Stekel, all he says is that the breach was caused by " matters which it is hardly possible to make public." The very reticence of this phraseology is what makes it so offensive. The reader might imagine that on one of the Wednesday evenings Stekel had been caught pocketing the spoons! Even

WILHELM STEKEL

more spiteful is the passage in which Freud refers to "Stekel, so serviceable to begin with, and afterwards so utterly untrustworthy." If Freud or one of his more immediate pupils finds it necessary to quote Stekel (such quotations are made as seldom as possible), the quotation is always accompanied by an expression of regret that this abominable name has to be introduced.

For my part, I am greatly indebted to Wilhelm Stekel. Alone among the psychoanalysts he has continued to befriend me during the years in which outward, and perhaps inward, circumstances have prevented my making any notable contribution to psychoanalytical science. I agree, therefore, that I may be prejudiced in his favour, and that I am not in a position to give an unbiased opinion in this affair of Stekel versus Freud. Still, I shall explain matters as I see them.

I need not dwell on Stekel's services in the diffusion of Freud's ideas throughout the German press. He no longer contributes in this way to periodicals. At the outset he was one of those who were immeasurably impressed by Freud's researches. Who could help being amazed by them? Even Janet, who described Freud's discovery as a bad joke, was, fundamentally, no less astonished than Freud's own disciples. It was those that were devoid of critical faculty, those that swallowed everything or rejected everything in block, who displayed poverty of intelligence. The faithful disciples were never able to get over their initial astonishment. Stekel recovered from it. He shook off the hypnotic influence that had emanated from Freud's imposing personality. This was the cause of the trouble.

When I say that Stekel criticised some of Freud's contentions, I am telling only half the story, and the less weighty half. The most important thing about Stekel seems to me to be the confidence with which he has moved along the roads first opened up by Freud. Thus Stekel unrestingly exploited the new scientific domain, and this aroused the hostility of the other disciples, and ultimately the hostility of the master himself—the man who, somewhat hesitatingly, had been the first to enter these dark recesses and to illuminate them with the torch of his research. Stekel is so fully convinced of the soundness of what he has accepted from among the Freudian doctrines, that he continues to build on this foundation without troubling himself about questions of principle, critical objections, and queries as to method.  His relationship to Freud may be compared with the relationship of the epoch of Rubens to the epoch of Michelangelo. For Michelangelo the perspective foreshortening of the human body always remained a problem. In the case of Rubens, the mastery of all these foreshortenings had become a self-evident presupposition of the painter's art. There was no longer any struggle to secure the draftsman's technique; wherefore, at times, the self-confidence of Rubens' work annoys the beholder.

Stekel was once described by a hostile critic as a man who carried something demoniacal in his waistcoat pocket. He is, in fact, so intimately acquainted with the daimons of the dream that he will face a combat with them fearlessly. Freud had to take a great deal of trouble to prove the general thesis that the dream has a hidden meaning, and his mission was to defend the discovery of the dream language against a world of enemies. Stekel's mission was different. He is quite unconcerned about those who refuse to admit that dreams have a meaning. He sets forth boldly to navigate the subterranean waters, and has made a whole series of discoveries in the field of dream interpretation. At first, even Freud's pupils laughed at many of these; but, undeterred by the mockery of the dull-witted, he has succeeded in making dream symbolism, which Freud had only hinted at, the very centre of dream interpretation. He was the first to recognise the death symbolism of the dream.[1] Not until 1922 did Freud accept Stekel's notion of death symbolism, with a proviso that showed the acceptance to be distasteful.[2] I can remember Stekel's first contributions to the discussions of the Psychoanalytical Society. He explained the significance of "right" and "left" in dreams; referred to the bisexuality of dream symbols; was the first to explain dreams of return to the father; and so on. Whenever he announced such discoveries, he was told that they were "exaggerations" which could only bring discredit upon psychoanalysis. The Zurichers, when they criticised the Viennese "far-fetched interpretations," were thinking especially of Stekel.

The fact is that Stekel has an unrivalled gift for dream interpretation. He does not confine himself to the narrow path pointed out by Freud, but discloses the significance of the dream by a peculiar form of insight which many people speak of as intuition. Having interpreted thousands upon thousands of dreams, he has become to a certain

---

[1] Refer back to the examples given on pp. 82–3 and 103.
[2] "Imago," viii, 1.

extent independent of the data contributed by the dreamer. Those who know how unwilling, owing to the resistance, the patient usually is to give the necessary associations to his dreams, will understand the value of this faculty of Stekel's. Of course, the method has its dangers, and it is easy to go astray. No matter. The misses count for nothing; the hits remain.

Thus an analysis by Stekel involves an active participation of the patient. Again and again, the latter feels that the shafts hit the mark, until at length he is impelled to disclose that which, when the passive form of psychoanalysis is alone practised, is often withheld until analyser and analysand have both lost patience. This explains Stekel's practical successes. Freud is a man of genius, but Stekel is a better dream interpreter than Freud. Stekel describes himself as the dwarf standing on the giant's shoulders. Now that he is banned by the orthodox Freudians, he sometimes amuses himself by reinterpreting a dream published, with an interpretation, by Freud or by one of the faithful. When this happens, Stekel's reinterpretation always has so remarkable a verisimilitude, that the original interpretation promptly falls to the ground. On p. 144 I gave Stekel's reinterpretation of a dream of Monroe Meyer's.

Here is another instance of reinterpretation. One of Freud's patients, a woman, dreamed of her deceased father, who appeared, and said to her in a menacing tone: "It is half-past eleven, it is a quarter to twelve." Freud tells us that the dreamer had been one of the auditors of an observation to the effect that something of primitive man (Urmensch) lingers on in us all. When the father spoke of half-past eleven (halb zwölf Uhr) and a quarter to twelve (dreiviertel zwölf Uhr), the dreamer, in virtue of one of those puns which are common in dreams, was making of her father an Uhrmensch (clock-man), i.e. Urmensch (primitive man)—this being a wish-fulfilment, the fulfilment of her wish that he might be living on in her, and therefore not be really dead.

Stekel's explanation of the dream was very different. The twelfth hour is the last hour. The father appears in order to warn the child. He says nothing more than that it is time, high time—half-past eleven, a quarter to twelve—to begin something, or finish something, or repeat something.

This critic made himself such a nuisance with his reinterpretations that the orthodox Freudians began to hesitate before publishing their interpretations, which were often strained. Much of what they wring from dreams by a process which amounts to distortion, vanishes into nothingness in the light of Stekel's intuition.

The reader will readily understand that the Psychoanalytical Society must have found a person with such uncanny talents a very inconvenient member. Imagine a circle of arithmeticians, laboriously working out difficult sums with the aid of pencil and paper; but among them is a master of mental arithmetic, who jumps to the right solution with perfect ease. This is very annoying to the plodders; and is, in fact, unscientific, for the scientist is not content with mere results, but wants to bear the burden and heat of the day on the way thitherward. It would require a good deal more patience than Freud and his disciples possess, to tolerate a man with Stekel's talents in their company.

Add to this, that Stekel does not merely unravel

the dream symbolism, but that he likewise adroitly disinters the actual conflicts from the patient's unconscious. In an astonishingly short time, during which he is mainly concerned with the study of the patient's dreams, he will often be able to tell the latter in plain words what the conflicts are. When he makes a mistake, which of course happens now and again, he is always ready to dismount and try a fresh horse. In this way he advances as a skilful man, and one who knows other men—far outstripping those who become analysts because they are really aloof from the world, and are incompetent, man to man, and without machinery, to find their way into a sick soul.

I concede the point that Stekel is commonplace when compared with Freud. This is because he is in closer touch with the everyday world than such a man as Freud, who stands on a peak apart. But inasmuch as the experiences that determine our illnesses are for the most part everyday and trivial, a physician who is at home in the trivial world will often cure us quickly where the titan will fail.

Of late years there has been much talk concerning the "active method" of psychoanalysis. The Swiss analysts mean by this what they also term "psychosynthesis," which has been discussed on pages 188-190. Freud considers that we are quite active enough if we persistently strive to overcome the patient's resistance and to disclose the transference. Also, says Freud, we must as far as may be lead the patient into a situation in which he will find his illness inconvenient; but this is a form of activity to which life imposes narrow limits.[1] Stekel understands by

[1] *Sammlung*, v, No. 3.

active psychotherapeutics a persistent bombardment of the patient by the active unravelling of his complexes. This method is certainly dangerous, and in unskilled hands quite impracticable. Furthermore, analyses thus conducted have no demonstrative force to confirm the accuracy of psychoanalytical laws, since they are based on an assumption that these laws are accurate. For a long time yet we shall have to counter the arguments of opponents who know nothing whatever of psychoanalysis. In so far as such persons are teachable, they can only be taught by practical experience. Besides, even Freud has not yet furnished us with a complete and entirely convincing analysis.

Stekel decided to adopt an active method of psychoanalysis because experience had shown him that passive analyses, those in which the physician interferes to a minimum extent, drag on too long. Very lengthy analyses are undesirable, were it only because few patients can spare time and money for them; but there are additional objections. In course of time, the transference upon the analyst assumes such a form that the patient gets a fixation upon the doctor. Furthermore, where can the patient find any one to take him so seriously as to be willing to listen and interpret for an hour day after day without end? Psychoanalysis, in such instances, itself becomes a disease, replacing the neurosis, which perhaps has already lasted for years. Stekel will not continue an analysis longer than a few months—from three to six. Nothing more can be done with anyone who is not cured within that space of time. In some cases, when progress has been arrested, we have tried the effect of exchanging patients. I have taken over Stekel's analysands, and he has still more often done the same for me. In this way we have tried to outwit the transference, usually with good results.

Analyses extending back into the days when the patient was in his mother's womb are a heroic undertaking. Freud's incomparable patience, thanks to which he has made some of his most splendid discoveries, is a glorious achievement of the human spirit. But this is not a road along which all the lesser analysts should try to follow him. The interests of pure science and those of medical practice are in conflict here, as Freud himself has frequently admitted.

Stekel is a practitioner, not a systematist. He juxtaposes the data of his experience without feeling impelled to force them into the framework of a system. His works are comprehensive. Doubtless, in composing them he has certain directives; but he is always willing to abandon these directives for new ones, and to respond to fresh stimuli. Thus he never loses touch with the multiform pulses of life. His lack of metaphysical tastes will displease a good many readers. But each man must follow his own bent. If Stekel has no leanings towards metapsychology, and is disinclined to formulate a system, this is because his talents lie in other fields. Whereas the rigidly orthodox Freudians seem to be drawing more and more away from medicine and from the direct observation of nature, Stekel goes on studying cases, more cases, and nothing but cases, concerning which he has already published hundreds upon hundreds of reports. The number sounds preposterous. It is in truth not quite so large as the foregoing statement suggests. Many individual cases appear more than once in his records, being contemplated from different aspects. Nevertheless, the volcanic character of his working powers can be neither denied nor imitated.

Stekel's books are easier to understand than most of the publications of the orthodox Freudians. For a good many years, now, doctors and others who have taken to the study of Freudian psychoanalysis, have reached that study by a circuitous route (if it be circuitous)—by the reading of Stekel's works. Able thinkers who have no intimate connexion with Freudianism, form the impression that of all Freud's pupils, Stekel is the most successful, and is the logical inheritor of psychoanalysis. An enormous work by Stekel, planned for ten volumes, is now in course of issue. Seven of these volumes, comprising about four thousand pages, have already been published. Never before, unless it be in the fictional series of such writers as Balzac and Zola, has any one attempted to present so complete a picture and to effect so far-reaching an analysis of all human passions. The work is a psychoanalytical encyclopædia. No analyst can ignore this monument.

The contempt with which the orthodox Freudians regard, or rather, feign to regard, Stekel is in amusing contrast with these facts. I learn from Stekel that, after the expulsion of Adler, Freud said to him: " I have made a pygmy great, but I have overlooked a giant close at hand. A single one among the many dream symbols you have discovered is worth more than the whole 'Adlerei' put together." No doubt Freud will have forgotten this utterance But Stekel has an agate bowl which Freud sent him from Carlsbad in 1911. It was accompanied by a letter containing the words: " I cannot conceive that anything could ever come between us." Very soon afterwards he was to write of Stekel as " so serviceable to begin with, and afterwards so utterly untrustworthy." What a cruel turn of fate! It does indeed seem to be predestined (I have no thought of irony) that trees shall not grow too far heavenward. How vast an influence these two men might have exercised on one another in the way of reciprocal stimulation! I know, of course, that Freud's figure is one of those which loom athwart the centuries, so that I can hardly speak of Stekel in the same breath. But I know, likewise, that Freud's character received a permanent twist from his relationship with Nephew John (supra, pp. 15, 19, and 45)—and that never, while life endures, will Freud be able to shake off this Old Man of the Sea.

Jung and Adler were ambitious, and they did not feel strong enough to win laurels from psychoanalysis in the field preempted by Freud. That is why they tried to divert the current of Freudian doctrine into new channels. But Stekel has both feet firmly planted upon the ground of psychoanalysis. He is ready and willing to go on working at the edifice whose foundations have been well and truly laid by Freud. He has cleared away some of the minor outworks, and this erstwhile disciple will not enter the ring where Freud's libido theory is housed. He works with the concepts of repression, resistance, and transference. He interprets dreams by methods which he has, indeed, elaborated, but which would have been unthinkable had it not been for the previous work of Freud. For Stekel, likewise, psychosexual infantilism and the sexuality of childhood remain matters of preponderant importance. In such circumstances, no unprejudiced person can fail to admit that Stekel's work is the legitimate offspring of Freud's teaching. The word " legitimate " may have an unpleasant connotation. I borrow it from Freud, who has used it several times in connexion with the growth of psychoanalysis.[1]

It was somewhere about 1910 when Freud's pupils began to promote the master to the rank of Pope, and Stekel ran counter on several occasions to the dogma of infallibility. He denied that anxiety could be the direct outcome of preventive intercourse, without the intermediation of a mental conflict (supra p. 48). He also denied the primary injuriousness of masturbation. Stekel does not believe that there are any " actual neuroses," in the sense in which the term is used by Freud. When I add that in the matter of homosexuality Stekel considers that congenital influences are practically inoperative, I have mentioned the third of the three points on which Stekel already differed from Freud more than ten years ago. In all three respects, Stekel's view comes as a deliverance. He delivers man from the doom of hereditary taint, inasmuch as he contends that relief can always be given by psychoanalysis. Since all human beings masturbate, Stekel's energetic insistence on his view that masturbation is harmless, removes an ancient incubus from those who learn his opinions.

Towards 1910, Freud said that Stekel was inclined to overstrain psychical explanations. Freud was nurtured in the physiological, the organic, school of medicine, and has not been able to free his mind

[1] Cf. Sammlung, vol. iv, pp. 69 and 80.

completely from the influence of early teachings. He tells us of mental conflicts in the unconscious. But he does not dare to be radical; he does not dare to cut the soul loose from all its moorings in the organic. Where he has shown timidity, Stekel has shown courage. Nevertheless, the theories which ten years ago led to a breach with Stekel are in favour to-day, provided they are put forward, not by Stekel, but by Groddeck—a man who kicks over all the traces of critical restraint.[1]

Stekel describes illnesses which we might term "actual neuroses," if that name were not already bespoken. He concentrates his attention upon the patient's actual mental conflicts. He knows that everyone cherishes a secret ideal in the unconscious, and that every one harbours a protest against reality. This secret ideal, this real character of the individual, is formed in early childhood; the Oedipus complex, narcissism, and the castration complex, contribute in varying degrees to its formation. Moreover, in many cases one can only happen upon the actual ideal in the unconscious by approaching it, as it were, from the rear, when we have made a great detour through the patient's childhood. But the most important matter in psychoanalysis is the tension between the secret wishes and the manifest life. The Oedipus complex lies hidden in us all; but, with few exceptions, what unfits us for life is some actual conflict.

One of Freud's younger followers recently declared that brief analyses, though they might relieve symptoms, could never cure the neurotic temperament. This profound saying is doubtless true!

[1] Das Buch vom Es.

Let me remind the reader of the melancholiac who was unconsciously mourning the loss of his eldest daughter, recently married. When, after a brief analysis, I made this man realise the nature of the conflict which was unfitting him for daily life, it is undeniable that I had merely relieved a symptom, had dispelled his melancholy mood. If I had wanted to immunise the patient's nervous mechanism against the possibility of relapse, a very protracted analysis would have been essential—and even then success would have been doubtful. Still, the precise causative factors will not recur; this father will not again have to give in marriage the eldest daughter whose youthful charms were, in his unconscious, a substitute for the fading beauties of a wife no longer found alluring. The practitioner may, as a rule, be well content if he can relieve such distressing symptoms. The other alternative is that adopted by the analyst who was unable to cure an attack of writer's cramp. But the analysis went on for a very long time, until ultimately the patient lost his sense of illness, and was able to put up with the symptom.

What had happened in that case ? The analyst had failed to discover the secret mental conflict which the writer's cramp symbolised. On the other hand, he had induced a vigorous transference, had installed a second neurosis to take its place beside the writer's cramp. The second neurosis may be called by the name of the analyst. The patient finds himself able to put up with his illness because thereby he can show his gratitude to the beloved analyst, who has taken such an infinite amount of trouble. Is that the sort of " cure " on account of which any analyst should wish to plume himself ?

Stekel, in his persistent search for the actual conflict, has come across the faith in the "great historic mission," which reaches its acme in the Messianic neurosis. Incredibly large is the number of persons, modest to all outward seeming, who secretly believe themselves to have a great historic mission. The paucity of their actual achievements is often in ludicrous contrast with the splendour of their imaginings. They suffer from the severe tension between what they do and what they would like to do. The resemblance between this formulation and Adler's is obvious.

Quite peculiar to Stekel, however, is, I believe, the discovery of a mechanism which is definitely opposed to repression. He terms it the "annulling mechanism" (Annullierungsmechanismus). Repressed ideas are unknown to the conscious, but they operate though they are unknown. On the other hand, there are ideas known to the conscious which remain inoperative because the unconscious does not recognise them, disowns them, annuls them. For instance, there are married men who, of course, know perfectly well that they are married, whose dreams show that in the unconscious they are unmarried. The unconscious has annulled the wife. A moment's reflection shows us that this mechanism is continually at work in our daily life. When two persons whose lives are ostensibly intertwined associate in a moody silence, it is obvious that each has annulled the other. In this dangerous way, one will annul the other for a long time, until, in accordance with the will of the unconscious, each comes to mean nothing to the other even in the realm of consciousness.

Another great service of Stekel's, one whose

importance grows increasingly manifest as the volumes of his great work succeed one another, is the elaboration of the idea that everyone, and in particular every neurotic, has a peculiar form of sexual gratification which is alone adequate. "Normal" sexual intercourse does not carry with it any guarantee that it furnishes adequate sexual gratification. That is how we answer our neurotic patients when they tell us that the sexual theory must be false, seeing that they have practised normal sexual intercourse and are none the less "nervous." Sometimes, the practice of normal sexual intercourse may be positively harmful, may engender nervous troubles, if it should conflict in some way with the form of sexual gratification which is unconsciously felt to be alone adequate. Thus Stekel (he does not stand by himself in this) has explained Don Juan and Casanova, and also the Messalina types among women, as persons eternally ungratified, living and dying in the vain search for the conditions of adequate sexual gratification.

But what Stekel was the first to recognise was that, in these cases, larval homosexuality is the predominant factor. People hardly realise, as yet, that unconscious homosexuality is tending more and more to become the undertone of our epoch. Women must no longer be women; they must become men, and we talk of "feminism." Their inborn rotundity of form no longer pleases; they must be lean and sinewy like men. They must cut their hair short. If possible, they must discard what used to be regarded as a hereditary feeling, the sense of shame. Far be it from me to play the moralist. I am not appraising these things, but merely recording them. The masculinisation of woman is of old date, and its primary determinant was need. Well-to-do women had no other occupation than to love themselves and their husbands, and to bring up their children. Need, poverty—and the oldest manifestation of this was at the coming of the Ice Age—constrained them to work like men. But the masculinisation of women to which I am now referring has nothing to do with the hunger need. Sexual need is the offspring of our altered conditions of life, which have shattered all settled relationships. The old moral codes, Christianity, the morals of family life—how much longer are they likely to endure? A great revaluation is in progress. But it is not altogether agreeable to live in the No Man's Land between two ethical worlds. We can no longer believe in the old; and yet we shrink from the new, being still entangled in the old. We swim in the waters of a huge wave; we suffer from unceasing tensions between can, may, must, shall, and will. That is why the age in which we live is under the evil star of neurosis.

Psychoanalysts used to regard the repression of sexuality as the only cause of neurosis. Stekel has drawn attention to the Satanists (the leading figure, the most tragical figure, among them is that of Nietzsche), who perish from the working of their inward and suppressed moral and religious feelings.

The ostensible cause of the breach between Freud and Stekel, in so far as I know anything about it, is too trifling to be worth recording. But the real cause bulks all the more largely. If Freud had paid keener heed, he would have realised that the Zurichers' attacks on Stekel were really aimed through the pupil at the master. In like manner, Freud was breaking with a part of himself when he abruptly severed all relationships with the man who had been his collaborator since 1896. Stekel could do without pricks of conscience everything which Freud was censured for doing, above all by the German intellectuals. Stekel could be one-sided, could generalise particular observations, could fail to pay attention to the phenomenology of the mind, could ignore the data of philosophy. But Freud was tormented by his conscience, was tormented by an unescapable ego-ideal which had been introduced into his mind by such teachers as Meynert and Brücke. He wanted to shake off part of his own ego, and succeeded in doing this when he began to hate Stekel. Projection explains the affective hatred with which, for years now, Freud has regarded his ex-disciple. To him Stekel seems unduly carefree, too regardless of criticism, in a realm which Freud discovered—without persistently believing in it.

After the expulsion of the fragment of the ego which is symbolised by Stekel, Freud turned to metaphysics, to what he calls metapsychology. He turned with a fervour which implied a longing to make up for lost time, and entered a domain into which Stekel, a man utterly averse from metaphysics, will certainly not follow him. There Freud is safe from the instrusion of that other ego, which to him has now become a thing of evil, as to the Christianised pagans the household gods they had formerly worshipped became evil demons.

CHAPTER FIFTEEN

FREUDIAN MECHANISMS

THE transferability of the libido is, perhaps, the most important principle of our mental life. Everything that comprises " Freudian mechanisms " is based upon it. That towards which the libido is directed becomes bright and congenial, and that from which the libido is withdrawn grows dark. It even flows out of the otherwise circumscribed individual, flows afar, and conquers the world. It returns from afar, laden with experiences like the bee laden with honey; is reabsorbed; becomes the ego, that fiction which in primitive philosophy was taken for reality.

Freud teaches that there is a super-ego, which arises through identification with the father-imago. But something more than the super-ego (also termed the ego-ideal) originates through identification. Freud will not shrink much longer from regarding the entire fiction of the ego as an identification with the father, the mother, and the whole living environment. At first everything is imitated; subsequently, that which is constructed by imitation is loved as the ego (narcissism), and through self-love it is detached from the environment (differentiated).

A missionary to the Indies in whose good faith I have full confidence told me of the following experience. It happened when he was preaching in an Indian village. He noticed that his congregation, which was listening devoutly, suppressed a laugh. Turning round to look for the cause of the merriment, he saw that a large monkey had taken up its position behind him, and was imitating all his gestures. On another occasion, when he came to unlock the door of his church, he found a monkey in the pulpit, making as if to preach, while half a dozen other monkeys were sitting in the choir wagging their heads. Thus the animals were imitating men's incomprehensible doings. What distinguishes them from men is merely their incapacity to construct an ego on the basis of such an imitation. Their mental activity is like a photograph which has not yet been fixed. Man's advance upon the lower animals has been the development of this capacity for fixation. That is why Goethe says of the human being: "He can give durability to the fleeting moment."

The "tu," likewise, is only recognised through love. Without love there is no tu, for in the image of the ego-fiction we create the tu as a fiction of the second grade. That which we do not love, is for us a third person, an alien He or She. Freud would probably not hesitate to identify the He and the She with those figures which loom in our environment from birth onwards, gigantic, seemingly eternal, and at first incomprehensible—to identify the He with the father and the She with the mother. He and She are there before we have built up our ego. We swallow parts of these incomprehensible structures, and out of them we make our ego. The rest of the He or the She, except for an incomprehensible residue, is transformed by love into a tu.

As soon as we realise that we live amid fictions, and that we cannot even count upon the apparently incontestable reality of the ego and the tu, we understand and can find a justification for every doubt, on the one hand, and every superstition, on the other. The savage constructs a world for himself after his own image. He lends his ego, not only to the tu, the whole living creature, but also to the tree, the spring, the wind, which he thus endows with a spirit like his own (animism):

> Wo jetzt nur, wie unsere Weisen sagen,
> Seelenlos ein Feuerball sich dreht,
> Lenkte damals seinen gold'nen Wagen
> Helios in stiller Majestät.
> Diese Höhen füllten Oreaden,
> Eine Dryas lebt' in jenem Baum,
> Aus den Urnen lieblicher Najaden
> Sprang der Ströme Silberschaum.[1]

Inasmuch as the savage thus breathes the breath of life into lifeless matter, and inasmuch as out of the divisible he creates the indivisible (the individual), he exercises a godlike omnipotence. Only because we have lost faith in it, do we ourselves lack this omnipotence; but in reality there lingers on in us all a certain measure of faith in the " omnipotence

---

[1] Where now, as our sages tell us,
Nothing but a soulless ball of fire moves,
Of old, Helios, in his majesty,
Drove his golden chariot.
These heights were peopled by Oreads,
A Dryad dwelt in that tree,
The silver waters of the streams
Flowed forth from the urns of graceful Naiads.

—From Schiller's Die Götter Griechenlands.—Here, in truth, we have passed beyond the level of animism, and climbed up on to that of religion. Freud draws an apt distinction between the three stages: animism, religion, and science.

of thought."[1] Folk-lore is full of evidences of this faith (the evil eye, the superstitious belief that certain actions are unlucky, etc.). Inwardly, too, we are convinced of our immortality. Although we know full well that our life has its term, we cannot make up our minds to give credence to this doom. One of the greatest minds of all the ages assures us that our essence, at least, is indestructible.[2] How little we have advanced beyond the stage of animism is made especially plain by our recognition of an ego—which Nietzsche rejected as "a leading astray by grammar." The greater part of our fancied omnipotence has had to yield to the dictates of inexorable logic; but the faith lives on in the unconscious, and from that secure vantage-ground it continues to operate.

Here is the dream of a man suffering from obsessional neurosis: "I say to my father, 'This child is not viable.' We draw near, and see that the child is dead. My father says sadly to me, 'If you know that you have such a power, why do you use it?'"

The source and the limits of our omnipotence are found in the transferability and detachability of the libido. At the bounds where this capacity ends, there lurk doubt, anxiety, and death. The saying, "Where faith is, there love is," can for our purposes be inverted thus: "Where love is, there faith is." Freud considers that all doubt originates in doubt of love. Thus Hamlet writes to Ophelia:

---

[1] The phrase was used by one of Freud's patients. Cf. Sammlung, iii, 2; cf., also, Totem und Tabu.

[2] Schopenhauer, in Ueber den Tod und die Unzerstörbarkeit unseres Wesens an sich.

> Doubt thou the stars are fire;
> Doubt that the sun doth move;
> Doubt truth to be a liar;
> But never doubt my love.

What would be left unshaken, if I had to doubt your love ?[1]

Since all love arises out of parental love, this doubt of love begins with the child's first doubt of the parents. It begins with a doubt of that first He or She who is the measure of all things for the growing boy or girl. Such doubts destroy a child's faith in the gods.

> Da ich ein Kind war, . . .
> kehrt ich mein verirrtes Auge
> zur Sonne, als wenn drüber wär'
> ein Ohr zu hören meine Klage,
> ein Herz wie meins,
> sich des Bedrängten zu erbarmen.[2]

Not only can an affect be displaced; it can be transformed into its opposite. Freud considers that the paranoiac's delusion of persecution arises from such an inversion. The mechanism works in several acts. Act One: the paranoiac loves a heterosexual partner. Act Two: the homosexual inclination is repressed as forbidden. Act Three: its return into consciousness is hindered by two checks. The first of these is: "He does not love me, but hates and persecutes me." The second is: "I do not love him, but hate him because he persecutes me."

[1] *Sammlung*, iii, Chapter Two, first edition, 1913, p. 191.
[2] When I was a child, . . .
I turned my wandering gaze
towards the sun, fancying there to find,
an ear to hear my plaint,
a heart, like mine,
to pity the distressed.

This is a typical Freudian mechanism. Judas is a paranoiac. So is Alexander the Great, when he throws his spear at Clitus. So is Saul in his maltreatment of David. Definite insanity is seen only in exceptional instances; but none except the dullest, or the most clear-sighted, of human beings are free from the influence of this mechanism. I am not sure whether the inclination out of which paranoia issues is always homosexual. Perhaps any forbidden trend can engender the same mechanism. Every inclination can do it and every aversion as well.

One of my patients was a butcher, who believed that his cook was mixing powdered glass with his food. He was also afraid that inadvertently he might poison his customers by supplying them with tainted meat. He would often run after them, wishing to buy back the meat they had just purchased. When one of his children was bitten by a dog, which was really quite free from the suspicion of rabies, he was frenzied with alarm; and although the Pasteur treatment was promptly applied, he continued to dread the onset of hydrophobia. Though generally regarded as a most kind-hearted and good-natured fellow, he would sometimes look at people in a way that made their flesh creep. During the course of the analysis, when selecting something to fidget with from among the various objects on my writing-table, he invariably showed a preference for a huge paper-knife. This is what Freud terms a " symptomatic act." My patient's unconscious was full of murderous thoughts, and betrayed itself thus.

During the last few months he had lost about forty pounds in weight, the ostensible trouble being an affection of the gall-bladder. This is why he had come to me for treatment. He suffered from sleeplessness, was continually thinking about his illness, and was depressed and suicidally inclined. In his relations with his wife he suffered from relative impotence. His illness had made him quite incompetent to look after his business. There was no organic disease in the gall-bladder; the trouble was nothing but hypochondria.

The suicidal inclinations had two distinct causes.

In the first place, they were the outcome of homicidal inclinations towards the wife, inclinations transferred upon his own ego. The dread of injuring his customers was a displaced homicidal idea. The dread of the cook, who was a substitute for the wife, was an inversion; he imagined that she wished to kill him, whereas really he wished to kill her.

The determinants comprising the second group were connected with the patient's twin brother. The two men had jointly inherited the business from their father. After my patient's marriage, there were persistent quarrels. In the end the brother broke off the partnership, was paid for his share of the business, and opened a rival establishment. When I add that the patient had left an efficient manager alone in the house with his wife while he himself was visiting one sanatorium after another, the reader will secure a fuller insight into the homosexual elements in the case, and into the working of Hebbel's Candaules motif.

In this case, a whole series of Freudian mechanisms was operative. The lost sexual object was the brother. The libido that had been attached to him had been withdrawn into the patient's own personality (melancholia). Through the gall-bladder trouble, which may after all have had a fraction of organic substratum (this being what Freud terms a "somatic response"), this portion of libido had been symbolised within the patient's own body and had undergone fixation there (hypochondria). He wished for the death of his wife because it was on her account that the breach with the beloved brother occurred.

No one thinks of suicide unless he has wished for another's death. His suicide is the punishment for the death wish. That conclusion was forced upon Freud and Stekel by their analytical experience,[1] and Stekel has illustrated it by reports of numerous cases. This explanation throws a remarkable light on many of the suicides sung by the poets. Neurotics, in especial, are in grave peril when any of their near and dear ones die. If the neurotic was very fond of the deceased, there was always an admixture (usually unconscious) of hatred in the passion. The neurotic's tempestuous love, the love that seems so exaggerated to a dispassionate observer, is also hatred, the love and the hatred being counterparts separated out by breaking up the neutral feeling of indifference. Every night in his dreams the neurotic kills the beloved. When the beloved spouse, father, brother, or friend, actually dies, the unconscious, confident of its own omnipotence, holds itself responsible for the death. A widow kills herself beside her husband's grave. Who understands this? The men of India understood it when, by the institution of suttee, they endeavoured to protect themselves against their wives' ill-wishes.

A young married woman, apparently attached

[1] Diskussionen der Wiener psychoanalytischen Vereinigung : Ueber den Selbstmord, Wiesbaden, 1911.

to her husband, becomes affected with feelings of self-reproach, thoughts of suicide, and ideas that the world is going to rack and ruin. Her husband has just returned home from a long stay in hospital. He comes back cured. During the months of his absence, his wife has held up valiantly, but now she falls ill in her turn. Every one imagines that her illness is due to nervous exhaustion, the result of prolonged anxiety about her husband's health. But for happy people there is no such thing as nervous exhaustion. What is hidden from every one, and even from the sufferer, is that she has secretly been hoping that she would soon be quit of her husband. Her illness is due to his recovery. The death wish has turned back upon the wisher.

No doubt, these are detestable mechanisms; but a thing does not cease to exist because it is detestable. In the case of the butcher, the illness began one day when his wife had a miscarriage and a flooding. Thereupon the suppressed death wish tended so forcibly to thrust its way into consciousness that the man's moral sense could only be satisfied by shifting the wish on to himself. The wish for his wife's death became a suicidal impulse.

The mind, at its deeper levels, is not only malicious; at these levels, the law of retaliation prevails with inexorable force. An eye for an eye and a tooth for a tooth would seem to have been the most primitive, the most elemental, notion of justice. The conscience of the unconscious is so strict that it is apt, in accordance with the law of retaliation, to sentence the offender to suicide for crimes that have been committed only in the imagination. The neurotic's symptoms usually furnish a close imitation of the offence that has to be atoned for. The patient who was doing penance for the supposed premature burial of his sister (supra pp. 90 et seq.) suffered from dyspnœa, an obsessive urge to inhale dust, a sense of suffocation, and syncopal attacks. The only way of understanding and unravelling the neurotic's symptoms is to call to our aid the principle of retaliation (substitution).

Offences committed against the neurotic patient by others, real or imaginary offences, are likewise imitated. The neurotic behaves like a child. " When the doctor examines a child's throat, or performs some trifling operation on the little patient, this alarming experience will certainly be rehearsed the next time the child is at play." [1] I knew a boy who wanted to go to the Danube to watch the steamboats. His father refused to let him go. The youngster got into a rage, and said: " When I grow up, I shan't let my children go and look at the steamboats, so there ! "

It is but one step from comedy to tragedy. I was acquainted once with a young man who was illegitimate. In every place where he chanced to be living, he would have a love affair, with consequences, and would trouble himself as little about his own illegitimate children as his father had troubled about him. Such is the curse of bad actions. The unconscious repays evil with evil, but not on the evildoer more than another—any one will serve its turn. In this respect it resembles the jealous God who visits the iniquity of the fathers upon the children unto the third and fourth generation.[2]

---

[1] Freud, Jenseits des Lustprinzips, p. 13.
[2] Cf. Freud, Das Ich und das Es, p. 56.

Very remarkable is the mechanism which works so as to win pleasure without incurring blame (Stekel). When a woman who is sexually assaulted faints, the working of such a mechanism is obvious. She ought to resist to the uttermost for the sake of her " honour." The faint relieves her of this responsibility.

A great many husbands would gladly be rid of their wives, a great many lovers would gladly be rid of their mistresses without feeling themselves to blame. One of the favourite mechanisms in such cases is for the man to make himself so disagreeable that the woman is moved to break the tie. He is bearish; comes late to appointments, or does not come at all. In a manner which may be more or less artful according to the extent to which hysteria underlies his conduct, he will undermine the intimacy until the other party takes the initiative in a separation.

The Freudian mechanisms lead us through Hades. The reader's progress through the land of the shades has been swifter than that of Dante when Virgil guided him through the Inferno. But in this brief passage it will have become plain that the psychoanalytical Hades is no less vast and no less terrible. The last Freudian mechanism I have to describe will show the " Genealogy of Morals " in a new light. Whence do conscience and self-condemnation spring? What is the origin of the consciousness of guilt which flourishes alike in neurotics and in the healthy, nowadays, as weeds sprout among the corn?

During the greater part of his life, Freud wrote of the unconscious as if it were solely bestial. It is difficult to say how far Nietzsche's outlooks may have

FREUDIAN MECHANISMS

influenced Freud in this matter. Nietzsche's superman is one who kills from pure delight, one to whom the sense of guilt is unknown. This " blond beast " (but why blond; why a Siegfried, and not, rather, a negro ?) corresponds to the Old Man of the Freudian primitive horde. To the Old Man everything is permissible. Like Cronus, he devours his own children; he kills his wives to intensify the titillation of his senses. He can blame others, but is himself free from blame. His children revolt. Those who had no rights, those who were ever at fault, slay the Old Man, tear him limb from limb, devour his remains, and themselves become Fathers of primitive hordes. But they lack the perfect self-satisfaction of the original Old Man. With his flesh they have assimilated a fraction of his menacing personality, and throughout their lives this eyes them askance and creates in them a consciousness of guilt. Since they killed their father, they know the fate that awaits them at the hands of their own children. For this reason they suppress the " instinct of freedom " (Nietzsche); and they do this, not only in their children, but also in themselves, hoping that freedom may be shuffled out of the world. " This instinct of freedom, forcibly made latent; this suppressed instinct of freedom, thrust into the background, prisoned in the inner man, and ultimately able to find vent only within itself—this, and nothing else, is in its beginnings what we know as a bad conscience." [1] Nietzsche's blond beast who murders from pure delight without a sense of guilt, and Freud's Old Man of the primitive horde, are kindred visions. Their poetical value is considerable, but their scientific value is small. Popper-

[1] Nietzsche, Zur Genealogie der Moral.

Lynkeus writes: " I can only see what exists now. I do not know what used to exist in former days."

The deduction is that the genealogy of morals, as worked out by Freud ontogenetically from a study of the individual childhood of each one of us, is far more important than a mythological and imaginative reconstruction of the primitive horde. The child's first ideal is the father (it would be more prudent to say, " the parents "); the great, strong, omnipotent, and omniscient father. The little boy would like to have the splendid qualities of his father. He tries to play the father, to identify himself with the father, to become incorporated with the father. Inevitably these attempts fail. In a subsequent phase of development, the boy feels that the father is a rival in the mother's love, a rival of whom he would fain rid himself. " When Father dies, I shall marry Mother ! " The formation of the Oedipus complex has begun. But the boy finds it hard to enter into the lists with one who up to now has been regarded as the embodiment of omnipotence and morality. He therefore despoils his father of all these qualities; and the sublime outward ideal is transformed into an inward ideal, which lives and works in the unconscious throughout life. Beside the ego, there is created another fiction, the super-ego. This super-ego is the swallowed father (the parents, authority). Ethics, religion, moral judgments, all develop out of the super-ego.

Freud describes; he does not appraise. In this respect he differs from Nietzsche. But, of course, he cannot prevent others who listen to his teachings from forming judgments of value. We have to enquire what religious or ethical system is most accordant with the genealogy of morals as described by Freud. Immediately we think of the teachings of Confucius, for whom reverence towards fathers and forefathers was the one and only transcendental law.

"Honour thy father and thy mother; that thy days may be long in the land which the Lord thy God giveth thee." With this ordinance the Jews, likewise, made the law of filial piety supreme among their commandments. We must not forget that Freud, one of the most notable geniuses of our day, was born and trained in a Jewish environment. Every one knows how important a part the family plays in Jewish life.

The prevalence of antisemitism creates in the minds of the Jews a passionate "Why?" In favourable circumstance, this urgent questioning may have results of considerable scientific importance. It has certainly a good deal to do with the genesis of the revolutionary sentiments which are so widespread among the Jews.

Freud relates: "I must have been about ten or twelve years old when my father began to take me with him on his walks, and to tell me his views concerning things in general. On one occasion, when he wished to show me that I was living in better times than those of his own youth, he said to me: 'When I was a lad I went for a walk one Sabbath through the streets of Freiberg, in my best clothes, and wearing a new fur cap. A Christian came by, knocked my cap into the mud, and cried, " Jew, get off the pavement ! "—' What did you do ? '— ' I stepped into the roadway and picked up my cap,' said my father quietly. To me, the boy whose father was leading him by the hand, the conduct of the big strong man seemed anything but heroic. In my imagination, I contrasted the situation with one much more to my taste. I recalled the scene when Hannibal's father had made his son swear upon the altar eternal hostility to Rome. Thenceforward, Hannibal had a place in my fantasies." [1]

Hannibal, the Semitic general, became the revolutionary-minded lad's favourite hero, because Hannibal had made himself dreaded by the Romans. Another heroic figure that has always loomed large before Freud's imagination is that of Cromwell, the regicide.

When Freud's own children were growing up, their father's mind was much exercised by the question how he could save them from the sense of inferiority, whose dangers were so well known to him. He appears to think that the nationalist idea is a good antidote to the sense of inferiority. For many years, now, he has been a member of the Jewish freemason's lodge Bene Brith. May there not be good reason to suppose that the cult of filial piety, after the Confucian model, would be a better, a nobler, a more aristocratic way of counteracting the sense of inferiority—one much less open to objection? For ages the Jews have instinctively followed this road. Nationalism is a mere imitation, and an imitation that follows the path of a transient historical phenomenon. Affectionate veneration for the parents, on the other hand, above all while they are still living, is the conscious acceptance of a deep-seated unconscious mechanism—a bridge leading from the ego-ideal to its origin. We are paying our primal creditors when we discharge our debt to our parents.

[1] *Traumdeutung*, p. 158.

CHAPTER SIXTEEN
BIPOLARITY

APART from its overwhelming inclination to use metaphors and symbols, the language of the dream differs in other respects from the language of consciousness. In the dream, there is no sharp distinction between alternatives. To consciousness, a thing must be either A or not-A; must be either black or white; must be either two or three. To conscious thought, it is either day or night, and not day and night at one and the same time. In the dream, these alternatives seem to be harmoniously combined. Freud has shown that, in the dream, black often signifies white, the small represents the great, up means down; in a word, that opposites may symbolise one another. In 1909 he referred to a pamphlet that had been published in 1884 by Abel the philologist. Abel had shown that in primitive tongues (just as in the dream) opposites can be denoted by the same word. Thus, in the hieroglyphic writing of ancient Egypt, the same character may represent both light and darkness. Per se, therefore, this character denotes merely a certain degree of lightness or darkness in the abstract, and we have to learn from the context whether the word signifies light or dark on this particular occasion. The report of the linguistic expert confirmed Freud in his view that in dreams we are using an archaic language, one which fulfils the needs of the dream, but has become inadequate for the needs of our waking life.

I am told that Abel's views are out of date. However this may be, the unification of opposites certainly plays its part in our mental life, in great things as well as small. To describe the phenomenon, Stekel speaks of the " bipolarity " of all mental happenings. Bleuler, says Stekel, wishing to describe a similar phenomenon (whose full import was hidden from Bleuler), made use of the word " ambivalency." Ambivalency is a much less apt term than bipolarity, but the orthodox Freudians make it a point of honour to use only the former term, in the hope that Stekel's better expression will lapse into oblivion. One inconvenience of this yielding to the impulse of hatred has been that the orthodox Freudians have failed to clarify their own ideas on the subject, so that they cannot use the concept of bipolarity with the requisite precision. The term ambivalency was borrowed from chemistry. Certain elements can combine with two different elements. They are ambivalent. In like manner, the idea of a person can be associated in our minds with two different feelings. The soul of Brutus is simultaneously filled with love and with hatred towards Cæsar. Adler terms this " the alternation of impulses " (Triebverschränkung). But the word ambivalency fails to connote that the twofold feelings with which our ideas are linked, are polar opposites: love and hate; pleasure and pain; attraction and repulsion. A much better image can be drawn from the electromagnet, whose soft iron core is neutral in the quiescent state; but when the current passes, the polar elements undergo separation, so that a

BIPOLARITY

magnet comes into being. Mental phenomena are bipolar, like those of magnetism. Freud's latest speculations imply that by a bipolarity of similar kind, life must first have originated out of the neutral grey of the non-living.

In 1920, Freud astonished the world by the announcement that in all living creatures there is active, in addition to the pleasure principle (which, since the days of Hellenic culture, has been known as Eros), another principle: "What lives, wishes for a return to death." Dust unto dust. In living matter there is the death instinct as well as the life instinct. When Freud made this communication to a listening world, he was suffering from the shock of the death of one of his daughters. For years, too, he had been full of anxiety concerning the fate of one of his nearest and dearest, who was with the fighting forces. Here is Freud's lament over his daughter's grave: "One who is under the universal doom of death, but has first of all to lose his dearest, would rather be subject to the working of an inexorable natural law, to the august $Ἀνάγκη$, than to the working of a chance which might have been avoided. Maybe, however, this belief in the inner necessity of death, this belief that death is due to the working of a natural law, is merely one of the illusions which we have created ' to help us in bearing the burden of existence.' "

Freud, in a personal letter, makes the following remarkable comment on the foregoing passage. " That seems to me most interesting, and I regard it as a warning. Beyond question, if I had myself been analysing another person in such circumstances, I should have presumed the existence of a connexion between my daughter's death and the train of thought presented in my book *Jenseits des Lustprinzips*. But the inference that such a sequence exists would have been false. *Jenseits* was written in 1919, when my daughter was still in excellent health. She died in 1920. In September 1919, I had sent the manuscript of this little book to be read by various friends in Berlin. It was finished, except for the discussion concerning the mortality or immortality of the protozoa. ' What seems true is not always the truth.' "

Stekel, who was accustomed to work with the concept of bipolarity, had discovered death instincts decades before in dreams, and had recognised them to be the bipolar counterpart to the ferment of life. Again and again have the great poets told us how death keeps vigil just behind life, and that death is closely akin to love. Every one of us who has ever lived through a severe illness must have known the longing to pass into that sleep which knows no waking. The yearning for death is no more than the alternative form in which the yearning for life makes itself known to consciousness. That is why Indian philosophy, and Schopenhauer its greatest occidental representative, disavow suicide. Life is not overcome by self-slaughter. The death instinct is an affirmation of life, being life's bipolar complement. The death instinct has nothing to do with death.

It lies beyond my competence to say what death really is, for I am not a nirvanist like Schopenhauer and the Indians. That vision can only be seen with the eyes of the mystic. I incline to the view of the Greeks, who regarded death as a pure negative, as nothing, as non-existent in the world. But there is a real entity, which is closely bound to that nonentity.

BIPOLARITY

It is anxiety, dread. Dread of death and longing for death form a bipolar couple; and they also combine to form a single pole, whose opposite pole consists of longing for life and dread of life. Obviously, the relationships are somewhat involved. Life, with its infinitely dichotomised bipolarity, arises through a continuous bipartition of simplicity. How far we are able to follow such ramifications into the thicket of mental happenings, will depend upon our individual talent for mathematics.

Those who take exception to the idea that death and dread of death are two utterly distinct things, or, rather, to the notion that death forms no part, whereas the dread of death forms the totality, of what we subsume under the idea of death, may be invited to consider the way in which melancholiacs ring the changes upon death and the dread of death. Sufferers from this form of mental disorder live in a perpetual dread of death. They cannot endure the persistent dread, and to escape it they rush into death. Thus, it is wrong to say that they have a dread of death; they have dread, and dread engenders death. But when dread engenders death, what greater contrast to love can we conceive, seeing that love engenders life?

Thus we come back to an outlook which Freud had as early as 1895, when he described the condition which he termed " anxiety neurosis." Anxiety and love are opposites belonging to the same stock; they are bipolar manifestations of the same primal entity. The best way of grasping their mutual relationships is through Plato's figure of the two-in-hand. [1]

Although, since Plato's day, so many other thinkers

[1] Supra, pp. 127–128.

have given their thoughts to the world, the world comes back ever and again to the marvellous parable of the great poet-philosopher who was Christ's forerunner. We are sitting in a cave with our backs towards the outlet. Behind us realities move to and fro. Still farther away behind us, perhaps outside the cave, is a source of light, and all that we know of the moving realities consists of the shadows cast on the walls of the cave. The gods alone can see the realities as they are in themselves.

Now that we have become accustomed to regard consciousness as merely a part of the mind, to look upon it, in a sense, as a screen upon which the unconscious casts shadows, we are coming very close once more to the parable of the men in the cave. None but the gods can see all that goes on in the depths of the unconscious. It suffices for us if we can unriddle a few of the laws of the unconscious. One such law is that of bipolarity. We love ourselves, and dread ourselves; we die, because we live. We love a tu, and hate it; we hate, because we love. We seek pleasure, and none the less make pain for ourselves, that we may win more pleasure by the road of pain. These opposites are inseparable. One who would avoid the pain of life, must likewise renounce its pleasure. So runs the rede, bipolar into infinity.

When we say that death is a negative,[1] we are very far from that which lives in the folk-mind and in the images of the dream. In the dream, as in folk-tales, death always appears as an active personality.[2] The symbolism of death is also at work in

---

[1] Freud writes: "Death is an abstract idea of negative content, one for which an unconscious expression is not to be found."

[2] Cf. the dream recorded on p. 82.

BIPOLARITY

dreams of a return to the mother's womb, the dreams that exclaim : " Back to the mother from whom thou camest." Once more there are signified here both He and She—the father and the mother. Those who have given us life are, in bipolar fashion, the daimons of death. We shall be gathered to our fathers, says Holy Writ.

Freud's metaphysic thus undergoes modifications which bring it wholly into the paths of Plato. The law of the eternal recurrence of the similar (Plato and Nietzsche) makes its demands upon us, asking our life of us. Aforetime we were not, and in a future time we shall not be; even as we were not throughout the ages before we were born. In the end, Freud comes to the thought that all life has arisen out of the tearing apart (polarisation) of a non-living substance. In this connexion he recalls a parable which Plato puts into the mouth of the satirist Aristophanes. Plato's intention was to make fun of the sophists, whose theories were brilliant but lacked solid foundation. This raillery at the sophists was to provide a background against which the glorious teachings of Socrates could stand out in finer relief. But lovers take the parable seriously, and it is all that many of the readers of Plato's *Symposium* retain in their memory. Aristophanes tells us that originally every human being had four arms and four legs. They were double creatures throughout, as if two of the human beings known to us were fused. Zeus cut these double creatures asunder, as we slice a pear into two halves, and, ever since, the severed portions have been roaming about, devoured with longing for reunion. When they have the good luck to find one another, these parts are filled with love for one another; they intertwine their limbs. Thus, in their affectionate embrace they temporarily re-establish the condition which used to be an enduring one.

The cleavage into masculine and feminine unceasingly complies with the great law of bipolarity. Neither a man alone nor a woman alone is a complete human being. Only in association are they members of the human species. That they may exist at all as individuals, each one of them is bipolar, i.e. bisexual. Many plants and many of the lower animals are bisexual, both male and female organs being possessed by the same individual. In the higher types of organic life, the sexes become distinct. However, just as a radical in organic chemistry cannot exist in isolation, but necessarily enters into combination, so neither sex can exist alone, for each contains elements of the other. This bisexuality, this compulsory hermaphroditism, is the negative opposed by the non-sexual earlier age to the present which has undergone sexual differentiation. That is why I wrote: " The libido frees itself from sexuality by way of bisexuality." And also: " Eros has no sex."

Much might be written about this matter, but we are hard upon the boundary, and perhaps beyond the boundary, where science merges into mysticism, and where the investigator grows ill at ease. Is it possible for us to decide whether the law of bisexuality is subordinate to that of bipolarity? The relationship may be the converse of this. Perhaps, as Freud declares: " Sexual behaviour has a prototypical power, a power which transfigures all the other reactions of the human being."[1] If this be so,

[1] Sammlung, vol. iii, p. 190.

BIPOLARITY

everything that is bipolar is formed after the model of man and woman, He and She. In this sense, at any rate, we may interpret Freud's declaration that the libido is masculine whereas anxiety is feminine. Life is masculine and death is feminine. On the plane of the intelligence, this means only that the former is positive and the latter negative; but the mystic will see more in the formulation.

As regards anxiety, I pointed out a good many years ago that, just as in the case of pleasure (supra p. 113), there are two contrasted types of anxiety manifestation. One form of anxiety is equable, so that, in view of its unarticulated persistence, anxiety of this type may be termed feminine. On the other hand, there is an anxiety paroxysm which rises to a climax of horror and ends in death. The curve representing its course is comparable with the curve of the crescent type of pleasure, masculine pleasure.

" I believe," says Freud, " that it is time to break off." He adds : " The reader may ask to what extent I am myself convinced of the soundness of the foregoing hypotheses.[1] My answer will run, that I am neither convinced myself, nor invite others to believe them. Perhaps it would be better to say that I do not know how far I believe them . . . But an investigator can give himself up to a train of thought, can follow such a train as far as it will lead him, solely out of scientific curiosity ; or, if you like, as devil's advocate—which does not mean that he has sold himself to the devil."

[1] Jenseits des Lustprinzips, p. 55.—The phrase has been interpreted as implying that Freud is extremely sceptical concerning the stability of the edifice of his own doctrines. This is a malicious misunderstanding. Freud is merely referring to some of the more fanciful thoughts in the book just named.

These sentences embody the real Freud. All great spirits are animated by the longing to look, once at least, into the eyes of reality, instead of for ever being content with the study of appearance; with the longing to see Plato's οὐσία, the inner being, the intimate essence of things. In Freud's mentality, the mystical gift of the seer is continually at war with the need for mechanical description. " Freudian mechanisms " would be a barren term for a barren thing unless behind them there was something other than mechanism, something alive; something which Freud has again and again suppressed, until, as if in spite of himself, and amid reiterated excuses, it forces itself into his latest utterances. No one need believe these latest utterances (such is Freud's implication); he does not know how far he believes in them himself! Herein lies the explanation of Freud's acerbity, which has grown with the passing of the years. He is afraid of his own supreme talents, and throughout all his life as an investigator he has been imposing a curb upon himself. One who, by temperament, is a seer, has been ardently devoting himself to the study of exact science, by the ordinary methods of scientific investigation. That was why Freud was so greatly disturbed about the little matter of the cocaine. That was why, at any earlier date, he heroically determined to study medicine, though his natural bent was towards the abstract sciences. This accounts, too, for his flight to Paris. It accounts for his remarkable feeling of happiness in the physiological laboratory, though the work there was not really congenial. He tells us that Brücke used often to be annoyed with him for coming late. How would Freud interpret such remissness? He would tell us that it was due to resistance. We are not late for an appointment that we really wish to keep. But the dissection of Ammocœtes [1] was not the sort of work to arouse the interest of a seer.

Great men often suppress their natural inclinations, and devote themselves with ardour to some alien occupation. Perhaps the mystery of genius is, in part, to be explained in terms of bipolar tension, the persistent struggle between the two poles, which are ever trying to break away from one another, and yet are eternally bound together, neither being thinkable without the other. Beyond question, herein lies the secret of success. Nietzsche, the revaluer of all values, Nietzsche, the antichrist, was, in the inner man, a conservatively-minded cleric. Karl Marx, the dialectician, the expounder of the circulation of commodities and of the materialist conception of history, was an ardent idealist, ethically inspired, filled with emotional longings. Schopenhauer denied the value of all earthly things because, for internal reasons, he could not win the supreme good the world offers—woman. Here are three instances among many. All the splendour and all the activity of such great ones are dependent upon this fascinating cleavage of the individuality, which every one feels, to which every one of us is subject.

Thus has it come to pass that Freud has enkindled the world. Many believe that psychoanalysis is destined to change the whole aspect of the universe. But the day for a final judgment on Freud has not yet come. He still lives among us, still works, and

---

[1] Die Traumdeutung, p. 252.—Ammocœtes is a rare fish. Freud had to dissect it in Brücke's laboratory. He wrote a monograph on this fish. (See Bibliography.)

no one can foresee the potentialities of a man of genius. Some praise him to the skies, and some revile him. I am not so arrogant as to believe that I have found the golden mean. Full well do I know that this essay upon Freud and his teachings is subjective through and through. I myself am bipolar in my attitude towards Freud. I, like others, have had personal differences with Freud, and have suffered therefor. Once, for me, as for all his pupils, he was a father-imago. He tells us that the death of the father is the most important event in a man's life. But perhaps there is another event no less important than the loss of the father. A son has been born to me! I no longer need a father, now that I am myself a father! Thanks to this gift, I have won sufficient strength to enter the field of psychoanalysis again, after many years of partial exile. As the first fruits of my renewed analytical activities, I present this book:

SIGMUND FREUD

1923

Seen through a Temperament.

GLOSSARY

The glossary contains all the psychoanalytical terms used in this volume, and also a few of the psychiatric and ordinary psychological terms likely to be unfamiliar to the general reader. Many of the psychoanalytical definitions are borrowed, or slightly modified, from Ernest Jones' *Papers on Psychoanalysis*. The translators are also indebted to the *Glossary for the Use of Translators of Psychoanalytical Works* recently published by the International Psychoanalytical Press, giving approved English equivalents of German psychoanalytical terms. The German term is, in many cases, given in brackets immediately after the English term in the glossary that follows.

abreaction. " The process of working off a pent-up emotion by living through it again in feeling or action." (Jones.) Verbal form, to **abreact**.

actual neuroses. " The symptoms of an actual neurosis —headache, sensation of pain, an irritable condition of some organ, the weakening or inhibition of some function—have no ' meaning,' no signification in the mind. Not merely are they manifested principally in the body, as also happens, for instance, with hysterical symptoms, but they are in themselves purely and simply physical processes; they arise without any of the complicated mental mechanisms we have been learning about." (Freud, *Introductory Lectures*, p. 323.) —Sometimes spoken of (in contradistinction to **psychogenic neuroses**) as **somatic neuroses**.

affect. " Feeling. The essential constituent of emotion." (Jones.)

alternation of impulses [Triebverschränkung]. See **ambivalency**. See also text, p. 250.

ambivalency. "The existence of opposed feelings—e.g. love and hate." (Jones.) Stekel conveys this idea by the use of the term **bipolarity.** Adler speaks of the **alternation of impulses** [Triebverschränkung]. See also text, p. 250.

amnesia. Forgetfulness, loss of memory. **Infantile amnesia** is loss of memory of the experiences of infancy and early childhood. See also **cryptomnesia.**

anagogic. This term (whose derivative meaning is "leading upwards"), ordinarily used to denote "spiritual or allegorical interpretation," was applied by Silberer to the moral or "uplifting" trends of the unconscious.

analysand. A person who is being psychoanalysed.

annulling mechanism [annullierende Mechanismus (Stekel)]. A mechanism in virtue of which ideas known to the conscious remain inoperative because the unconscious disowns and annuls them.

anxiety hysteria [Angsthysterie]. Term coined by Freud in 1908 to denote phobias (morbid dreads) engendered by the same kind of psychological determinants as ordinary hysteria.

anxiety neurosis [Angstneurose]. Functional nervous disorder in which anxiety, i.e. intense morbid dread, is the most conspicuous and persistent symptom.

autoerotism [Autoerotismus]. Sexual excitement and/or sexual gratification occurring independently of actual relations with another individual, and self-induced, either physically or mentally. (Adjective, **autoerotic.**)

autosuggestion. The process in the unconscious in virtue of which the thought of an action arouses an impulse to perform the action; or in virtue of which the expectation of a result leads an individual to contribute towards bringing about the result. The original thought and expectation and the impulse or action are above the threshold of consciousness; the autosuggestive link is below the threshold. See **heterosuggestion, suggestibility,** and **suggestion.**

GLOSSARY

bipolarity. See **ambivalency.** See also text, p. 250.

Candaules motif. Candaules, king of Lydia, exhibited his wife in a state of nudity to Gyges. The psychoanalytical explanation is that such actions are determined by unconscious homosexuality. See text, pp. 213 and 240.

castration complex [Kastrationskomplex]. "The idea of injury to the penis, testicles, or clitoris." (Jones.) See also Chapter Eleven, for a detailed discussion of this matter.

cathartic method. The purging of the effects of a pent-up emotion by bringing it to the surface of consciousness. This term was applied by Breuer to the technique which was subsequently perfected as psychoanalysis.

cathexis [Besetzung]. "Charge of energy. Investment (of an idea) with feeling and significance." (Jones.)— In the text, "Besetzung" has usually been rendered by "investment" or "charge."

censor and **censorship.** Figurative names given to the forces at work in the mind whereby a memory or an impulse is repressed into the unconscious, and whereby its reappearance in consciousness is prevented. Also called the "endopsychic censor." See **repression.**

claustrophobia. See **phobia.**

coitus interruptus. Sexual intercourse in which the male organ is withdrawn before the ejaculation of semen (as a method of birth control).

complex. "A group of emotionally invested ideas partially or entirely repressed." (Jones.) In current parlance, the notion of repression into the unconscious is not a necessary part of the concept "complex." Thus, in this sense, a "hobby" is based upon a complex, although there may be no repression whatever. But Freud defines **complexes** (*Introductory Lectures*, p. 90) as "circles of thoughts and interests of strong affective value . . . of whose influence at the time nothing is known . . . unconscious."

conation. The striving of the individual towards self-realisation and self-expansion; a fundamental characteristic of life.

cryptomnesia. Literally, "hidden memory," i.e. "forgetfulness." But it connotes the idea that the act of forgetfulness has an unconscious motive. See **amnesia**.

delusion of reference [Beziehungswahn]. The delusion that every objective happening has a personal bearing. A symptom of paranoia. Delusion of persecution and delusion of grandeur are sub-varieties. Minor degrees of delusion of reference constitute a quasi-universal human characteristic.

dementia paranoides. A form of **dementia præcox** resembling **paranoia,** but differing in that the delusions are less completely systematised.

dementia præcox. Many of the commoner types of insanity at puberty and during adolescence are classed under this head. See **schizophrenia**.

dream distortion. The modifications effected in the dream ("manifest content") in order to conceal from the conscious the underlying thoughts and wishes of the unconscious ("latent content").

ego-ideal. "A critical faculty [Instanz] within the ego, which even in normal times takes up a critical attitude towards the ego, . . . may cut itself off from the rest of the ego and come in conflict with it." This **super-ego** is the source of the moral conscience, the censorship of dreams, self-observation; and it is the chief influence in repression. See Freud, *Group Psychology and the Analysis of the Ego*, p. 69.

ego impulse. In Freud's earlier theory of sex, "auto-erotism and object love were contrasted with the non-sexual impulses of the personality, grouped together under the name of ' ego impulses.' " (Jones, *Papers on Psychoanalysis*, 3rd ed., p. 47.)

GLOSSARY 265

Electra complex. Excessive attachment, sexually tinged, of the daughter to the father. The feminine counterpart of the **Oedipus complex** (which see). See also **fixation**.

erogenic zone. "An area of the body stimulation of which gives rise to erotic sensations." (Jones—who uses the form " erotogenic.")

exhibitionism [Zeigelust]. The exposure of some part of the body usually concealed, in most cases the genital organs, with accompanying sexual excitement. The person performing such an act is an **exhibitionist**.

extrovert. One whose **libido** (which see) or vital impetus or psychic energy tends mainly outwards. Thus the extrovert is predominantly a man or woman of feeling or action. The state of being an extrovert is called **extroversion**. See **introvert**.

fetichism. A fixation and limitation of affect, in virtue of which, by a perversion, an individual's sexual libido undergoes concentration upon a " fetich " (hair, underclothing, etc.) instead of being directed towards the whole personality of the beloved.

fixation [Fixierung]. Short for " fixation of affect." The arrest of an affect at a more primitive stage than that normally corresponding to the individual's age and development. Especially used of the fixation of a daughter's sexual affection upon the father (" father-fixation," see **Electra complex**); and of the fixation of a son's sexual affection upon the mother (" mother-fixation," see **Oedipus complex**).

heterosuggestion. The unconscious realisation of an idea suggested by another. Also the act of suggesting an idea to another. See **autosuggestion** and **suggestion**.

homosexuality. Love for a member of the same sex. See **inversion**.

hypochondria. A form of **melancholia** (which see) in which fixed ideas (partly or wholly unfounded) as to the existence of bodily disorder predominate.

imago. "This word is taken from the title of a novel by Carl Spitteler. . . . It denotes an interior type, a type moulded upon real persons (in especial upon the father or the mother), which, from the depths of the subconscious continues to guide our actions and to stimulate our sympathies and our antipathies." (Baudouin, *Psychoanalysis and Æsthetics*, p. 220.)

individual psychology. Adler teaches that those who have to deal with difficult children must try to discover the nature of the **inferiority complex** (which see) by which these children are affected. The sufferers must be guided in directions where they will be able to substitute a feeling of superiority for the feeling of inferiority. Adler speaks of his method as "individual psychology." It should be noted, however, that in *Massenpsychologie und Ich-Analyse* Freud uses the term **individual psychology** in a sense of his own, quite different from Adler's, as contrasted, to a certain extent, with "mass psychology" (translated by James Strachey as "social psychology" or "group psychology").

infantilism. Arrest of development at an infantile stage; and, especially, fixation at an infantile stage of feeling. See **fixation.**

inferiority complex. The complex which results from the thwarting of man's natural urge to self-expansion, and which (when repressed into the unconscious) impels him to try to achieve power along some other line than that in which his conation is blocked. (Adler's terminology.) See also **masculine protest.**—Adler regards a sense of **organ inferiority** (physical inferiority in one respect or another) as a leading cause of the "inferiority complex."

inferiority of the organs (Adler) [Minderwertigkeit der Organe]. See **inferiority complex.**

initial pleasure [Vorlust]. The pleasure attending all the stages of the sexual act that precede its climax.

GLOSSARY

inspectionism [Schaulust]. The craving to inspect, and the pleasure induced by inspecting, some part of the body usually concealed, in most cases the genital organs, belonging to another person than the **inspectionist**. The inspectionist act is attended by sexual excitement. In some instances the inspectionist craving takes the form of a longing to witness another engaged in some intimate bodily function (such as urination or defæcation) usually performed in private. Synonymous terms are **voyeurism** and **scoptophilia** or **scoptolagnia**. The counterpart of **exhibitionism**, which see.

introvert. One whose **libido** (which see) or vital impetus or psychic energy tends mainly inward. Thus the introvert is predominantly a thinker. The state of being an introvert is called **introversion**. See **extrovert**.

inversion, sexual. A synonym for **homosexuality**, but Freud prefers the term " inversion." It " may be either objective, only the sex of the love-object being changed, or subjective, where the the attitude (masculine or feminine) is inverted as well." (Jones.)

libido. Sexual hunger; the mental aspect of the sexual instinct. But by psychoanalysts the term " sexual " is used with wide connotations, so that " libido " becomes almost synonymous with " psychic energy," with conation, and also with what Bergson terms the " vital impetus." Thus Jung unifies all instinctive energy under the term " libido."

masculine protest [der männlicher Protest]. The **inferiority complex** (which see) leads to a desire for superiority —a " wish to be a complete man," the " masculine protest." Adler regards the idea of inferiority as associated with femininity.

masochism. Voluptuous (sexual) enjoyment experienced when suffering mental or bodily pain, usually inflicted from without; the counterpart of **sadism** (which see).

melancholia. Mental disorder in which emotional depression predominates.

Messianic neurosis [Christusneurose]. The neurosis of those who believe they have a mission to save the world.

narcissism [Narzissmus]. The concentration of interest (and especially sexual interest) upon one's own body and one's own personality in general. (From the myth of Narcissus.) Some Freudian writers shorten the term to " narcism." Adjective **narcissistic** [narzisstisch].

nuclear complex. The **Oedipus complex** (which see) is sometimes spoken of as the " nuclear complex." In women, of course, the **Electra complex** (which see) will then be considered the " nuclear complex."

Oedipus complex. Defined by Ernest Jones as " the (usually unconscious) desire of a son to kill his father and possess his mother." Many would prefer to define it, less uncompromisingly, as excessive attachment, sexually tinged, of the son to the mother. The counterpart in women is the **Electra complex** (which see). See also **fixation**.

organ inferiority (Adler) [Minderwertigkeit der Organe]. See **inferiority complex**.

palpationism [Betastungslust]. The desire to handle, and the pleasure induced by handling, the genital organs, or the accessory sexual zones (**erogenic zones**) of another person than the **palpationist**. The palpationist act is attended by sexual excitement.

pansexualism. The investment (**cathexis**) of the whole body—skin, mucous membranes, muscles, intestines, sense organs—with sexual desire and gratification. This is regarded as characteristic of sexuality in very young children.

paranoia. A form of insanity characterised by systematic delusions.

paranoid dementia. See **dementia paranoides**.

parapraxis [Fehlleistung]. A generic term for slips of tongue and pen, blunders, forgettings, errors, and faulty acts, due to unconscious urges that counteract the desire in the conscious.

GLOSSARY

pedication. Immissio membri in anum. Often misspelled " pædication " from a partial confusion with " pæderasty." The root of the latter word is the Greek term for " boy." The root of pedication is the Latin " pedex " or " podex," the fundament.

penis anxiety. A form of the **castration complex** (which see). A dread that the penis will be cut off. See text, p. 161.

penis envy. The form the **castration complex** (which see) takes in girls. See text, p. 161.

phobia. A morbid dread. An intensification of " anxiety," and relating to a particular object or situation or group of objects or situations, as, e.g., to being " shut in " **(claustrophobia).**

phylogenesis. The development of the race or species. Adjective **phylogenetic,** pertaining to the development of the race.

pleasure principle [Lustprinzip]. The tendency to seek immediate pleasure (and shun immediate pain) regardless of the future cost. It conflicts with the **reality principle,** which see.

projection. When an individual, failing to recognise certain processes as mental, as subjective, ascribes them to the outer world, he is said to **project** these mental processes, and the act of doing so is termed " projection."

psychoanalysis. A study and analysis of man's unconscious motives and desires as shown in various nervous disturbances and in certain manifestations of everyday life in normal individuals. Ernest Jones defines it briefly as " the study of unconscious mentation."

psychogenic. Psychically engendered, i.e. due to psychological, not material, determinants. **Psychogenic neuroses** are thus contrasted with **actual neuroses** or **somatic neuroses.**

psychoneuroses. These are contrasted with **actual neuroses** (which see).

rationalisation. " The invention of a reason for an attitude, or an action, the motive of which is not recognised." (Jones.)

reality principle [Realitätsprinzip]. The principle whose function it is to adapt the organism to the exigencies of reality, to subordinate the imperious demand for immediate gratification, and to replace this by a more distant but more permanently satisfactory one. It is thus influenced by social, ethical, and other external considerations that are ignored by the **pleasure principle** (which see).

regression. Two meanings in Freudian terminology: " (1) Resolution of an idea into its sensorial components instead of the usual passage onwards in the direction of action. (2) Reversion of mental life, in some respects, to that characteristic of an earlier stage of development, often an infantile one." (Jones.)

relative impotence. The sexual impotence of a man who is impotent in relation to a particular woman while potent in relation to others.

repetition compulsion [Wiederholungszwang]. The urge to repeat an experience of any kind. See text, p. 95.

repression [Verdrängung]. " The keeping from consciousness of mental processes that would be painful to it." (Jones.) See also **censor**.

resistance [Widerstand]. " The instinctive opposition displayed towards any attempt to lay bare the unconscious; a manifestation of the repressing forces." (Jones.)

sadism. Voluptuous (sexual) enjoyment on inflicting, or witnessing the infliction of, bodily or mental pain; the counterpart of **masochism** (which see).

schizophrenia. A more modern name for **dementia præcox** (which see).

scoptolagnia and **scoptophilia** [Schaulust]. See **inspectionism**.

GLOSSARY

screen-memory [Deckerinnerung]. A memory which crops up as a cover, a screen, to conceal another (associated) memory, which the repressive forces are able in this way to keep concealed.

somatic neuroses. Neuroses that are not **psychogenic**, but are due simply to bodily processes. See **actual neuroses**.

sublimation. The employment of energy belonging to a primitive instinct in a new and derived, i.e. non-primitive, channel. E.g. the use of sexual energy ("**libido**," which see) in "intellectual" love or creative work.

suggestibility. The liability to be influenced by **suggestion** (which see).

suggestion. A general name for **autosuggestion** and **heterosuggestion**, which see.

super-ego. The same as **ego-ideal**, which see.

superiority complex. The individual's emotionally tinged conviction that he excels others in one or many respects. Often an unconscious reaction against the **inferiority complex**, which see.

terminal pleasure [Endlust]. The pleasure attending the climax of the sexual act.

transference [Uebertragung]. "Two meanings: (1) displacement of affect from one idea to another; (2) specifically, displacement of an effect, either positive or negative, from one person on to the psychoanalyst." (Jones.)

unconscious. "Two meanings: (1) all mental processes not in consciousness at a given moment; (2) specifically, those that cannot be brought into consciousness by any effort of the will or act of memory. The former includes the latter, which is the typical psychoanalytical sense." (Jones.)

voyeurism. See **inspectionism**.

BIBLIOGRAPHY

ADLER, Alfred, Praxis und Theorie der Individualpsychologie, Bergmann, Munich, 1920.—English translation by Paul Radin, Individual Psychology, Kegan Paul, London, 1924.

ADLER, Alfred, Ueber den nervösen Charakter, Bergmann, Wiesbaden, 1912, third edition, 1922.—English translation by Bernard Glück and John E. Lind, The Neurotic Constitution, Kegan Paul, London, 1921.

ADLER, Alfred, Das Problem der Homosexualität, Munich, 1917.

ADLER, Alfred, Organ Inferiority and its Psychical Compensation, Nervous and Mental Disease Publishing Co., New York and Washington.

ARIOSTO, Ludovico, Orlando Furioso.

BAUDOUIN, Charles, Psychoanalysis and Æsthetics, Allen and Unwin, London, 1924.

BÖRNE, Ludwig, Die Kunst, in drei Tagen ein original Schriftsteller zu werden.

BREUER, Josef, and FREUD, Sigmund, Studien über Hysterie, Deuticke, Leipzig and Vienna, 1895; third edition, 1921.

BREUER, Josef, and FREUD, Sigmund, Ueber den psychischen Mechanismus hysterischer Phänomene, "Neurologisches Zentralblatt," Nos. 1 and 2, 1893.

Diskussionen der Wiener psychoanalytischen Vereinigung: Ueber den Selbstmord, Wiesbaden, 1911.

EXNER, Sigmund, Entwurf zu einer physiologischen Erklärung der psychischen Erscheinungen, Leipzig and Vienna, 1894.

FERENCZI, S. Entwicklungsstufen des Wirklichkeitssinnes, an article in the "Internationale Zeitschrift für aerztliche Psychoanalyse," 1912.

BIBLIOGRAPHY 273

FLIESS, Wilhelm, Der Ablauf des Lebens, Grundlegung zur exakten Biologie, Leipzig and Vienna, 1906.

FRAZER, James George, Totemism and Exogamy, 4 vols., Macmillan, London, 1910.

FREUD, Sigmund. See also BREUER.

FREUD, Sigmund, Ueber den Ursprung der hinteren Nervenwurzeln im Rückenmark von Ammocœtes, Vienna, 1877.

FREUD, Sigmund, Beobachtungen ueber Gestaltung und feineren Bau der als Hoden beschriebenen Lappenorganen des Aals, Vienna, 1877.

FREUD, Sigmund, Ueber Spinalganglien und Rückenmark des Petromyzon, Vienna, 1878.

FREUD, Sigmund, Ueber den Bau der Nervenfasern und Nervenzellen beim Flusskrebs, Gerold, Vienna, 1882.

FREUD, Sigmund, Ueber Coca, Vienna, 1885.

FREUD, Sigmund, Zur Auffassung der Aphasien, Deuticke, Vienna, 1891.

FREUD, Sigmund [with Oscar RIE], Klinische Studien ueber die halbseitige Cerebrallähmung der Kinder, Perles, Vienna, 1891.

FREUD, Sigmund, Zur Kenntniss der cerebralen Diplegien des Kindesalters (im Anschluss an die Little'sche Krankheit), Deuticke, Vienna, 1893.

FREUD, Sigmund (with Josef BREUER), Ueber den psychischen Mechanismus hysterischer Phänomene, " Neurologisches Zentralblatt," Nos. 1 and 2, 1893.

FREUD, Sigmund (with Josef BREUER), Studien ueber Hysterie, Deuticke, Leipzig and Vienna, 1895 ; third edition, 1922.

FREUD, Sigmund, Die infantile Cerebrallähmung, Hölder, Vienna, 1897.

FREUD, Sigmund, Die Traumdeutung, Deuticke, Leipzig and Vienna, 1900 ; second edition, 1909 ; third edition, 1911 ; fourth edition, 1914 ; fifth edition, 1919 ; seventh edition, 1922. There are numerous translations.— English translation by A. A. Brill from third German edition, The Interpretation of Dreams, Allen and Unwin, London, 1913.

FREUD, Sigmund, Ueber den Traum (in Grenzfragen des Nerven- und Seelenlebens, a series by various authors), Bergmann, Wiesbaden, 1906; third edition, 1921.—English translation by M. D. Eder, On Dreams, Heinemann, London, 1914.

FREUD, Sigmund, Zur Psychopathologie des Alltagslebens (Vergessen, Versprechen, Vergreifen), Karger, Berlin, 1901; ninth edition, 1923.—English translation by A. A. Brill, Psychopathology of Everyday Life, Fisher Unwin, London, 1914.

FREUD, Sigmund, Der Witz und seine Beziehung zum Unbewussten, Deuticke, Leipzig and Vienna, 1905; third edition, 1921.—English translation by A. A. Brill, Wit and its relation to the Unconscious, Fisher Unwin, London, 1916, and Kegan Paul, London, 1922.

FREUD, Sigmund, Bruchstück einer Hysterieanalyse, Karger, Berlin, 1905.

FREUD, Sigmund, Drei Abhandlungen zur Sexualtheorie, Deuticke, Leipzig and Vienna, 1905; second edition, 1910; fifth edition, 1922.—English translation by A. A. Brill, Three Contributions to the Theory of Sex, third revised edition, Nervous and Mental Disease Publishing Co., New York and Washington, 1918.

FREUD, Sigmund, Sammlung kleiner Schriften zur Neurosenlehre, five vols., Deuticke, Leipzig and Vienna, 1906, etc.

FREUD, Sigmund, Der Wahn und die Träume in W. Jensen's "Gradiva," Deuticke, Leipzig and Vienna, 1907; second edition, 1912.—English translation by Helen M. Downey, Delusion and Dream, etc., Moffat, Yard and Co., New York, 1917, Allen and Unwin, London, 1921.

FREUD, Sigmund, Ueber Psychoanalyse (Lectures delivered at Clark University, Worcester, Mass., U.S.A., in September, 1909), Deuticke, Leipzig and Vienna, 1910, sixth edition, 1922.

FREUD, Sigmund, Ueber den Selbstmord, insbesondere der Schüler-Selbstmord (A Discussion at the Viennese Psychoanalytical Society, in which Freud participated), Bergmann, Wiesbaden, 1910.

BIBLIOGRAPHY

FREUD, Sigmund, Eine Kindheitserinnerung des Lionardo da Vinci, Deuticke, Leipzig and Vienna, 1910; third edition, 1923.—English translation by A. A. Brill, Leonardo da Vinci, a psychosexual Study of an infantile Reminiscence, Moffat, Yard and Co., New York, 1916, Kegan Paul, London, 1922.

FREUD, Sigmund, Die Onanie (A Discussion at the Viennese Psychoanalytical Society, in which Freud participated), Bergmann, Wiesbaden, 1912.

FREUD, Sigmund, Totem und Tabu, einige Uebereinstimmungen in Seelenleben der Wilden und der Neurotiker, Heller, Vienna, 1913; second edition, 1920; third edition, 1922, Internationaler Psychoanalytische Verlag. —English translation by A. A. Brill, Totem and Taboo, Routledge, 1919, Moffat, Yard and Co., New York, 1918.

FREUD, Sigmund, Vorlesungen zur Einführung in die Psychoanalyse, Internationaler Psychoanalytischer Verlag, Vienna, 1918.—English translation by Joan Rivière, with a Preface by Ernest Jones, Introductory Lectures on Psychoanalysis, Allen and Unwin, London, 1922.

FREUD, Sigmund [another edition of the Vorlesungen], Vorlesungen zur Einführung in die Psychoanalyse, Die Fehlleistungen, Der Traum, Allgemeine Neurosenlehre, Taschenausgabe, Internationaler Psychoanalytischer Verlag, Vienna, 1922. (For English translation see above.)

FREUD, Sigmund, Preface to Theodor REIK's Probleme der Religionspsychologie, Leipzig and Vienna, 1919.

FREUD, Sigmund, Introduction to S. Ferenczi's Zur Psychoanalyse der Kriegsneurosen, 1919.—English translation, Psychoanalysis and the War Neuroses, by S. Ferenczi and Ernest Jones, with an introduction by Sigmund Freud, International Psychoanalytical Library, London and Vienna, 1921.

FREUD, Sigmund, Jenseits des Lustprinzips, Internationaler Psychoanalytischer Verlag, Vienna, 1920.—English translation by C. J. M. Hubback, Beyond the Pleasure Principle, International Psychoanalytical Library, London and Vienna, 1922.

FREUD, Sigmund, Massenpsychologie und Ich-Analyse, Internationaler Psychoanalytischer Verlag, Vienna, 1921; third edition, 1923.—English translation by James Strachey, Group Psychology and the Analysis of the Ego, London and Vienna, 1922.

FREUD, Sigmund, Das Ich und das Es, Leipzig, 1923.

    Translations not precisely corresponding in respect of contents to the German originals mentioned in the bibliography of Freud's works are :

FREUD, Sigmund, Selected Papers on Hysteria and other Psychoneuroses, translated by A. A. Brill, third, enlarged, edition, New York, 1920.

FREUD, Sigmund, Reflections [on War and Death], translated by A. A. Brill and Alfred B. Kuttner, Moffat, Yard and Co., New York, 1922.—The German original, Zeitgemässes über Krieg und Tod, appears in the fourth volume of Sammlung, etc. (see above).

FREUD, Sigmund, The History of the Psychoanalytic Movement, Nervous and Mental Disease Publishing Co., New York, 1916.—The German original, Zur Geschichte der psychoanalytischen Bewegung, appears in the fourth volume of Sammlung, etc. (see above).

FÜRSTNER, C., Article in vol. vii of Die deutsche Klinik, edited by Ernst von Leyden and Felix Klemperer, Urban and Schwarzenberg, Vienna, 1906.

GOETHE, Johann Wolfgang, Faust.

GOETHE, Johann Wolfgang, Fragment über die Natur, 1781-1782, Colto's edition, vol. xxxix, p. 3.

GRODDECK, Georg, Das Buch vom Es, Psychoanalytische Briefe au eine Freundin, Internationale Psychoanalytische Verlag, Leipzig, 1923.

JONES, Ernest, Das Problem des Hamlet und der Oedipuskomplex, 1911, being No. 10 of Schriften zur angewandten Seelenkunde (translated into German by Paul Tausig), edited by Sigmund Freud, Deuticke, Leipzig and Vienna.—The English original, A psychoanalytic Study of Hamlet, forms Chap. I in Essays in Applied Psychoanalysis, The International Psychoanalytical Press and Allen and Unwin, Vienna and London, 1923.

BIBLIOGRAPHY

JONES, Ernest, Papers on Psychoanalysis, third edition, Ballière, London, 1923.

JUNG, Carl Gustav, Die Bedeutung des Vaters für das Schicksal des Einzelnen, Deuticke, Vienna, 1909.

JUNG, Carl Gustav, Psychologische Typen, Rascher, Zurich, 1921.—English translation by H. Godwin Baynes, Psychological Types, or the psychology of individuation, Int. Libr. of Psych., Phil., and Sci. Method, London, 1923.

JUNG, Carl Gustav, Wandlungen und Symbole der Libido, Deuticke, Leipzig and Vienna, 1912; English translation by Beatrice M. Hinkle, The Psychology of the Unconscious, Moffat, Yard and Co., New York, 1916, Kegan Paul, London, 1921.

LESSING, Gotthold Ephraim, Nathan der Weise.

LYNKEUS, see POPPER.

MAEDER, A. Ueber das Traumproblem, Vienna, 1910.

NIETZSCHE, Friedrich Wilhelm, Menschliches, Allzumenschliches, Schmeitzner, Chemnitz, 1878.—English translation, Human, All-Too-Human, being vols. vi and vii of Oscar Levy's edition of the complete works, Foulis, Edinburgh and London, 1909-13.

NIETZSCHE, Friedrich Wilhelm, Zur Genealogie der Moral, eine Streitschrift, Leipzig, 1887.—English translation by Horace B. Samuel, The Genealogy of Morals, a Polemic, being vol. xiii of Oscar Levy's edition of the complete works, Foulis, Edinburgh and London, 1910.

PLATO : Phædrus, The Republic, Symposium.

POPPER, Josef (wrote under the pseudonym of " Lynkeus," and usually now spoken of as " Popper-Lynkeus "), Phantasien eines Realisten, Reissner, Dresden and Leipzig, 1918.

RANK, Otto, Das Inzestmotiv in Dichtung und Sage, Grundzüge einer Psychologie des dichterischen Schaffens, Deuticke, Vienna, 1912.

RANK, Otto, Der Künstler, Ansätze zu einer Sexual-Psychologie, Heller, Vienna, 1907.

ROSTAND, Edmond, Cyrano de Bergerac.

SADGER, Isidor, Die Lehre von den Geschlechtsverirrungen (Psychopathia Sexualis), auf psychoanalytischer Grundlage, Deuticke, Vienna, 1921.

SADGER, Isidor, Friedrich Hebbel, ein psychoanalytischer Versuch, Deuticke, Vienna.

SCHERNER, Carl Albert, Entdeckungen auf dem Gebiete der Seele, vol. i, Das Leben des Traumes, Schindler, Berlin, 1861.

SCHILLER, Johann Christoph Friedrich, Die Künstler, Die Götter Griechenlands.

SCHOPENHAUER, Arthur, Ueber den Tod und die Unzerstörbarkeit unseres Wesens an sich.

SHAKESPEARE, William, Romeo and Juliet, Hamlet, Julius Cæsar.

STEKEL, Wilhelm, Die Sprache des Traumes, Bergmann, Wiesbaden, 1911; second edition, 1921.

STEKEL, Wilhelm, Fortschritte der Traumdeutung, " Zentralblatt für Psychoanalyse," iv, 1914.

STEKEL, Wilhelm, Koitus im Kindesalter, " Wiener medizinische Blätter," April 18, 1896.

STEKEL, Wilhelm, Nervöse Angstzustände und ihre Behandlung, third edition, Berlin and Vienna, 1921.—English translation by Rosalie Gabler, Conditions of Nervous Anxiety and their Treatment, Kegan Paul, London, Dodd, Mead, and Co., New York, 1923.

STEKEL, Wilhelm, Störungen des Trieb- und Affektlebens, Urban and Schwarzenberg, Vienna, 1912 et seq.; Vol. II, Onanie und Homosexualität; Vol. V Psychosexueller Infantilismus; Vol. VI, Impulshandlungen; Vol. VII, Fetischismus.

WEININGER, Otto, Geschlecht und Charakter, Vienna and Leipzig, 1903.—English translation, Sex and Character, Heinemann, London, 1906.

WITTELS, Fritz, Alles um Liebe, Berlin, 1912.

WITTELS, Fritz, Der Juwelier von Bagdad, Berlin, 1914.

WITTELS, Fritz, Die sexuelle Not, 1910.

WITTELS, Fritz, Tragische Motive, Berlin, 1911.

INDEX

ABEL, 249, 250
Ablauf des Lebens, Grundlegung zur exakten Biologie, 273
ABRAHAM (patriarch), 126
ABRAHAM (psychoanalyst), 135, 201
Abreaction, 38, 261
Acheron, 16
Active Method, 222–3
Actual Neurosis, 47, 50, 51, 227, 228, 261, 269, 270
Adequacy of Sexual Gratification, 231
ADLER, 114, 124, 132, 138, 139, 140, 145–59, 161, 165, 166, 176, 177, 178, 181, 193, 203, 206, 216, 225, 226, 230, 250, 266, 267, 268, 272
Adlerei, 225
Affect (defined), 261
Affect, Fixation of,
  See
    Fixation
Aggressive Impulse, 148, 157
Agoraphobia, 95
Ahnfrau, 90
Aida, 90, 92
ALEXANDER THE GREAT, 89, 239
" Alienist and Neurologist," 200
Alles um Liebe, 113, 171, 193, 197, 278
Allgemeine Neurosenlehre, 275
Alternation of Impulses, 250, 261, 262
Alti Castrati, 163
Ambition, 199
Ambivalency, 44, 45, 250, 261, 262, 263
  See also
    Bipolarity
Ammocœtes, 259
Amnesia (defined), 262
Amnesia, Infantile, 111, 262
Anæsthesia, Hysterical, 29
Anagogic Trend, 193, 262
Anal Phase of Sexuality, 108
Anal Zone, 199
Analysand (defined), 262
Analyse der Phobie eines fünfjährigen Knaben, 111
Analyst-Fixation, 223, 229
Angsthysterie, 262
Angstneurose, 262
Animism, 236, 237
Annulling Mechanism, 230, 262
Antinarcissism, 207
Antisemitism, 163, 164, 247
Anxiety, 46–58, 253, 257
  See also
    Dread
Anxiety Hysteria, 262
Anxiety Neurosis, 46–58, 253, 262
Anxiety, Objective, 52
Anxiety Paroxysm, 257
Aphasia, 35
Appearance and Reality, 258
Apulia, 76
Arcady, 174
ARIOSTO, 130, 272
ARISTOPHANES, 255
ARISTOTLE, 131

Armada, 28
Art, Genesis of, 170–2
Art of becoming an original Writer in three Days, 87
ARTEMIDORUS, 88, 89
Autoerotism, 112, 125, 200, 207, 208, 210, 262, 264
  See also
    Narcissism
Autosuggestion (defined), 262

BACH, 133
BALZAC, 225
Batastungslust (defined), 268
BAUDOUIN, 266, 272
BAYNES, 277
Bedeutung des Vaters für das Schicksal des Einzelnen, 131, 277
BEHRING, 26
BELLA VON M., 208–9, 212
Bene Brith, 248
Beobachtungen über Gestaltung und feineren Bau der als Hoden beschriebenen Lappenorganen des Aals, 273
BERGSON, 267
Berlin, 201
BERNHEIM, 36, 38, 39, 40, 41, 49
Bernheim's Experiment A, 39, 85
Bernheim's Experiment B, 41, 49, 85, 86, 90
Besetzung (defined), 263
Beyond the Pleasure Principle, 275
Beziehungswahn (defined), 264
Bible, 88, 143, 255
BINET, 34
Bipolarity, 79, 94, 120, 126, 195, 203, 241, 249–60, 262, 263
Birth, Memories of, 51, 52
Bisexuality, 101–4, 114, 124–8, 256
BLEULER, 135, 144, 250
Blond Beast, 245
Blunders,
  See
    Slips
BÖRNE, 19, 87, 88, 272
BOSWELL, 133
BREUER, 30, 35, 36–45, 46, 60, 75, 85, 100, 114, 122, 216, 263, 272
BREUER and FREUD, 36–45
Bridges, Fear of, 90, 95
BRILL, 47, 179, 273, 274, 275, 276
Bruchstück einer Hysterieanalyse, 94, 130, 274
BRÜCKE, 22, 23, 25, 27, 30, 41, 42, 46, 50, 233, 258, 259
Brückenangst, 90, 95
Brünn, 75
BRUTUS, 250
Buch vom Es, 194, 276
BÜCHNER, 30
Budapesth, 87, 135, 189
Buddhism, 184
" Bund," 106
Burghölzli, 136, 187

CÆSAR, 250
CALVIN, 187
Candaules Motif, 213, 240, 263
Capitol, 151
Carlsbad, 225
CASANOVA, 231
Castrates, Choir of, 163
Castration, 160
Castration Anxiety, 160, 161, 167
Castration Complex, 121, 150, 154, 156, 157, 160–75, 228, 263, 269
Castration, Discovery of, 167, 168
Castration Fantasies, 162–3
Castration Substitutes, 162
Catalepsy, 92
Cathartic Method, 38, 46, 263
Cathexis, 112, 155, 207, 208, 263, 268
Cave, Plato's Parable of, 254
Censor (defined), 263
Censorship (defined), 263
CHAMPOLLION, 73
Character formed in early Childhood, 228
CHARCOT, 27–35, 36, 38, 40, 41, 50, 51, 60, 86, 132
Charge, 155, 263
Child-Woman, 209–11, 212
CHRIST, 254
Christianity, 184–5, 189, 232
Christusneurose (defined), 267
Circumcision, 163
Civilisation, 148, 149, 197, 198, 202, 211
Civilisation, Origin of, 171–2
Claustrophobia (defined), 269
Cleanliness, 199
CLITUS, 239
Cocaine, 23–5, 258
Coitus interruptus, 48, 49, 51, 54, 55, 58, 263
COLUMBUS, 184
Common Sense, 153
Complex (defined), 263
See also particular complexes, as Castration Complex, etc.
COMSTOCK, 173
Conation, 264, 267
Conditions of Nervous Anxiety and their Treatment, 278
Conflicts, 21, 42, 46, 47, 48, 55, 107, 122, 174, 222, 228, 229
CONFUCIUS, 247
Conquest of the Mate, 56
Conscience, 194
Consciousness, Double, 85, 86, 91
See also
Multiple Personality
Constitution, Neurotic,
See
Neurotic Constitution
Content of Dream,
See
Latent Content
Manifest Content
Criminal Trends, 194–6
CRŒSUS, 211, 212
CROMWELL, 248
CRONUS, 245
Cryptomnesia, 87, 88, 102, 103, 104, 134, 154, 195, 201, 225, 262, 264
Cultural Overtones, 194
Cyclothymia, 206
Cyrano de Bergerac, 69, 277

Daimon, 33, 103, 180, 218, 255
DANTE, 244
Danube, 243
Darmstadt, 23
DARWIN, 25
DAVID, 239
Death akin to Love, 252
Death and Castration, 166, 167
Death Instinct, 251, 252, 253
Death, Negativity of, 254
Death, Symbolism of, 82, 83, 103, 219, 254
Death Wish, 241, 242
Deckerinnerung (defined), 270
Degeneration, 122
DELBOEUF, 34
Delusion and Dream, 274
Delusion of Persecution, 238
Delusion of Reference, 206, 264
Dementia paranoides, 162, 264
Dementia præcox, 138, 264
DEMOSTHENES, 145
Desexualisation of Eros, 203
Destruction of the World, 206
Determinism, 40, 98, 251
Deutsche Klinik, 30, 276
Dialogues of Plato, 128
Dichtung und Wahrheit, 16
Differentiation, 234
Diplegia, 35, 107
Diskussionen der Wiener psychoanalytischen Vereinigung, 241, 272
Dissociation, 34
Distortion,
See
Dream Distortion
Doctor-Fixation, 223, 229
DON JUAN, 231
Double Consciousness,
See
Consciousness
DOWNEY, 274
Dread, 253
See also
Anxiety
Dream Distortion, 61, 62, 76, 264
Dream Interpretation, 59–84, 88, 89, 152, 218–22, 226
Dreamer, The, 201
Drei Abhandlungen zur Sexualtheorie, 60, 110, 112, 114, 116, 125, 130, 142, 197, 200, 274

ECKERMANN, 133
EDER, 274
Educational Science,
See
Pedagogy
Eger, 76
Ego, 34, 159, 167, 234, 236, 237, 246
See also
Ego-Impulse
Narcissism
Ego-Fiction, 235
Ego-Ideal, 60, 128, 194, 233, 234, 248, 264
Ego Impulse, 148, 157–9, 183, 264
See also
Narcissism
EITINGTON, 135
Elective Affinities, 57

INDEX

ELECTRA, 115
Electra Complex, 115, 265, 268
  See also
    Mother Complex
Electrotherapeutics, 36
ELLIS, 200
Emasculation,
  See
    Castration
End of the World, 206-7
Endlust (defined), 271
Endopsychic Censor,
  See
    Censor
Entdeckungen auf dem Gebiete der Seele, 278
Entwicklungsstufen des Wirklichkeitssinnes, 171, 272
Entwurf zu einer physiologischen Erklärung der psychischen Erscheinungen, 30, 272
Equivalents of Anxiety, 47
ERB, 36
Erogenic Zone, 155, 199, 203, 265, 268
Eros, 105-28, 151, 169, 200, 203, 251, 256
  See also
    Sexual Theory
Essays in Applied Psychoanalysis, 276
Everyman, Parable of, 68-70
Exhibitionism, 113, 265, 267
EXNER, 30, 31, 272
Extroversion (defined), 265

Family as Forcing-House of Neurosis, 117
Father Complex, 60, 118, 122
  See also
    Oedipus Complex
    Father Ideal
Father, Death of, 59, 60
Father-Fixation, 42, 54, 265
Father Ideal, 119
  See also
    Father Complex
    Father-Imago
    Oedipus Complex
Father-Imago, 234, 246, 247, 248, 255, 260
Faust, 16, 33, 66, 67, 71, 98, 100, 118, 276
FAUST, 35, 71
FEDERN, 132
Fehlleistung, 99, 268
Fehlleistungen, 275
Feminism, 147, 231
  See also
    Woman's Question
FERENCZI, 51, 135, 136, 137, 138, 139, 171, 182, 183, 197, 198, 272, 275
Ferment of Life, 252
Fetichism, 113, 195, 265
Fetischismus, 114, 195, 278
Fixation (photographic sense), 235
Fixation (psychoanalytical sense), 42, 212, 265, 266, 268
  See also
    Analyst-Fixation
    Doctor-Fixation
    Father-Fixation
    Mother-Fixation
FLECHSIG, 76
FLIESS, 101, 102, 103, 104, 216, 273

Formulierungen über die zwei Prinzipien des psychischen Geschehens, 109
Fortschritte der Traumdeutung, 191, 278
Fragment über die Natur, 19, 276
FRAZER, 191, 273
FREDERICK THE GREAT, 80, 81
Free Will, 40, 98, 191
Freiberg, 247
Freud Craze, 137
FREUD, JOHN, 15, 19, 45, 226
FREUD (senior), 15, 21, 59, 60
FREUD, SIGMUND—
  early Years, 15-26
  Birth, 15
  Relationships with John, 15, 19, 45, 226
  Ambition, 19
  Combativeness, 19
  Choice of Career, 19 et seq.
  visits half-brother in England, 21
  becomes Demonstrator of Physiology under Brücke, 22
  discovery of Cocaine, 23-5, 258
  influenced by Meynert and by Kassowitz, 25-6
  studies in Paris under Charcot, 27-35
  as Seer, 33, 51, 258, 259
  is unmusical, 33
  as Cerebral Anatomist, 34, 35
  a born Revolutionist, 35, 43
  as Devil's Advocate, 35, 257
  his Collaboration with Breuer, 36-42
  Marriage, 42, 43
  personal Characteristics, 43-5, 129-44, 150
  visits Nancy, 38-41
  and the Anxiety Neuroses, 46-58
  and Dream Interpretation, 59-84
  Death of Freud senior, 59, 60
  discovers Repression and Transference, 85-7
  abandons Use of Hypnotism, 85, 86
  and the Sexual Theory of the Neuroses, 105-28
  visits United States, 136-7
  Relationships with Adler, 145-59
  and the Castration Complex, 160-75
  Relationships with Jung, 176-96
  and the Theory of Narcissism, 197-215
  Relationships with Stekel, 216-33
  cannot wholly break away from Organic Explanations of Disease, 227, 228
  and the Freudian Mechanisms, 234-48
  Enthusiasm for Hannibal, 247, 248
  Enthusiasm for Cromwell, 248
  a Freemason, 249
  and the Doctrine of Ambivalency, 249-60
  Death of Daughter, 251, 252
  complete Bibliography of Works, 273-276
FREUD's half-brother, 17, 21
Freudian Mechanisms, 124, 146, 148, 234-48, 258
  See also
    Annulling Mechanism
FRIEDJUNG, 133
Friedrich Hebbel, ein psychoanalytische Versuch, 213, 278
FÜRSTNER, 30, 276

GABLER, 278
Gaia, 113
GALVANI, 24
GÄRTNER, 24
Genealogy of Morals, 244, 246, 247
Genealogy of Morals, 277
Genetic Theory of the Libido, 180, 199
  See also
    Libido
Geneva, 135
GENGHIS KHAN, 184
Gephuraphobia, 90, 95
Germ-plasm, 59, 167
Geschlecht und Charakter, 103, 278
Glacial Epoch, 170, 171
Glossary for the Use of Translators of Psychoanalytical Works, 261
GLÜCK, 272
GOETHE, 15, 16, 19, 27, 33, 57, 88, 133, 235, 276
Götter Griechenlands, 236, 278
GRAF, 133
Graphology, 77
Grenzfragen des Nerven- und Seelenlebens, 274
Grief, 204, 205
GRILLPARZER, 90, 92
GRODDECK, 194, 228, 276
Group Psychology and the Analysis of the Ego, 264, 276
Group Psychology, 266

HABSBURGS, 17
HAECKEL, 30
HAGEN, 177
Hamburg, 42
HAMLET, 58, 237
Hamlet, 278
HANNIBAL, 248
HASENTREFFER, 130
HAUFF, 130, 211
He (Father-Imago), 235, 238, 255, 257
HEFFEL, 177, 213, 240
Heidelberg, 23, 24
Heine Strasse, 17
HEITLER, 23
HELENA, 71
HELMHOLTZ, 23
HERCULES, 131
Heredity, 122
HERODOTUS, 160
Hetaira, 211
Hetaira-Cult, 212–13
Heterosuggestion (defined), 265
Hieroglyph, 73, 249
HINKLE, 277
His Majesty the Baby, 215
History of the Psychoanalytic Movement, 149, 155, 179, 276
HITSCHMANN, 132
HOMER, 131
Homosexuality, 114, 136, 212–14, 227, 238, 240, 265, 267
Homosexuality, Larval or Unconscious, 231
Horde, Primitive,
  See
    Primitive Horde
HUBBACK, 275
Human, All-Too-Human, 277
Hydra, 178

Hypnosis, 31, 36, 37, 38, 39, 41, 42, 85, 86
Hypnosis, Stages of, 34
Hypnotism,
  See
    Hypnosis
Hypochondria, 202, 203, 204, 206, 240, 241, 265
HYRTL, 22
Hysteria, 28–30, 35, 48
  See also
    Anxiety Hysteria
Hysteria, Breuer's Classical Case, 37–8
Hysteria in the Male, 32
Hysteria, Möbius' Definition of, 37
Hysteria, Phases of, 33
Hysteron, 32

IBSEN, 76
Ice Age, 170, 171, 174, 185, 232
Ich und das Es, 60, 83, 102, 191, 243, 276
Identification, 109, 119–20, 207, 208, 214, 234
Imago (defined), 266
  See also
    Father-Imago
    Mother-Imago
"Imago," 219
Imitation, 234, 235
Impotence Complex, 80, 81, 122
Impulse,
  See
    Aggressive Impulse
    Alternation of Impulses
    Ego Impulse
    Moral Impulse
    Sexual Impulse
Impulshandlungen, 196, 278
Incest, 115–16
  See also
    Electra Complex
    Oedipus Complex
Incest Barrier, 192
Incretions, 29
Individual Psychology, 155, 156, 266
Individual Psychology, 272
Infantile Amnesia,
  See
    Amnesia
Infantile Autoerotism, 210
Infantile Cerebrallähmung, 273
Infantile Sexuality,
  See
    Sexuality of Early Childhood
Infantilism, 114, 164, 226, 266
Inferiority Complex, 124, 145–59, 161, 203, 212, 248, 266, 267, 268
Inferiority of the Organs, 146, 155, 266
Inferno, 244
Infra-Ego, 83
INGRES, 114
Initial Pleasure, 112, 113, 266
Inquisition, 172
Inspectionism, 113, 185, 186, 267
Instanz, 264
Instinctive Energy, 267
Institutional Disease, 117
International Psychoanalytical Association, 138, 140, 178
"Internationale Zeitschrift für aerztliche Psychoanalyse," 164, 171, 272
Interpretation of Dreams, 28, 61, 273

INDEX

Interpretation of Dreams,
    See
        Dream Interpretation
Interpretations, far-fetched, 219
Intimidation, Sexual,
    See
        Sexual Intimidation
        Castration Complex
Introductory Lectures on Psychoanalysis, 201, 261, 263, 275
Introversion, 201, 267
Intuition, 33
Inversion, 114, 265, 267
Investment, 112, 155, 201, 207, 263, 268
Inzestmotiv in Dichtung und Sage, 118, 277
It, the, 194
    See also
        Ich un das Es

"Jahrbüch für Psychoanalyse," 178, 197
JANET, PAUL, 28
JANET, PIERRE, 28, 34, 85, 132, 153, 166, 217
JEHOVAH, 28
Jenseits des Lustprinzips, 35, 96, 243, 252, 257, 275
JENSEN, 274
Jerusalem, 172
Jocasta, 115
JONES, 131, 261, 262, 263, 264, 265, 267, 268, 270, 271, 275, 276, 277
JOSEPH (Pharaoh's Factor), 74, 75
JOSEPH II, 17, 100
JOWETT, 128
JUAN, DON, 231
JUDAS, 180, 239
Julius Cæsar, 278
JUNG, 83, 114, 115, 131, 135, 136, 137, 138, 140, 158, 164, 176–196, 197, 198, 199, 216, 267, 277
Jungle Book, 76
Juwelier von Bagdad, 213, 278

Kaa, 76
KAHANE, 132, 216
Kaiser Josef Strasse, 17
KANT, 194
KASSOWITZ, 25
Kastrationskomplex (defined), 263
Kinderheimkrankheit, 117
Kindheitserinnerung des Lionardo da Vinci, 275
KIPLING, 76
KLEMPERER, 30, 276
Klinische Studien über die halbseitige Cereballähmung der Kinder, 273
Know thyself, 62
KOCH, 24
Koitus im Kindesalter, 107, 278
KOLLER, 24, 25
Kunst in drei Tagen ein Originalschriftsteller zu werden, 87, 272
Künstler, Der, 133, 171, 277
Künstler, Die, 71, 278
KUTTNER, 276

LAIUS, 115
Latent Content, 61, 77, 264
Leben des Traumes, 88, 278

Lehre von den Geschlechtsverirrungen, 164, 278
Leipzig, 17, 30
Length of Analysis, 223–4
Leonardo da Vinci, a psychosexual Study of an infantile Reminiscence, 275
LESSING, 18, 72, 277
LEVY, 277
LEYDEN, 30, 276
Libido, 54, 55, 158, 169–72, 176, 181, 182, 183, 199, 226, 234, 256, 257, 265, 267, 271
    See also
        Narcissism
Libido, Genetic Conception of, 180–1
Libido Theory, 114
    See also
        Sexual Theory
LIÉBEAULT, 38
Life Instinct, 251, 252, 253
LIND, 272
Living Corpse, 90
Lobositz, 80
London, 135
Love of Own Children as Narcissism, 214, 215
Love Passion, 201, 202, 204
Lunacy, 136, 201, 202, 203
    See also
        Specific Psychoses, as Melancholia, Paranoia, etc.
Lustprinzip (defined), 269
LUTHER, 101
LYNKEUS,
    See
        POPPER-LYNKEUS
M. R., 60
MACDUFF, 52
MACH, 53, 157
MAEDER, 83, 135, 178, 277
Manifest Content, 61, 264
MARIA THERESA, 17
MARX, 259
Masculine Protest, 147, 157, 161, 165, 180, 266, 267
Masculinisation of Woman, 232
Masochism, 172, 267, 270
Mass Psychology, 266
Massenpsychologie und Ich-Analyse, 141, 214, 266, 276
Masturbation, 48, 51, 55, 56–8, 111, 156, 186, 227
Mate,
    See
        Conquest of the Mate
Mechanism, annulling,
    See
        Annulling
Mechanism, Freudian,
    See
        Freudian
"Medizinische Klinik," 144
Megalomania, 203, 215
Melancholia, 136, 204, 205, 229, 240, 253, 265, 267
Memories of Early Childhood, 107–8
    See also
        Amnesia, Infantile
Memory, submerged, 154
    See also
        Cryptomnesia

Menschliches, Alzumenschliches, 62, 277
Mental Disorder,
  See
    Lunacy
MEPHISTOPHELES, 35, 100
MERCK, 23
MESSALINA, 231
Messianic Neurosis, 230, 268
Metaphysics and Science, 53, 54, 169, 199, 224, 233, 255
Metapsychology, 54, 142, 233
MEYER, 143, 220
MEYNERT, 25, 27, 31, 32, 46, 50, 233
MICHELANGELO, 218
Minderwertigkeit der Organe (defined), 266
Miserliness, 199
Mission, Great Historic, 230
Mistakes and Blunders,
  See
    Slips
MÖBIUS, 30, 37, 50
MOLESCHOTT, 30
MOLOCH, 184
Moral Impulse, 157, 194–6
Mother Complex, 118
  See also
    Electra Complex
Mother-Fixation, 185–7, 214, 265
Mother-Imago, 235, 238, 246, 247, 248, 255
Multiple Personality, 209
  See also
    Consciousness, Double
Munich, 191, 216
Mysticism, 256, 257, 258

NAECKE, 200
Nancy, 38, 39, 40, 41, 85
NAPOLEON, 69
Narcissiom, 121, 149, 154, 158, 197–215, 228, 234, 235, 268
Narcissism, Secondary, 208
NARCISSUS, 200, 268
Nathan der Weise, 72, 277
Nationalism, 248
NEBUCHADNEZZAR, 88
Necessity, 251
Nervöse Angstzustände und ihre Behandlung, 49, 278
Neurasthenia, 50
"Neurologisches Zentralblatt," 272, 273
Neurosis,
  See
    Actual Neurosis
    Anxiety Neurosis
    Messianic Neurosis
    Psychogenic Neurosis
    Psychoneurosis
    Somatic Neurosis
Neurotic Constitution, 148, 156, 176
  See also
    Adler
    Inferiority Complex
Neurotic Constitution, 153, 272
NIETZSCHE, 43, 62, 63, 88, 125, 145, 232, 237, 244, 245, 246, 255, 259, 277
Ninth Symphony, 198
Nirvana, 252
No Man's Land, 232
Normal Sexual Intercourse, Concept of, 57, 231

Notre-Dame, 27
Nuclear Complex, 116, 268
Nuremberg, 138, 140, 141, 148, 177

Obsessional Neurosis, 237
OEDIPUS, 115, 162
Oedipus Complex, 45, 57, 114–21, 152, 161, 162, 164, 165, 178, 185–7, 191, 192, 228, 246, 265, 268
  See also
    Father Complex
    Father Ideal
Old Maid, 106
Old Man, 139, 192, 245
Old Man of the Sea, 226
Omnipotence of Thought, 236, 237
On Dreams, 274
On the Right to separate from Neurasthenia a definite Symptom-Complex as Anxiety Neurosis, 47
Onanie, 275
Onanie und Homosexualität, 56, 114, 278
Onesidedness of Freud's Theories, alleged, 50, 233
OPHELIA, 237
Ophthalmological Congress in Heidelberg, 24
Ophthalmoscope, 23, 41, 42
Opposites, Unification of, 249, 250
  See also
    Bipolarity
Oral Phase of Sexuality, 108
Organ Inferiority, 146, 155, 266, 268
Organ Inferiority and its Psychical Compensation, 272
Orlando Furioso, 130, 272
Orphans especially prone to Neurosis, 117
OSTWALD, 53, 60
Over-Determination, 77

Pæderasty, 176
Palpationism, 113, 268
Pansexualism, 112, 125, 141, 268
Papers on Psychoanalysis, 261, 264, 277
Paralysis, Hysterical, 29
Paranoia, 136, 238, 239, 264, 268
Paranoid Dementia,
  See
    Dementia Paranoides
Parapraxis, 98, 104, 268
  See also
    Slips, Mistakes, and Blunders
Paris, 27, 36, 40, 42, 258
PASTEUR, 239
Peasant, The, 188
Pedagogy, 154, 155, 189
Pedantry, 199
Pedication, 160, 269
Penis Anxiety, 161, 269
  See also
    Castration Complex
Penis Envy, 161, 269
  See also
    Castration Complex
Persuasion, 41, 86
Perversion, 112, 113, 114, 116, 161, 172, 200
Perversion, Polymorphic, 112
PFISTER, 135, 144, 187
Phœdrus, 127, 128, 277
Phantasien eines Realisten, 277

INDEX 285

PHARAOH, 74, 88
Philosophy,
    See
        Metaphysics
Phobia, 48, 95, 262, 269
    See also
        Agoraphobia
        Claustrophobia
        Gephuraphobia
Phthisicus semper salax, 210
Phylogenesis, 168, 269
Plait-Cutters, 162
PLATO, 110, 113, 126, 127, 128, 253, 255, 277
Pleasure, Initial,
    See
        Initial Pleasure
Pleasure Principle, 109, 174, 251, 269, 270
Pleasure, Terminal,
    See
        Terminal Pleasure
Pleasure, two Forms of, 113
Polarisation, 255
    See also
        Bipolarity
Polymorphic Perversion,
    See
        Perversion
Pope, 227
POPPER-LYNKEUS, 62, 66, 77, 88, 245, 246, 277
Praxis und Theorie der Individualpsychologie, 145, 272
Precocity, 123
Primitive Horde, 45, 139, 165, 192, 193, 245
Primitive-horde Complex, 192
Primitive Man, 220, 221
Principle, Pleasure,
    See
        Pleasure Principle
Principle, Reality,
    See
        Reality Principle
Problem der Homosexualität, 145, 272
Problem des Hamlet und der Oedipuskomplex, 131, 276
Probleme der Religionspsychologie, 275
Projection, 233, 269
PROMETHEUS, 61
Protozea, Immortality of, 252
Psychic Energy, 267
Psychoanalysis, 20, 21, et passim.
Psychoanalysis and Æsthetics, 266, 272
Psychoanalysis (defined), 269
Psychoanalysis, Discovery of, 36–42
Psychoanalysis, its fundamental Task, 49
Psychoanalysis, "Politics" of, 137, 176
Psychoanalysis, revolutionary Potentialities of, 259
Psychoanalysis, Technique of, 87
Psychoanalytic Study of Hamlet, 276
Psychoanalytical Congress—
    first, 135–6, 177
    second, 138–41, 177
    third, 177
    fourth, 178
    fifth, 189

Psychoanalytische Bemerkungen über einen autobiographisch beschriebenen Fall von Paranoia, 197
Psychogenic (defined), 269
Psychogenic Neuroses, 28–30, 31, 37, 227, 261, 269
Psychology of the Unconscious, 178, 182, 183, 197, 277
Psychology, Traditional or Old, 130
Psychologische Typen, 188, 277
Psychoneurosis, 269
Psychopathology of Everyday Life, 274
Psychosexueller Infantilismus, 114, 278
Psychosis,
    See
        Lunacy
Psychosynthesis, 188–90, 222
    See also
        Active Method
Puns, 75, 221
PYTHAGORAS, 24

RADIN, 272
RANK, 118, 133, 171, 277
RAPHAEL, 20
Rationalisation, 39–40, 186, 205, 270
Realangst, 52
Realitätsprinzip (defined), 270
Reality and Appearance, 258
Reality Principle, 109, 174, 269, 270
Recurrence of the Similar, 95, 96, 104, 255
Reference, Delusion of,
    See
        Delusion
Reflections (on War and Death), 276
Regression, 116, 168, 174, 270
REIK, 275
REITLER, 132
Relative Impotence, 186, 240, 270
Religion, 182–3, 236, 246
Religion and Sexuality, 172
Renaissance, 184
Repetition Compulsion, 95, 270
Repression, 42, 49, 90 et seq., 148, 149, 173, 226, 232, 263, 264, 270
Repression and Transference, 85–97
Republic, 277
Resexualisation of Eros, 203
Resistance, 90 et seq., 148, 173, 222, 226, 259, 270
Retaliation, Law of, 165, 242, 243
Return to the Mother's Womb, 80, 120, 255
Revaluation of Values, 232, 259
Revolutionary Sentiments of Jews, 247
RIE, 273
RIKLIN, 135
Ritual Circumcision,
    See
        Circumcision
Ritual Murder, 163
RIVIÈRE, 275
Rocket, 94
ROKITANSKY, 22
Rome, 163, 191, 248
ROMEO, 174
Romeo and Juliet, 78, 278
RÖNTGEN, 24
Rosetta, 73
ROSTAND, 277

ROUSSEAU, 187
RUBENS, 218

SADGER, 76, 124, 132, 136, 138, 142, 164, 166, 167, 213, 278
Sadism, 113, 172, 267, 270
St. Helena, 69
St. Peter's, 163
Salpêtrière, 28, 31, 34
Salzburg, 135, 138, 141, 177
Sammlung Kleiner Schriften zur Neurosenlehre, 19, 33, 38, 42, 46, 63, 97, 107, 109, 111, 122, 124, 136, 139, 157, 159, 165, 197, 199, 211, 213, 215, 222, 227, 237, 238, 256, 274
SAMUEL, 277
SATAN, 130, 173
Satanists, 194, 232
SAUL, 239
Schaulust (defined), 266, 267
SCHERNER, 88, 89, 278
SCHILLER, 71, 179, 236, 278
Schizophrenia, 136, 264, 270
SCHOPENHAUER, 31, 53, 63, 70, 167, 181, 237, 252, 259, 278
SCHREBER, 136, 177, 206
Schriften zur angewandten Seelenkunde, 276
SCHRÖTTER, 68
Science and Metaphysics, 53, 54
  See also
    Metaphysics
Science and Mysticism, 256
Scoptolagnia (defined), 266, 267
Scoptophilia (defined), 266, 267
Screen-Memory, 19, 271
Seer, Charcot as, 32, 51
Seer, Freud as, 33, 51, 258, 259
Selected Papers on Hysteria and other Psychoneuroses, 47, 276
Self-determination, 191
Sentiment d'incomplétude, 153, 166
Sex and Character, 278
Sexual (psychoanalytical use of Term), 267
Sexual Impulse, 148, 157, 199
Sexual Intimidation, 156
  See also
    Castration Complex
Sexual Need, 106
Sexual Theory, 50, 51, 63, 78, 101-4, 105-28, 140, 141, 155, 156, 169-75, 183-8, 231
  See also
    Libido
    Narcissism
Sexuality of Early Childhood, 105-12, 226
Sexuelle Not, 106, 158, 209, 278
SHAKESPEARE, 78, 278
Shame, 231
She (Mother-Imago), 235, 238, 255, 257
Siegfried, 177, 187, 245
Siegmund, 134, 135
SILBERER, 68, 83, 193, 262
Slips, Mistakes, and Blunders, 98-104, 268
Social Instinct, 194-6
Social Psychology, 266
SOCRATES, 33, 255
Socratic Method, 130

Somatic Neurosis, 50, 51, 261, 269, 271
Somatic Response, 241
Song of Solomon, 172
Songes-mensonges, 61
Sophists, 255
Sorbonne, 28
South Sea Islanders, 192
Sperl Gymnasium, 18
Spermatozoa Dreams, 120
Sphinx, 114
SPITTELER, 266
Sprache des Traumes, 73, 83, 89, 278
STÄRKE, 164
STEINACH, 213
STEINER, 132
STEKEL, 17, 19, 48, 49, 56, 57, 72, 73, 75, 76, 82, 83, 89, 107, 112, 114, 120, 132, 138, 139, 140, 144, 151, 164, 165, 176, 177, 179, 187, 191, 195, 196, 212, 216-33, 250, 252, 262, 278
STEPHENSON, 94
STILICHO, 146
Störungen des Trieb- und Affektlebens, 114, 158, 278
STRACHEY, 266, 276
STRICKER, 24
Studien über Hysterie, 30, 38, 272, 273
Studies concerning Hysteria, 42, 46, 47, 75
Sublimation, 125, 126, 127, 184, 198, 271
Submerged Memory, 154
  See also
    Cryptomnesia
Substitution, 243
Suggestibility (defined), 271
Suggestion, 38, 39, 190, 262, 271
Suicide, Significance of, 241, 252
Super-Ego, 60, 83, 128, 193-5, 234, 246, 264, 271
  See also
    Ego-Ideal
Superiority Complex (defined), 271
Suttee, 241
Symbolism, 42, 74, 75, 88, 151, 166, 168, 219, 222, 249
Symposium, 110, 127, 255, 277
Symptomatic Act, 239
Syphilis, 184

Tarpeian Rock, 151
TAUSIG, 276
TAUSK, 68, 142
TAYLOR, 100
Terminal Pleasure, 112, 113, 271
Terre, La, 188
Thebes, 115
Thirty Years' War, 101
Three Contributions to the Theory of Sex, 274
TOLSTOY, 90
TORSTENSSON, 146
Totem und Tabu, 191, 192, 237, 275
Totemism and Exogamy, 191, 273
Tragische Motive, 171, 213, 278
Transferability of the Libido, 234
Transference, 42, 93 et seq., 148, 190, 206, 207, 222, 223, 224, 226, 271
Transference Neuroses, 206
Transmutation of Affect, 198, 202
  See also
    Sublimation

INDEX

Trauer und Melancholia, 136
Traum, 275
Traumdeutung, 15, 16, 17, 18, 19, 22, 27, 28, 32, 33, 43, 45, 59, 60, 67, 71, 73, 89, 98, 100, 101, 102, 107, 108, 115, 181, 215, 248, 259, 273
Triebverschränkung, 250, 261, 262
Tu, 235, 236, 254
Two-in-Hand, 127, 128, 253
Tyre, 89

Ueber Coca, 273
Ueber das Traumproblem, 178, 277
Ueber den Bau der Nervenfasern und Nervenzellen beim Flusskrebs, 273
Ueber den nervösen Charakter, 145, 272
Ueber den psychischen Mechanismus hysterischer Phänomene, 38, 272, 273
Ueber den Selbstmord, 241, 272, 274
Ueber den Tod und die Unzerstörbarkeit unseres Wesens an sich, 237, 278
Ueber den Traum, 274
Ueber den Ursprung der hinteren Nervenwurzeln im Rückenmark von Ammocœtes, 273
Ueber die allgemeinste Erniedrigung des Liebeslebens, 213
Ueber die Berechtigung von der Neurasthenie einen bestimmten Symptomenkomplex als Angstneurose abzutrennen, 46
Ueber Psychoanalyse, 274
Ueber Spinalganglien und Rückenmark des Petromyzon, 273
Uebertragung (defined), 271
Uhrmensch, 221
Unconscious, 40, 85, 90, 271
Unconscious as Source of Artistic Inspiration, 117–18
Unconscious Ideas, 30
Unconscious, Reflex from, 42
Unification of Opposites, 249, 250
See also
  Bipolarity
Uplift, 190, 262
Urethral Erotism, 199
Urmensch, 220, 221

Values, Revaluation of, 232, 259
Verdrängung (defined), 270
Vienna, 17, 18, 23, 27, 68, 157, 178
Vienna General Hospital, 23, 31, 130
Vienna University, 22
Viennese Medical Society, 32, 142
Viennese Psychoanalytical Society, 97, 132, 142, 148, 151, 155, 211, 219, 221, 274, 275
Viennese School of Medicine, 31, 34–5, 36
Viennese School of Psychoanalysis, 178, 219
VIRGIL, 244
Vital Impetus, 267
Vitzliputzli, 182

Vorlesungen zur Einführung in die Psychoanalyse, 55, 73, 129, 157, 201, 275
Vorlust (defined), 266
Voyeurism (defined), 266, 267

WAGNER-JAUREGG, 31
Wahn und die Träume in W. Jensen's "Gradiva," 274
WALLENSTEIN, 179
Wandlungen und Symbole der Libido, 178, 181, 277
Weimar, 27, 177, 216
WEININGER, 67, 103, 278
Widerstand (defined), 270
WIDMANN, 106
Wiederholungszwang (defined), 270
"Wiener medizinische Blätter," 107, 278
Will, 181
Will, Free,
See
  Free Will
Will-to-Power, 145, 147, 149, 151, 166, 181
See also
  Inferiority Complex
Wish-Fulfilment, 221
Wit, 32
Wit and its relation to the Unconscious, 274
WITTELS, 135, 213, 278
Witz und seine Beziehung zum Unbewussten, 32, 274
Woman's Question, 147, 209–11, 231–2
Womb, Return to,
See
  Return
Worcester University, 136
WUNDT, 130

ZARATHUSTRA, 63
Zeigelust (defined), 265
Zeitgemässes über Krieg und Tod, 276
"Zentralblatt für Psychoanalyse," 140, 191, 278
"Zentralblatt für Therapie," 23
ZEUS, 255
ZOLA, 188, 225
Zur Auffassung der Aphasien, 273
Zur Einführung des Narzissmus, 199
Zur Genealogie der Moral, 245, 277
Zur Geschichte der psychoanalytische Bewegung, 276
Zur Kenntniss der cerebralen Diplegien des Kindesalters (im Anschluss an die Little'sche Krankheit, 273
Zur Psychoanalyse der Kriegsneurosen, 275
Zur Psychopathologie des Alltagslebens, 21, 43, 60, 98, 100, 101, 107, 192, 274
Zurich, 135, 136, 201
Zurich School, 128, 135, 136, 176–96, 203, 219, 232, 233